Safe Behind Bars

Ellis Amdur, M.A., N.C.C., C.M.H.S.,
Sergeant Michael Blake and
Chris De Villeneuve, M.B.A./H.C.M., M.Ed., D.M.H.P.

Communication, Control, and De-escalation of
Mentally Ill and Aggressive Inmates

A Comprehensive Guidebook for

Correctional Officers in Jail Settings

An Edgework Book
www.edgework.info

Notes and Notices

Safe Behind Bars: Communication, Control, and De-escalation of Mentally Ill and Aggressive Inmates for Correctional Officers in Jail Settings

By Ellis Amdur, M.A., N.C.C., C.M.H.S., Sergeant Michael Blake, and Chris De Villeneuve, M.B.A./H.C.M., M.Ed., D.M.H.P. © 2013

ISBN: 978-0-9823762-9-4

A Message to Our Readers

Edgework is committed to offering the best of what our years of experience and study have taught us. We ask that you express your respect for these intentions and honor our work by adhering strictly to the copyright protection notice you will find below. Please know that by choosing NOT to reproduce these materials, you are supporting our work and making it possible for us to continue to develop materials that will enhance both officer and public safety. We thank you sincerely for your vigilance in respecting our rights!

Notice of Rights

Limited Liability and Disclaimer

This book is informational only and is not to be considered an official policy manual. By purchasing this book, you agree that you will hold the authors and publisher harmless from all claims arising out of or related to your access or use of, or inability to access or use, this book or the information contained herein.

The information in this book is provided for general information only and provided "AS IS" to the fullest extent permitted by law, without express or implied, including, but not limited to, any warranty of fitness for a particular purpose. The authors and publisher make no warranties about the accuracy, completeness, or timeliness of the content, services, text, graphs, and links appearing in this book.

Credits

Photographs by: Dreamstime.com
Illustrations by: Shoko Zama
Design: Soundview Design Studio
Cover photograph by: Junichiro Aoyama, Wikimedia Commons

Contents

Published Works by Ellis Amdur (and Co-Authors) vii

In Gratitude For Expert Critique..ix

Foreword: Donald Leach xi

Introduction..xiii

Section I   The Mentally Ill Inmate: Inside the System 1

Chapter 1   Why Are Mentally Ill Individuals Repeatedly Incarcerated? 3

Chapter 2   Who Are the Mentally Ill in Jail? 11

Chapter 3   Life for the Mentally Ill in Prison 17

Chapter 4   What Do Mentally Ill Inmates Need? 21

Chapter 5   The Role of the Correctional Officer in Supervising Mentally Ill Inmates 25

Chapter 6   What Should Happen at Intake? 29

Chapter 7   Taking into Account an Inmate's Mental Illness During Write-ups and
               Disciplinary Hearings...37

Chapter 8   Drug Use by Mentally Ill Inmates 41

Chapter 9   Specialized Units 45

Chapter 10   The Role of Medical Staff Within the Jail 49

Section II   The Mentally Ill Inmate: "Outside"—The Other System 53

Chapter 11   In Between: Continuity of Care Requires Restoration of Benefits............55

Chapter 12   Mental Health Court and Diversion...57

Chapter 13   The Role of Probation as Part of an Overarching System of Custody and Care..........63

Chapter 14   Mental Health and Psychiatric Services on the "Outside" 65

**Section III   Core Requirements for De-escalation and Control of Agitated,
               Aggressive, and/or Mentally Ill Inmates** 69

Chapter 15   The Development of a Safety Mindset 71

Chapter 16   Training Your Intuition (Correctional Awareness) to Pick up Danger 79

Chapter 17   Honing Your Intuition Through Awareness of Personal Spacing 81

Section IV   Centering: Standing With Strength in Crisis Situations.......................85

Chapter 18   Introduction to Centering 87

Chapter 19   A Fair Witness: Peer Support Is a Survival Tactic 91

Chapter 20   It's not Personal Unless You Make It So 93
Chapter 21   Circular Breathing: Be the Eye in the Center of the Hurricane 99
Chapter 22   The Intoxication and Joy of Righteous Anger 105

Section V   Dealing With Those Who Have Unusual, Intense, and Eccentric Communication Styles...107
Chapter 23   Overview of Section V...109
Chapter 24   Rigid Personality: Asperger's Syndrome and Other Similar Disorders 111
Chapter 25   Tell It Like It Is: Communication With Concrete Thinkers 115
Chapter 26   Information Processing and Retention: Consolidating Gains....................117
Chapter 27   Coping With Stubborn Refusals 119
Chapter 28   Stuck: Coping With Repetitive Demands, Questions, and Obsessions 121
Chapter 29   The Need for Reassurance 123
Chapter 30   Dealing With Mood Swings 125
Chapter 31   They Aren't Moving: What to Do? 127
Chapter 32   Should a Correctional Officer Ever Apologize? 129
Chapter 33   Useful Tactics for Dealing With Symptoms of Paranoia and Persecution 131

Section VI   Recognizing the Strategies of Opportunistic and Manipulative Inmates......135
Chapter 34   Divide and Confuse: Borderline Personality Disorder and Splitting.........137
Chapter 35   Bad Intentions: Recognizing the Strategies of Opportunistic and Manipulative Inmates..141
Chapter 36   Tactical and Safety Considerations Related to the Supervision of the Psychopathic Inmate 145

Section VII   Communication With Inmates That Have Severe Mental Illness or Other Conditions that Cause Severe Disability.........149
Chapter 37   Overview of Section VII..151
Chapter 38   Struggling in a Fog: Dealing With the Symptoms of Disorganization.......153
Chapter 39   Latency: Dropping Stones Down a Well..157
Chapter 40   Withdrawal From Intoxicating Substances...159
Chapter 41   Psychosis: Delusions and Hallucinations 161
Chapter 42   Communication With Inmates Experiencing Delusions/Hallucinations....165
Chapter 43   Welcome to the Rollercoaster: Tactics for Dealing With Symptoms of Mania..........175
Chapter 44   Communication With Inmates With Dementia (The Elderly)....................181

Section VIII   Suicide...183
Chapter 45   Suicide in Jail 185
Chapter 46   The Basics of Intervention With an Inmate Who May Be Suicidal 189
Chapter 47   Essential Questions 193
Chapter 48   Self-Mutilation...199

Section IX **Recognizing Patterns of Aggression** 203

Chapter 49   The Cycle of Aggression 205

Chapter 50   Why Would an Inmate Become Aggressive? 211

Chapter 51   What Does Aggression Look Like? 215

Section X **De-escalation of Angry Inmates** 223

Chapter 52   Preemptive De-escalation 225

Chapter 53   Physical Organization in the Face of Aggression 227

Chapter 54   Tone and Quality of Your Voice 233

Chapter 55   Across the Spectrum of Anger..235

Chapter 56   Diamonds in the Rough: Essential Strategies for De-escalation of Anger 241

Chapter 57   Tactical Paraphrasing: The Gold Standard With Angry and Agitated Mentally Ill Inmates 247

Chapter 58   Big Mistakes That Seemed Like Such Good Ideas at the Time 255

Section XI **A Consideration of Communication With Mentally Ill, Emotionally Disturbed, and Drug Affected Incarcerated Youth: For Correctional Officers Who Work With Juvenile Offenders** 259

Chapter 59   Working With Incarcerated Youth...261

Chapter 60   No Brake Pads: A Consideration of the Impulsive Youth 263

Chapter 61   Contact Disorder: Fierce Youth 265

Chapter 62   Dynamite Under a Rock: Explosive Kids..269

Chapter 63   Opposition-Defiant Kids: "Even if You Make Me, I'll Still Make You Miserable" 271

Chapter 64   Post Traumatic Stress Disorder in Youth 273

Chapter 65   Pseudo-Nihilism...275

Section XII **Managing Rage and Violence** 277

Chapter 66   Preface to Rage and Violence...279

Chapter 67   Chaotic Rage: A Consideration of Rage Emerging from Various Disorganized States...281

Chapter 68   Terrified Rage...289

Chapter 69   Hot Rage...291

Chapter 70   Predatory or Cool Rage 303

Chapter 71   De-escalation of Developmentally Disabled Inmates 307

Chapter 72   Mob Rage: Feeding Frenzy 309

Chapter 73   Deceptive Rage: Snake in the Grass...311

Chapter 74   The Aftermath: What Happens to the Aggressive, Mentally Ill Inmate After an Aggressive Incident? 313

Chapter 75   Managing Threats to Your Family..315

Chapter 76   Conclusion..317

Appendices 319
Appendix A   The Question of Positional and Compression Asphyxia – by Dr. Gary M. Vilke 321
Appendix B   Suggested Response Protocol for Correctional Facilities Concerning
              Suspected Excited Delirium Incidents – by Lieutenant Michael Paulus 325

Endnotes 341
About the Authors 345

Published Works by Ellis Amdur (and Co-Authors)

Published by Edgework www.edgework.info

On the De-escalation of Aggression

EVERYTHING ON THE LINE: Calming and De-escalation of Aggressive and Mentally Ill Individuals on the Phone
A Comprehensive Guidebook for Emergency Dispatch (9-1-1) Centers
Ellis Amdur

FROM CHAOS TO COMPLIANCE: Communication, Control, and De-escalation of Mentally Ill, Emotionally Disturbed and Aggressive Offenders
A Comprehensive Guidebook for Parole and Probation Officers
Ellis Amdur & Alan Pelton

GRACE UNDER FIRE: Skills to Calm and De-escalate Aggressive and Mentally Ill Individuals in Outpatient Settings: 2nd Edition
A Comprehensive Guidebook for Health and Social Services Agencies, and Individual Practitioners
Ellis Amdur

GUARDING THE GATES: Calming, Control and De-escalation of Mentally Ill, Emotionally Disturbed and Aggressive Individuals
A Comprehensive Guidebook for Security Guards
Ellis Amdur & William Cooper

IN THE EYE OF THE HURRICANE: Skills to Calm and De-escalate Aggressive and Mentally Ill Family Members: 2nd Edition
Ellis Amdur

SAFE BEHIND BARS: Communication, Control, and De-escalation of Mentally Ill and Aggressive Inmates
A Comprehensive Guidebook for Correctional Officers in Jail Settings
Ellis Amdur, Michael Blake & Chris De Villeneuve

SAFE WITHIN THE WALLS: Communication, Control, and De-escalation of Mentally Ill and Aggressive Inmates
A Comprehensive Guidebook for Correctional Officers in Prison Settings
Ellis Amdur & Notable Consultants in the Field of Corrections

SAFE HAVEN: Skills to Calm and De-escalate Aggressive and Mentally Ill Individuals: 2nd Edition
A Comprehensive Guidebook for Personnel Working in Hospital and Residential Settings
Ellis Amdur

SAFETY AT WORK: Skills to Calm and De-escalate Aggressive and Mentally Ill Individuals
A Comprehensive Guidebook for Corporate Security Managers, Human Resources Staff, Loss Prevention Specialists, Executive Protection, and Others Involved in Threat Management Professions
Ellis Amdur & William Cooper

THE THIN BLUE LIFELINE: Verbal De-escalation of Mentally Ill and Emotionally Disturbed People
A Comprehensive Guidebook for Law Enforcement Officers
Ellis Amdur & John Hutchings

On Martial Arts

HIDDEN IN PLAIN SIGHT: Tracing the Roots of Ueshiba Morihei's Power
Ellis Amdur

Published by Freelance Academy Press, Inc. www.freelanceacademypress.com

DUELING WITH OSENSEI: Grappling with the Myth of the Warrior Sage
Ellis Amdur

OLD SCHOOL: Essays on Japanese Martial Traditions
Ellis Amdur

In Gratitude for Expert Critique

The following professionals have closely reviewed this book. With each draft, we corrected errors of fact, added new information, and fine-tuned the manuscript. One of the qualities of a good correctional officer is the understanding that the task supersedes protecting someone's feelings; therefore, we have appreciated all the direct criticism.

All responsibility for this book, however, must lie in our hands. Any errors, in particular, are our responsibility. Given that lives can be on the line in work such as this, please don't hesitate to contact us if you believe that any part of this book is inaccurate or requires additional material. The book will be revised, if needed, in future editions.

Deputy Sheriff Mike Hoekstra is a seven-year veteran of the Washoe County Sheriff's Office in Reno Nevada. He has spent many of those years specifically working with mental health inmates in the detention area. Along with working directly with the psychiatric staff, he has also completed many training courses including a weeklong Crisis Intervention Team (CIT) training. He is a member of the CIT, helping inmates to move forward to the many facilities and resources available to the mentally ill in the State of Nevada. He is currently assigned to the mental health unit in the Washoe County Detention Center and works directly with some of the most violent and high-risk inmates in the facility.

Executive Lieutenant Adam Hopkins is a twenty-three year veteran of the Washoe County Sheriff's Office in Reno Nevada. In this capacity he is responsible for running the Detention Bureau of approximately 200 commissioned personnel and approximately 1100 inmates. He has both Patrol and Detention experience both as a deputy and supervisor. Hopkins received his Bachelor in Science in Education from New Mexico State University in 1987. He is a certified Excited Delirium Instructor, and is the ranking instructor for Excited Delirium in Northern Nevada. He has extensive experience working with the mentally ill in both public and private psychiatric facilities as well as in the Detention setting. Hopkins is also the President of Lumicore Training, LLC, where he teaches on the topic of Excited Delirium and Agitated Chaotic Episodes, as well as other topics relevant to Law Enforcement and related fields.

Sergeant Danny D. Kaiser was hired with Clark County Sheriff's Office in 1981 as a Correction Officer, and in 1986 was appointed to work with the Jail Transport Team. He worked on the Sheriff's Office Health and Wellness committee, and was elected by his peers to serve as a shop steward. Corrections Officer Kaiser was promoted to Sergeant in 1994, and in 1995, became the supervisor for the Jail's Security Response Team. In 1996, he was appointed to work in the Internal Affairs Unit. During Sgt. Kaiser's civil service career he was also a citizen-soldier, serving 7 years on active duty, and then 20 years with the Oregon Air National Guard with the 142nd Security Forces Squadron. Sgt. Kaiser's Unit was mobilized after 9/11, and he spent the next 14 months back on active duty. After demobilization in 2003, he retired from the Air National Guard, and return to Jail Operations with the Sheriff's Office. In 2007, Sgt. Kaiser was appointed to the Sheriff's Office Training Unit, and for the next 4 years worked with Ellis Amdur to train and educate all of the Sheriff's Office members in working with and safely managing both the public and inmates who might find themselves in mental health crises. In 2007, Sgt. Kaiser was selected as the Sergeant of the Year. Sgt. Kaiser current position is in Operations, supervising and managing inmates with the Sheriff's Office.

Donald L. Leach II (Author of the Foreword)

Donald (Don) was the Administrative Officer, Senior (Deputy Director) for the Lexington-Fayette Urban County Division of Community Corrections, Lexington, Kentucky from 1996 to 2008. After serving in the Marine Corps, he graduated from the University of Kentucky in 1978 with a degree in Social and Political Theory, graduate work in Theory of Geography and holds a doctorate degree in Public Administration (Unaccredited). He began his employment with the Division of Community Corrections as a Deputy Jailer in 1984. Don has designed, developed, and supervised the Division's pre-service and in-service training programs, management information systems, and offender classification systems. He has developed contracts for a range of privatized jail services. Since 1993, he has served as a jail management consultant for agencies such as the National Institute of Corrections, the American Jail Association, Voorhis-Robertson Justice Services, the U.S. Department of Justice and the Ministry of Justice, Netherlands. Don also provides specialized consulting and expert witness services to individual jurisdictions across the United States. He has been active in implementing statewide jail risk management initiatives in South Carolina, Virginia, and Wisconsin. He has served as a First Vice President on the American Jail Association's Board of Directors.

Officer Drew Smetana has worked for the Clark County Sheriff's Office in Washington State for over twenty years. During his time with the department, he has been a Field Training Officer, a member of the Security Response Team, and has had extensive training and experience in High Risk Prisoner Transport. He is also a Custody Officer of the Year award winner.

Sergeant Darren Stewart has worked for the King County Jail in Washington State for nineteen years. His past assignments include Field Training Officer, Recruitment Coordinator, Jail Renovation Project Manager, Policy and Procedure Development Sergeant and he currently manages the King County Jail's training unit. He has earned credentials as a Firearms Instructor, Taser Instructor, Less Lethal Weapons Instructor, Correctional Emergency Response Instructor and Crisis Intervention Team Instructor.

FOREWORD

Donald Leach

In the very first paragraphs, the authors tell us in forthright terms exactly why we need to make this book a part of our operational philosophy guiding us in decisions regarding training, administration and the operation of our jails. Managing the mentally ill in jails, which were never designed nor intended to be acute medical and mental health care institutions, is a role thrust upon us as jail administrators. This "mission creep" is moving jails from a criminal justice function to a public health function. This movement makes a book of this depth and breadth ever more critical to the proper housing, supervision, and service provision for those placed in our charge.

It is a paradigm shift that needs to take place, but a shift guided by the knowledge the authors provide herein to ensure that we undertake our responsibilities in a humane and secure manner. Understanding the nature of mental illness, and the commensurate management issues is a critical first step. The authors provide insight and guidance that helps ease the difficulty that corrections historically demonstrated in making that first step.

The authors' use of real life experiences enhances the ability to relate to the topical subject being addressed. Those of us who have spent our careers in corrections will be able to relate to the examples, and identify individuals whom we have had in our care that exemplify them. This is where the value of the authors' experiences in dealing with the mentally ill in the community and correctional setting readily shines through. If you are new to the profession, learn from these illustrations; if you are an old hand in corrections, critique your own actions.

For at least the foreseeable future, public service budgets will continue to get hammered. The need to "do more with less" will only increase. Community mental health services have long been in a state of crisis, a situation that is destined to get worse. Fallback placement of the mentally ill has been, and will continue to be, the jail. The knowledge offered by the authors in this book could, and should, form the foundation for mental health training to new and on-line law enforcement staff in jails, prisons, and the community. In the absence of other resources, being informed is the best weapon in our arsenal in order to manage the mentally ill in the community and in our institutions.

Corrections and law enforcement have long held a paradigm involving a force response to a mental health problem. It is my belief that such a force response has been driven by fear, which arises from misunderstanding and ignorance. This seems especially true of our actions and reactions to inmates who are seriously mentally ill. This book will serve to buttress a change in the correctional and law enforcement paradigm from one focused on "control" to one concerned with care.

Introduction

This book is designed to address the unique challenges facing Institutional Correctional Officers (referred to as "correctional officers" in this text) assigned to supervise mentally ill inmates incarcerated in local jail settings. It is intended to increase officer and inmate safety by introducing specific identification and response strategies to manage distressed, threatening or aggressive inmates quickly and safely. The strategies and techniques presented in this book are to be used as a foundation upon which the individual correctional officer, and indeed entire agencies, can improve outcomes and increase safety.

The behaviors of mentally ill individuals can be quite bizarre. Through understanding such behaviors, you will become more skillful in assessing if an inmate is truly dangerous, and in many situations, you will have the ability to calm and deescalate such an individual. Often, you will find your presence alone prevents a situation from escalating, with inmates complying with directives willingly, with some even anxious to meet your approval or gain your respect.

Throughout this book we speak of officer safety. Officer safety is a subject that goes far beyond managing to survive a shift uninjured. In addition to the threat of violence, correctional officers routinely face serious job-related pressure including a lack of adequate staffing, mandatory overtime, rotating shift work, etc. However, dealing with bizarre, profoundly distressed and perhaps dangerous mentally disordered inmates can exponentially add to the rigors of the job. If correctional officers have confidence that they know the best way to communicate with these most confusing and sometimes dangerous inmates, their very stressful job will become less so, and therefore, safer in the bargain.

It is the hope of the authors, whose professional experiences encompass over sixty-five years of interaction in face-to-face encounters with mentally ill and emotionally disturbed individuals, that this book will be invaluable in readying both newer officers and experienced veterans for such encounters. You may find, however, that reading this book is not sufficient. For those interested in more hands-on training, the authors, in varying capacities, offer direct instruction, traveling to your location to provide not only basic de-escalation training, but advanced training in such areas as strategic communication with individuals with character disorders or anti-social traits, and tactical safety in the field. We also offer consultation services designed to formulate the best strategies to enhance officer, staff, and inmate safety.

This book is part of a series of guidebooks authored or co-authored by Ellis Amdur for people who must face aggressive individuals. Other books in these series are specific to those who work as emergency dispatchers, police officers, security professionals, parole/probation officers, hospitals, state and federal prisons, and social services personnel. The centerpiece of the series is a version for families who live with mentally ill family members. Please refer to the website www.edgework.info for more information on all of these books.

SECTION I

The Mentally Ill Inmate:
Inside the System

CHAPTER 1

Why Are Mentally Ill Individuals
Repeatedly Incarcerated?

Incarceration or Treatment: Are They Necessarily in Conflict?

The general public, and in fact, many correctional employees do not want to know about the inmates — only that they are secured and serving their time. They want justice (if not punishment) and safety. Most citizens will vote to fund education or pay to put more law enforcement officers out on the road, but are unlikely to willingly fund making jails and prisons a more "livable" place, much less funding what can be very expensive treatment and housing for mentally ill inmates.

The fields of mental health and corrections are, by definition, at odds with one another. Unfortunately, the purposes and goals of these systems often collide, particularly in regards to the individual with mental illness who breaks the law. We simply do not have a system that offers the best care for the mentally ill inmate as well as ensuring public safety at an optimum level.

Especially for small jails, having a therapist or case manager on staff, even during regular work hours, is considered a luxury. State facilities generally have the budget to fund long-term treatment for inmates, but small county or municipal facilities do not. It takes time, insight, and unfortunately, sometimes a law suit for agencies to acknowledge the need for mental health care inside their facilities.

Without the realization that, generally speaking, treatment for inmates pays off in behavioral dividends for the line correctional officer, inmates are subjected to repeated (albeit usually necessary) uses of force or sanctions for their disorderly behavior. Furthermore, such untreated inmates are often victimized in general population units or they victimize others. This leaves the institution little choice, but to house them in behavioral management units, where, isolated from other inmates, they are unable to participate in any programs, and separated from all but the barest of human interactions. The correctional facility may meet its obligation to the public by securing the inmate for the prescribed amount of time, but these inmates are then released back into the community, often untreated and dangerous, soon to re-offend.

The Correctional Officer Meets the Mentally Ill Inmate—Something not in the Basic Job Description

There is a range of reasons why someone chooses the field of corrections. For some, it's serving their community; for others it's being able to enforce the law. Many officers enter the field of corrections as a stepping-stone to placement as a law enforcement officer. Unfortunately, no one mentions the mentally ill until they are already hired.

Smaller correctional facilities do not require advanced degrees to work in corrections, and many of the officers have not been educated on even the basics about how and why a mental illness manifests itself. Unless the facility dedicates expensive training time specifically for dealing with mentally ill inmates, officers may never gain the skill or knowledge to successfully deal with potentially one of the most difficult and dangerous populations unless they do it on their own.

Concrete skills, such as Taser™, defensive tactics, threat identification, and cuffing are often easier to learn than "soft skills" of communication and body language, the latter being an almost constant requirement in correctional institutions. Just as with physical skills, you must strive to train your verbal responses into "pseudo-instinct, where you don't have to think before you effectively react, something that takes practice. It is not a matter of simply knowing the "right" thing to say; experts at de-escalation must have the fluidity to move from one style into another if the first doesn't work.

Should Jails Even Be Treating the Mentally Ill?

Whenever there are budget shortfalls, the focus of a law enforcement agency devolves to the expenditures of the agency, forgetting that law enforcement has an ethical obligation to the community it serves. How can you protect your community if you are laying off officers, reducing or eliminating training, and not even providing necessary equipment? Lean times require cutting the extras, and funding the well-being of mentally ill inmates is often one of the first things to be pared away.

From insufficient budgets to untaught educational requirements, the correctional industry does not adequately foster the appropriate treatment of the mentally ill inmate. To be sure, one can easily assert that jails should not even be involved in the treatment of such individuals. However, since no-one else is taking the responsibility of caring for the misdemeanant mentally ill, much less those who commit felonies and are awaiting adjudication, it naturally falls to the jail systems to take care of this population.

Even with good intentions and a will to implement a program on behalf of the inmate, it is hard to set up a long-term treatment plan when jails do not even provide long-term incarceration. Many of our most troubled and hard-to-manage mentally ill inmates never commit felonies which would facilitate their movement into the state or federal prison system, where there are multiple mental health professionals on staff as well as twenty-four hour medical care. Misdemeanant mentally ill inmates are often arrested for trespassing or domestic violence charges, for failing to pay a restaurant bill or theft of property. Many are brought in on drug charges. These offenses generally do not carry long enough sentences to get the inmate to a prison facility. Instead, they become caught in a dysfunctional loop of arrest, equivocal stabilization and release back into the community, untreated and without supervision, then back to jail once again.

Structural Issues

Listed below are a number of long standing issues that often lead to the mentally ill inmate not receiving a comprehensive adequate level of care.

- **Physical Plant Problems.** Many of the older jails were designed for incarceration purposes alone. All too often, there is a lack of dedicated space in jails for the care and treatment of the mentally ill. In such situations, general population housing is converted for the use of the mentally ill, often lacking appropriate clinical space, step-down or intermediate care units and/or programs.

- **Inadequate Infirmaries.** Many facilities have medical staff and programs, but these are generally focused on general population inmates and are usually not capable of providing crisis level mental health treatment. Most treatment takes place in the unit where the inmate is housed, unless they are contagious or present a potential for victimization from other inmates. Many older facilities do not contain air handlers that can maintain the proper temperature level within the facility to maintain the quality of many medications that are heat sensitive.

- **Access Issues.** All of the clinical resources in the world will be of little value if the inmate cannot access the resources they need. Count time, lockdowns, feeding, recreation, therapy, and locked doors and wings contribute to inmates being unable to physically travel to areas of the jail to routinely access services, as well as interfering with clinical staffs' access to them. Providing scheduled, uninterrupted clinical time requires the jail to dedicate an officer or two to moving the inmates from their units to the clinic.

The Revolving Door

Mentally ill inmates are in the wrong place, with the wrong people, and given the severe overcrowding that is endemic in most jails in the United States, are lost among the numbers. Beyond the funding and structural issues that have already been described, these problems are exacerbated by:

- **Lack of Staff.** There is rarely enough correctional staff to protect them, to manage their behaviors, and to create a milieu that will actually ameliorate their symptomology.

- **Lack of Training.** Few jail systems have adequate mental health training for correctional officers, even though they spend more time with their mentally challenged inmate populations than with general population inmates.

- **Lack of Mental Health Professionals.** There are rarely enough mental health professionals available. In order to provide service to the mentally ill in today's jails, appropriate numbers of psychiatrists, psychologists, therapists, medical records staff, and pharmacists are necessary to allow for a constitutional level of service (see below). This is particularly true in large jails where the inmate population can total several thousand, and fifteen to twenty percent of that population is mentally ill. In many institutions, therapist positions often go wanting or are filled with poorly qualified personnel. "Therapy sessions" can be little more than a roll-call walk through a jail block or tier(s) by a counselor.

- **Treatment With Only Medication.** All too often, medication is the only assistance routinely available. In some cases, older less effective drugs are utilized due to budgetary concerns.

Figure 1.1 How scheduling can impede care
In many jails, scheduling requires that prisoners receive and take medications in the early evening, even though those specific medications should be taken just before a patient goes to sleep. This results in an inmate who is drowsy and unable to follow direction, who is then viewed as non-compliant.

- **Staff Turnover.** Turnover among correctional and clinical staff can be destabilizing for the mentally ill. Information that is known to help an inmate can be lost when staff transfer out or leave.

- **Insufficient Level of Care.** Mental health care in jails rarely provides specialized facilities to provide a licensed hospital or clinical correctional level of care for the most seriously ill. If there are court ordered evaluations that need to take place in licensed care, the waiting list is long and it can take a month or more for the inmate to be transferred. This translates into longer incarceration times.

- **Inadequate Assessment and Information Management.** Poor screening tools and assessments, and inadequate data management and tracking can all be factors in misidentifying or being unable to provide adequate care and treatment. Furthermore, some mental health and medical practitioners' interpretation of HIPPA laws has made it even more difficult to get access to protected health information. Although there is a clear exemption in HIPPA for law enforcement, many medical and mental health professionals are resistant to releasing information on their patients to law enforcement officers.[1]

- **Disruption of Care Due to Transfers.** The regular movement and unit-transfers of prisoners within large jails makes continuity of care nearly impossible.

- **Mental illness May Not Be Noticed.** Because many, if not most, jail populations are comprised of young adults within age ranges where chronic mental illnesses first begin to appear, many prisoners begin to develop signs of illness after they are already incarcerated and unfortunately are not readily diagnosed. This is further complicated by the rampant use of drugs among incarcerated inmates. Long term methamphetamine use, in particular, can cause causes drug-induced psychosis indistinguishable from such major mental illnesses as schizophrenia and schizoaffective disorder, but even marijuana use can exacerbate latent mental illness within a vulnerable individual.

- **Disciplinary Methods Can Be Destructive.** Disciplinary methods can be destructive to a mentally ill inmate's stability. The use of segregation or isolation units as either a disciplinary or protective measure can have an adverse effect in the mentally ill unless, unusually, the segregation unit is either within a licensed clinical correctional facility, or has a comprehensive mental health program for those segregated inmates. When held in segregation or isolation, even under strict clinical protocols, mentally ill inmates tend to "act out" and engage in self-destructive acts such as the destruction of personal property, or the cell and its furnishings, feces smearing, as well as self-mutilation and even suicide.

This lack of proper care may begin a cycle of disruptive behavior that is exacerbated by isolation, causing more psychological distress and disruptive behavior, all the way to his or her eventual confinement in an acute care treatment bed where they may become more stable. Ironically, stabilization is often followed with a transfer to an unlocked general population setting, resulting in the inmate decompensating again. For the mentally ill, the jail not only becomes a warehouse with a revolving door aspect between segregation units and the general population, but also can become an incubator for decompensation and further psychiatric breakdowns.

Things do not improve upon release. Because jail mental health programs are often not well coordinated with local mental health care providers, many, if not, most of the mentally ill persons leaving jail receive little, if any, aftercare. Even that which is offered is often poorly coordinated with the jail; resulting in changes to their medications and treatment patterns at each agency they are placed.

Inadequate pre-release planning, and a lack of adequate community resources, such as primary care and treatment, makes the possibility of a successful reentry to the community a highly unlikely event for the mentally ill parolee. Worse, and truly absurdly, much of the onus for the continuity of treatment falls upon the inmate who, released from a structured environment, must cope with life within the community where there is no schedule or predictability, and where ostracism, the lack of opportunity or ability to garner gainful employment, homelessness and poly-drug and/or alcohol abuse pretty much guarantee continued interruptions in treatment. All too often, the released inmate, whether on parole or freed outright, soon degenerates to community crimes to eat or more likely, to maintain one or more addictive habits. Soon, they are arrested for one or more new criminal offenses or for violation(s) of their parole conditions and find themselves back within the jail system.

The Need for a System of Interagency Cooperation

There must be continuity of care as well as purposeful boundaries and rules so that an inmate/client is confronted with the same plan of action from one agency to the next. Continual re-enforcement of medication and treatment schedules as well as rules to live by ("You can't go to Denny's restaurant, they have a no-trespass order against you, remember?") would serve this population in better ways that the turbulent cycle within which they are now enmeshed.

Aside from the lack of continuity, we are creating a complicated system that guarantees that mentally ill inmates will fail in their endeavors to get better by giving them opposing or differing goals. Inmates who cannot handle their own appointment calendar are not going to be able to balance their probation appointment and pay schedules along with their mental health appointment schedule and medication management. If their probation contains provisions to keep them on their medications (usually a court order is required here), there must be a substantial amount of cooperation between agencies so that this can actually occur.

Instead of each agency having to deal with the same inmate over and over, why not come together for arrest and pre-release planning, and deal with the inmate only once? Pooling resources together to offer training to all agencies would reduce costs and put into place the needed skills for each officer and mental health worker. Time put in on the front end of a situation almost always pays off at the other end:

- **No Duplication of Services.** One plan means that services will not be duplicated, and different individuals will not waste time "reinventing the wheel," resulting in the reduction of man-hours spent on a single individual. If one agency's plan conflicts with the next (for instance from jail to probation) then everyone's time has been wasted.

- **The Inmate's Time Is Not Wasted.** Inmates realize that you place a value on their time as well as your own. This builds trust.

- **Reduced Training Costs.** A reduction in training costs will result when there is a system-wide dissemination of useful mental health or law enforcement knowledge and tactics. Everyone educates everyone else.

- **Limits Manipulation Opportunities for Inmates.** When all providers are in contact with one another, manipulative inmates/offenders have less opportunity to set various stakeholders at odds with one another.

Figure 1.2 Author's Experience: A Success Story

David was frequently incarcerated in a local county correctional facility. He could be violent, and was continually off and on community supervision following convictions for a string of misdemeanor crimes—usually involving trespass or obstructing law enforcement. Each incarceration was extended, due to multiple referrals to state mental facilities for evaluations. Although David was known to be a methamphetamine user along with his diagnosed mental illness, he was never sent to a treatment facility. He frequently was returned to jail on probation violations for using methamphetamine.

Each time he was sent for an evaluation, he was usually (re)diagnosed, often differently from before, stabilized with medications, and then sent back to the correctional facility where he immediately decompensated. Upon release, he would return to the community, where his protective payee for his state benefits was his mother, also a known meth user. If his mother paid for a place for David to live, it was usually in a local motel known for hourly rates and a brisk drug trade/trafficking area.

David's last two arrests showed a pattern of increasing danger. In the first, he was taken down by Taser and nearly shot while being arrested for a mere parole violation; in the second, his arrest was prompted by calls from the community of a man playing tag with the cars on the local highway—except he was not in a car.

The jail facility called an informal meeting with the in-house mental health team, incarceration team, community mental health team and his probation team—all of whom had been dealt with David individually for years. None, apart, could get him stabilized.

Together they made an action plan to send David to a state facility for long-term stabilization, to have his protective payee changed to mental health professionals, and for his most recent charges to be dropped. He was to remain on community supervision. After his long-term stabilization, he was released to a therapeutic group home. He has not been incarcerated for the past three years.

Eighth Amendment Issues

According to the letter of the law, we are badly failing mentally ill inmates. Jail officials are obligated under the Eighth Amendment[2] to provide prisoners with a system of ready access to adequate mental health care:

- There must first be a systematic program for screening and evaluating inmates in order to identify those who require mental health care.
- Treatment must entail more than segregation and close supervision of the inmate/patient.
- Treatment requires the participation of trained mental health professionals who must be employed in sufficient numbers to identify and treat in an individualized manner, those treatable inmates suffering from serious mental disorders.
- The provider must maintain accurate, complete and confidential records of the mental health treatment process.
- Prescription and administration of behavior altering medications in dangerous amounts by dangerous methods, or without appropriate supervision and periodic evaluation is an unacceptable method of treatment.
- A basic program for the identification of inmates with suicidal tendencies is a necessary component of any mental health inmate treatment program.

Actionable harm resulting from jail staff not following Eighth Amendment requirements include:

- Failure to follow-up on prisoners with known or suspected mental health disorders.
- Failure to provide adequate numbers of qualified mental health staff.
- Housing mentally ill prisoners in segregation without adequate mental health access.
- Failure to transfer mentally ill prisoners to more appropriate facilities.
- Improper use of restraints.
- Excessive use of force against mentally ill inmates.
- And finally, jail officials and correctional staff who fail to provide protections and treatment for the mentally ill may be seen at both the state and federal level of court to be "deliberately indifferent" to the care and treatment of their charges.

Deliberate indifference is defined as being aware there is a problem, but doing nothing to alleviate it. It is manifested by jail administration/staff when they recklessly disregard a substantial risk of harm to the prisoners who are their responsibility. In the context we are using, it is applied to the mental health needs of prisoners, but jail staff should be aware that its definition is applicable to **any** jail process or function which impacts those rights assigned to the incarcerated under the auspices of the Eighth Amendment.

Figure 1.3 Deliberate Indifference

Deliberate indifference in the eyes of the court bears a higher threshold than negligence and requires that the jail official knows of and disregards an excessive risk of harm to the prisoner. The proof of a jail official's knowledge of a substantial risk to the prisoner's mental health is established by either **circumstantial evidence;** for example, it may be inferred that prisoners' mental health is deteriorating with such evidence as weight loss, self-mutilation, suicide, etc., or by **direct evidence** in documents such as requests for interviews, sick call slips, psychiatric records, grievances, appeals, etc.

Jail officials and staff cannot escape liability if the evidence shows that the official(s) declined to verify underlying facts that were strongly suspected to be true, or declined to confirm instances of risk that were strongly expected to exist.

Remedies for such violations have resulted in federal oversight of jail mental health programs, and can also result in monetary judgments against jail departments and staff.

CHAPTER 2

Who Are the Mentally Ill in Jail?

The vast majority of people with mental illness are productive members of their communities. Incarceration of a small minority of this population is usually the end of some series of events that also included the failure to take care of themselves. They may come into the jail dehydrated. Often they are homeless and have been living in abandoned buildings or on the street. Needless to say, hygiene has usually not been one of their priorities. Some are violent for a myriad of reasons, some of which we are only now beginning to understand. On the other hand, mental illness does not affect intelligence. (Try to convince someone with a quantum physics degree that there are not demons in his room or better yet, that you aren't a demon!) When we look at behavior rather than diagnosis, incarcerated mentally ill inmates roughly divide into five populations:

- **Chronic Mentally Ill Inmates.** These are inmates, typically diagnosed with schizophrenia, schizoaffective disorder and/or bipolar disorder, who commit a string of misdemeanor crimes, and regularly frequent the same jail. Officers usually know them by name, and know what interventions work with them and what do not.
- **Developmental Delayed Inmates.** This population of inmates has developmental disabilities (intellectual/developmental disabilities or fetal alcohol syndrome, for example) that affect their cognitive abilities and maturity levels. They may also have mental illnesses beyond their developmental disability. They are usually booked in on domestic violence charges or custodial assaults.
- **Violent Mentally Ill Inmates.** These inmates are highly violent and aggressive. They generally fall into one of two categories: those that are experiencing hallucinations or delusions, and those inmates that will not cooperate with the simplest of directives because they resist your control. The first tend to be psychotic (**Chapters 41/42**), whereas the latter are primarily paranoid (**Chapter 33**).
- **Crisis Inmates.** These are the inmates who would otherwise be productive society members but due to some crisis, have stopped taking their medications or had a breakdown in their life, causing deterioration in their level of functioning.
- **Victim Mentally Ill Inmates.** These mentally-ill inmates are usually actively involved in criminal activities such as prostitution or theft, and are often controlled by another person, usually a non-mentally ill criminal, who uses them as a source of income.

In this chapter we are going to take a closer look at each of these populations and how such individuals tend to end up incarcerated. Of course, these categories are a general overview of the most prevalent populations. Because mental illness manifests itself differently in each person, there are inmates that will not fit into these five categories, or may fit into more than one. Given changing circumstances, inmates may shift from one category to another.

The Chronic Mentally Ill Inmate (Chronic MI Inmate)

This inmate is generally not overtly aggressive, but can be if they feel threatened or pressured. They frequently lack support or even contact with their family and friends, and are frequently homeless. They often don't like or believe in the value of medications, or sometimes, because they think they are cured, discontinue taking prescribed medications. They get booked in on a string of misdemeanor charges ranging from trespassing, domestic violence assaults, or custodial assaults. Another frequent charge is "dine and dash" or in some jurisdictions, quaintly known as "defrauding an innkeeper," meaning going into a restaurant, having dinner, and then refusing to pay.

Correctional officers know these inmates by first names, and often know their families. When these inmates are brought in to the booking window, officers will often change places or calls will go out on the radio to get an officer that the inmate likes to book them. Conversely, some officers will try to stay out of view because the inmate doesn't like them, and escalates when they see them. Officers will know on which of these inmates that pepper spray does or does not work, or what verbal interventions either calm them down or enflames them. They sometimes know that the inmate's family will bail them out, or put money in their commissary account for them.

The Chronic MI Inmate will often spend more time in jail than an inmate who is not mentally ill who commits the same crime. Conversely, there are times that such charges will be dropped: small jurisdictions cannot afford the lengthy mental health evaluations and treatments required to "restore" an inmate to competency. Faced with an enormous bill for psychiatric care, smaller agencies sometimes dismiss the charges to avoid the bill.

When the Chronic MI Inmate goes to court, their attorney will almost invariably request a mental health evaluation. If this is granted, the speedy trial rule is signed away as the state mental health hospitals are crowded, and there is a back-log of inmates waiting for evaluations. If the defense or prosecution does not like the outcome of the state evaluation, they can ask for a private doctor to complete a second evaluation, hoping to dispute the first. Each evaluation can take weeks if not months to complete. By the time court reconvenes to decide competency issues (let alone guilt or innocence), the inmate may have done more time in the jail than if they had just pled guilty in the first place. The benefit of this scenario is that, de facto, the inmate does receive treatment, but it is doubtful the inmate views being incarcerated for up to a year as a benefit. Rather than a year's worth of incarceration time, in which treatment is "bootlegged in," were the inmate placed in an appropriate psychiatric facility with effective outpatient follow-up, they would likely stabilize far sooner.

Attorneys often avoid these clients, or put off working on their case. These inmates often have their own ideas about their cases—essentially making it up as they go along, while completely believing everything they say. One of the authors refers to this as "speaking into being" meaning, "if I said it, it's real." This is clinically referred to as "magical thinking." If they tell you they were wrongly arrested, you are never going to convince them otherwise, even if you have the warrant or citation in your hand. If they feel that you have wronged them in even the slightest way, you will only get back in their good graces if another person does something worse (in their mind) to take the spotlight off of you—and that might not work either. You might stay on their "enemies list" for life. Sometimes you will have no idea what caused them to turn on you. You may have dealt peacefully with them for years, but suddenly, for no apparent reason, it's your turn to be the bad guy.

Some such inmates are often brought to jail naked, at best wearing underwear, or when they are booked in, they soon strip off their uniforms. Inmates who are this severely ill are generally isolated due to disruptive behaviors at booking, and they tend to stay naked in their isolation cells until they are released. Some inmates use blood, urine and feces to cover their cells, and sometimes themselves, sometimes for months on end. Even more horribly, some eat their own excrement. This behavior works to their advantage by decreasing exposure to other inmates and providing them with their own cell. It is also a manifestation of the absolute destitution and horror they experience isolated in a locked cell while in the throes of mental illness, or conversely, when exposed to the aggressive chaotic environment of general population. They often have to be moved from their cells with force so the officers can clean it. These inmates are then pushed into showers as they refuse to clean themselves. (How many days can you leave an inmate smeared in his or her own fecal matter before it becomes negligence? And how many such occurrences does it take before officers become burned out, or worse, regard such inmates with contempt or even hatred?). Some officers are more stressed by these inmates than any others: one can feel completely helpless in dealing with them, yet one is forced to witness and experience humanity at its most repulsive. To make matter worse, these profoundly ill people are also some of the highest risk inmates for self-harm and aggressive behavior.

The Developmentally Delayed Inmate

These inmates, moderately to severely cognitively impaired, are frequently booked on Domestic Violence Assault or Custodial Assault charges. Developmentally Delayed Inmates are often taken care of by aging parents or they are placed in an adult care facility. They often strike out against the people closest to them when aggravated—family and other caregivers. Developmentally Delayed Inmates, appear childlike. They are easily victimized, rarely treatable, and often lack a basic understanding of the world beyond their own home—let alone jail.

There are many social, environmental, and physical causes of developmental disabilities, although for some a definitive cause may never be determined. Treatment of developmental delays in a corrections facility is about behavior management. Consider this statement, "All behavior is functional." Their behavior is often the root of the problem: getting upset, yelling, hitting and intimidation may have garnered attention in a family home, group home or community living facility, but in a corrections environment this behavior can be devastating. In most states, the system for developmentally disabled individuals is even more underfunded and under-resourced than the mental health or corrections systems. The resources for training and interventions in the jails is limited and for these reasons few if any officers want to manage them.

They will be incarcerated within your facility, and regardless of their treatability, these inmates can be prepared for in advance, through specialized training and programming Your jail can work with other agencies to set up release planning for them as well. This requires liaison beyond the mental health system, establishing working relationships with the various agencies associated with the care, housing and treatment of the developmentally disabled.

The Violent Mentally Ill Inmate (Violent MI Inmate)

Violent Mentally Ill Inmates make up one of the smallest portions of incarcerated mentally ill inmates. This is fortunate because these inmates consume time and resources quickly. If a local agency is unlucky enough to have two or more of these inmates incarcerated at the same time the majority of officers' time will be taken up with them, to the detriment of all other inmates in the jail.

Violent MI Inmates often come in to jail dehydrated, violent, and fighting. They may not have slept for days and will go on for more days in jail without sleeping, eating, or drinking. This drains even more resources. Medical intervention may be necessary when the inmate becomes physically compromised. Time and resources will be taken up at the judicial level, too, if a court order is needed to use chemical restraints (injectable medications) for the inmate's well-being. Officers will more than likely have to wrestle the inmate to the ground in order to give them the medications.

Other Violent MI Inmates simply will not comply with the simplest directive because they choose not to. Whether or not they are hearing voices or perceiving hallucinations through other senses, they are very paranoid **(Chapter 33)**, and very angry towards anyone they perceive as having authority over them or in any way controlling them. These inmates will get offended at the slightest thing, "Why are you looking at me like that?" "Why did you look away when you were talking to me?" "Is that a smirk on your face?" "Get out of my room!" "Don't touch my stuff!" "Don't touch me!" Anything and everything will set them off. For the person dealing with them, there is no right answer; nothing will please this inmate or calm them.

Violent MI Inmates are unimpressed by consequences. If you take away their books, they may write on their uniforms. If you take away their pencils, they may rip their uniforms. If you take away their uniforms, they may rip apart their cells. If you restrain them in chains, they may try to kill themselves. If you put them in a restraint chair, they may urinate and defecate all over themselves and the chair and try to spit on you and bite you. Sometimes they will take bites out of their own flesh. When you try to take them out of the chair and clean them up, they will fight you. If you leave them naked in a cell, they flood the cell. If you turn off the water they may plug their toilets with fecal matter. When you come into unplug it, they may throw fecal matter, urine, and/or blood on you. If you don't try to unplug it or tell them to unplug it, they may smear the room and themselves with fecal matter. They may even eat it.

Violent MI Inmates are some of the highest risk inmates in any correctional population. If they can't hurt another person, they may just as readily hurt themselves. These inmates will often have multiple "use of force" events involving a Taser™ or pepper spray whereas most inmates will, after only one use of force with either of these less-than-lethal weapons, decide that they do not want to re-experience it.

The Crisis Mentally Ill Inmate (Crisis MI Inmate)

This population of inmates is the polar opposite of the Violent MI Inmates. Crisis Mentally Ill Inmates are functioning members of their community with treatable mental illnesses, or sometimes an immediate crisis that causes them to reach a "breaking point." They usually have homes, jobs and families. They may have a nurse practitioner, doctor or treatment team who monitors their medication and mood. However, a crisis in their life sends them into a spiral. In other instances, they quit taking their medications for any one of a number of reasons. They usually get arrested for a misdemeanor—theft, trespassing, driving under the influence, sometimes for a domestic violence charge—and they end up in jail.

Crisis MI Inmates are ill equipped to deal with real criminals or the jail environment. They are at risk for victimization in correctional facilities, and above and beyond their current charge, would not normally be leading a life of crime. Crisis MI Inmates can receive secondary trauma simply from the booking and jail processes. (Imagine going through a strip search while in a psychotic or suicidal state!) More often than not, once they are stabilized, they are shocked and appalled at their behavior and subsequent incarceration. Even if they have more than a single episode of incarceration, it is usually for non-violent misdemeanors.

Crisis MI Inmates usually have families who are deeply worried for them and who bail them out as soon as possible. Because this occurs before they are stabilized, this may not be a good solution either. They might be better served in a crisis care facility, and when released, be under the guidance of a probation officer or case manager until they truly restore themselves to stability.

The Victim Mentally Ill Inmate (Victim MI Inmate)

Victim Mentally Ill Inmates aren't as common as some of the other types of mentally ill inmates in correctional facilities, but they are certainly one of the saddest for professionals to deal with. These inmates usually have mental illnesses that are treatable, and could live very stable and fruitful lives; however, without a family to help or an honest protective payee, manipulative criminals easily prey on them. For example, many people with mental illness cannot be gainfully employed, but receive monthly SSI or Veterans' checks. The government funds that are meant to help a debilitated member of our society have instead placed a very large target on those needing it, visible to anyone of the many criminals who want to make a dollar or have the perverse urge to control and corrupt the life of another person.

The easiest way to control such a vulnerable person is through love or drugs—or both. Criminals isolate Victim MI Inmates from family and/or other support people. The criminal enlists his victim to steal from their family, their friends, to borrow money and never repay it. Soon the criminal is the only person the mentally ill person has access to. All information coming in or going out of the relationship is carefully monitored and sifted by the criminal—after all, knowledge is power. They also control their prescription medication (if they allow the person to take them) and any other drugs: generally, they sell the prescriptions on the street. The criminal eventually will turn the Victim MI Inmate to criminal activity, generally prostitution for women and burglary or theft for men. The cycle of crime and jail begins. Without any support system to help them out of the cycle, they may soon slip beyond saving, despite all of our efforts. When these inmates are released from jail, it is their pimp or their dealer who picks them up because, tragically, that is the only person who is interested in their continuing welfare, and that is only as a source of income.

CHAPTER 3

Life for the Mentally Ill In Prison

Incarceration can be traumatizing to some, and irrelevant to others. For many, it is somewhere in-between. For some mentally ill inmates, jail may be the safest, most comforting place they know. For others, it is hell.

Mentally ill prisoners are generally at the lowest strata of the jail inmate hierarchy. They are often disheveled in appearance, destitute of funds to purchase inmate commissary commodities, lacking any resources including, sadly, even visits from family members, and unable to hold the higher paying jobs in jail, due to both emotional instability and impaired cognitive abilities. The mentally ill inmate is often unprepared to navigate the difficult and sometimes treacherous waters of a jail within the United States.

More often than not, Crisis MI Inmates do not possess the mindset or skills to successfully navigate the jail environment or the justice process. They frequently become Victim MI Inmates if a criminal gets their claws into them or if their family or support network cuts off contact with them.

For example, under-going a strip search—even for a mentally unimpaired individual—can be humiliating and frightening. For a person who is mentally ill or distraught, this can become a terrifying, emotionally scarring event. These inmates may not have ever been incarcerated, seen any violence first hand or ever been threatened beyond a heated text message or posting on Facebook. Because of jail culture, they often cannot even ask for help. For example, if a Crisis MI Inmate were threatened by a gang member, and reported the threat to a correctional officer, they would be marked as a snitch and then at risk from nearly all the inmates.

Crisis MI Inmates have to be separated from most general population inmates. General population inmates make fun of them, victimize them, steal from them, and/or beat them. On the other hand, they often exhibit behaviors that are annoying or frightening to other inmates. If properly processed and housed at intake, Crisis MI Inmates have the best chance of exiting the justice system without becoming career criminals through proper referral and treatment with the Medical and Mental Health Teams. With support from family or from case managers, these folks tend to get back on track.

Violent MI Inmates cannot operate within the parameters that society has decided upon, and more often than not, cannot even function inside a correctional facility. They break the rules wherever they are, and wherever they go. The simplest directive such as, "flush your toilet" is met with a verbal outburst, if not a physical one. These are the inmates that will hit and kick the walls if they can't hit you, even to the extent of breaking their own bones. They are not, however, usually at risk of victimization, unless placed in a general population unit where more than one inmate can gang up on them. Even then, the consequences may be dire for the attackers. This type of inmate, male or female, will often keep getting up and attacking, no matter what the cost to himself or herself.

For most mentally ill inmates, even the physical environment is an assault on their senses. It is a land of walls, uncompromising rules, and fluorescent lighting. It is too loud, too bright and too noisy. Couple this with insufficient "nourishing" human interaction (in the form of programs, medication management and therapy), and these inmates become more and more ill.

Specialized Housing

Because of these problems, many mentally ill inmates are placed in protective custody, administrative segregation or housed alone. Protective custody is when the inmate asked not to be housed with anyone else for fear of harm. Administrative segregation is when the facility decides to house the inmate separately because of one of the following reasons:

- The inmate would victimize others.
- Other inmates would victimize the inmate.
- The inmate would pose a serious threat to the security and safety of the institution (such as a local crime lord or someone involved in a very high profile case).

In any and all of the above situations, the inmate would be housed alone and not allowed to participate in programs that involve other inmates. This takes the mentally ill inmate from an over-stimulating and frightening environment to an under-stimulating, profoundly boring environment. Inmates that are left with very little day-to-day interaction soon learn to cherish any kind of attention or activity that is diversionary, be it positive or negative. It is often in these circumstances that mentally ill inmates engage in damaging and degrading actions such as self-mutilation, destruction of their cell and their own possessions, and feces smearing.

Long-term facilities try to "program" with the inmates. Counselors and other professionals meet with the inmate through the door to their cell. The inmates turn in written homework or journal entries. Some long-term correctional facilities actually have rolling cells, or inmate containment units. The inmates are placed in these rolling cells where they—and everyone around them—are safe. Several of the inmate containment units are brought together for programs with an instructor. This allows social interaction with other inmates and professionals who are trained to deal with extreme behaviors. Inmates who act inappropriately are simply wheeled out of the learning environment and class continues.

Can Mentally Ill Inmates Serve Their Sentences in the Community?

On the other hand, some inmates who are mildly affected by their illness can take part in work release or electronic home monitoring programs and work themselves out of jail fairly quickly.

- Crisis MI Inmates, in particular, can adapt to home monitoring and deferred programs.

- Victim MI Inmates may possibly benefit, but inmates on programs cannot make money for their pimps or dealers. Therefore, effective parole/probation of Victim MI Inmates <u>must</u> factor in protection from the controlling criminal, or they will surely fail.
- Violent MI Inmates rarely meet the needed criteria for most of these programs.
- Developmentally Delayed Inmates, on the other hand, can successfully serve their sentences in the community <u>if they have a support network or caregiver</u>.
- Chronic MI Inmates also are unlikely to meet the criteria for alternatives to incarceration unless they receive comprehensive wrap-around services. Often the main limitations for them succeeding are situational: homelessness and lack of effective treatment outside the jail setting.

CHAPTER 4

What Do Mentally Ill Inmates Need?

The purpose of classification is to ensure the safety of the community, institution, staff, and inmates. Classification deals with concrete facts: criminal history, current crime, and institutional behavior. Care must be taken to ensure, as much as possible, that security classification(s) do not over-ride treatment needs. The security classification determines where the level of care will be implemented; not what level of care is offered. Treatment requirements, as medical necessities, should be independent of security status or location as much as possible, even though there must be exceptions in locked wings or jail setting where lockdowns must frequently occur. Mentally ill inmates, therefore, should not be housed in disciplinary units (unless they are being disciplined). Even though the physical properties of the cells may be desirable for the mentally ill inmates, placing them in a disciplinary unit is punishing them because they are mentally ill.

Ultimately, good treatment enhances institutional security while good security enhances treatment. Any decisions regarding the nature, level, or type of security required during periods of treatment should be collaborative between security staff and clinicians, ensuring appropriate correctional staff and inmate safety as well as the inmates' therapeutic concerns.

In order to achieve a comprehensive mental health program within a jail setting, there a number of essential components:
- **Training and Consultation.** Mental health training appropriate to the role of particular staff is absolutely necessary and in some states mandated by correctional guidelines. Staff should receive routine training related to the signs and symptoms of the mentally ill, de-escalation tactics appropriate to specific behaviors, as well as an understanding of the policies and practices of the facility's mentally ill program. To the greatest extent possible, such training should begin in staff orientation followed by mandatory training at no less than an annual basis. For staff that routinely interact with mentally ill inmates, training modules for refresher purposes should occur more frequently. All training records should be maintained by a dedicated in-service training division.
- **A Suicide Prevention Program.** Training on the ability to recognize suicidal inmates and structured planning on dealing with the suicidal inmate are not only necessary, but also in many instances mandated by state or correctional guidelines.[3] The protocol for inmates who have expressed suicidal ideation or who have made a suicide attempt must be completely understood by all staff, including knowledge on how to access a mental health professional for assessment and planning.
- **An Acute Care Intervention Protocol.** The protocol for individuals in acute mental health crisis, including suicidal events, is handled by the correctional staff until the mental health counsel-

ors are on site. There must be a safe place to house and monitor a suicidal inmate until they have been medically cleared, signed a safety plan, or other case management options have been put in place. Padded cells with tear resistant clothing and bedding need to be available as inmates have hanged themselves with socks, underwear, sheets, and uniforms. Some facilities require twenty-four hour direct observation of suicidal inmates while others require seven-minute checks. Inmates who are actively trying to harm themselves must to be restrained in a safe and humane manner. Many options exist from cocoon boards to restraint chairs and benches. Inmates who are restrained must have their restraints checked, and must still be offered water, food, and access to toilet facilities. Training must include an understanding of how to assess if the inmate is calming or is becoming increasingly suicidal or agitated. Lastly, staff must establish the criteria that the inmate is required to meet to be deemed no longer suicidal or otherwise in crisis, and to return to previous housing. It is imperative that each step of the protocol is simple to follow, that staff has received training on the protocol and that it is followed to the letter in each and every instance.

- **Reintegration Planning**. Depending on the institution's clearing process, inmates who have contracted for their safety ideally should spend a few days in transitional housing before returning to their previous or new housing assignment. This transitional housing assignment should afford a higher level of monitoring by the correctional staff and more face-to-face time with case managers. This housing should also limit the amount of items that an inmate can have in their dorm (such as a "no-sharps" unit). As the inmate progresses, more items and privileges can be returned. This is not punishment, but a gradual return to what is normal for the inmate with the added precautions of additional observation from security and treatment professionals.

- **Stabilization Planning.** Jail populations are mercurial by nature and case managers are nearly always overloaded, operating without a concrete timeline for any of their clients. Their focus is on medication-management and an overall stabilization of each inmate. Long term care must be left to outside referrals.

- **A Special Needs Unit**. Such facilities are necessary for inmates who do not require inpatient treatment, but require a therapeutic milieu due to their inability to function adequately within the general population. Without the ability to fully fund such a treatment unit, the best many smaller institutions can provide is often separate housing—either in small dorms or single units—with increased accessibility to medical/mental health staff and increased security checks. If small jails have the option of establishing a contractual arrangement, they will often send such inmates to a larger jail in order to get more services for mentally ill inmates.

- **Outpatient Referral Services**. Case Managers try to send mentally ill inmates out the door with (at least) medication and referrals to outside case management. Sometimes the court will order that the inmate take their medication as part of their probation. How much medication an inmate will receive upon release should be contingent upon a reasonable estimate on how long it will take the inmate to be linked with services on the outside. This could range from one week to over a month's worth. Unfortunately, inmates are often released with a minimal amount, merely a few days, and once that runs out, they soon decompensate.

- **Discharge/Transfer Planning.** Adequate discharge planning is a fiscally sound process that goes a long way towards reducing recidivism and a costly return to jail following a violation of parole or an entirely new crime.[4] When transferring from one facility to another, jails should put together a package of information for the next facility including information on medical care and institutional behavior. However, although state facilities can afford to budget for release planning, small jails are not funded for it. If release planning is going to happen, it must be implemented as a cooperative endeavor between local agencies.

- **Evolving Issues.** Evolving issues include mental health input into the inmate disciplinary process; discharge planning for inmates with serious mental illness; management of inmates with inappropriate sexual behaviors; special requirements for the care of female mentally ill inmates; the development and use of quality improvement systems; inmate management information systems; and substance abuse treatment modalities.

- **Malingering.** While there is no doubt inmates in jail may use malingering as an attention getter and to receive extra services, inmates malingering a mental illness while *having* a serious mental illness are not uncommon. For example, inmates who have a history of overt suicidal manipulation are not infrequently high risk for actual suicide in the long term.

CHAPTER 5

The Role of the Correctional Officer in Supervising Mentally Ill Inmates

The Role of the Correctional Officer

Correctional officers work throughout the United States in both civil service and corporate (for-profit or private) institutions. These facilities vary greatly in the demographics of jail populations, and physical plants. Some organizations exist only to transport inmates from one institution to another, not operating any facility of their own. Inmate populations range from less than one hundred for some community-based facilities to over six thousand in mega-facilities such as those in California, Texas, New York, etc. Security levels in jail vary from minimum custody inmates incarcerated primarily for low-level drug and/or property crimes to high security units with inmates convicted of capital offenses such as murder, robbery, great bodily injury, rape, and a host of other violent crimes. Many jails also operate electronic home monitoring, work release and pretrial release programs. At the most extreme level, some jails (usually state-run facilities) include highly enhanced security-oriented programs at the maximum to super-maximum security level for validated high level jail gang inmates, and inmates with extremely disruptive violent histories. State facilities may also be called upon to house high-level gang officials from different states. Local jails tend to deal with all of these populations before they are either released/sentenced on misdemeanor charges or sent to state prisons to complete their sentences.

Jails may also include academic and vocational programming, work assignments, and medical and psychological services. Jails may be required to provide treatment for the mentally ill, therapeutic substance abuse programs, programs for the developmentally and medically disabled as well as Sometimes local jails will find grants to implement special treatment programs or other types of programs that enable the inmates to contribute and make restitution to the community such as graffiti or campground clean-up.

Figure 5.1 Author's Experience: Benefits of Giving Something Back

In one of the author's facilities, some of the minimum-security inmates were able to work outside the facility on supervised work crews. One of the most popular crews was the one that cleaned up the local campgrounds that hosted disabled and terminally ill children. The inmates would come back in the jail after working eight hours, dirty, tired, dragging their feet, but with the biggest smiles on their faces. This crew of inmates would brag about how much they had gotten done and they were very proud to be able to do that work for special needs children. It is important to note that the inmates never got to see the children enjoy the campground—they were never there when the children were present—but they still got the inner satisfaction of helping them out. The officer that ran the work detail was also proud to be the supervisor of that program.

Any program that gets offenders invested in their community is a program worth looking into. People that feel a bond and an obligation to their community are less likely to want to vandalize or harm that community. That's a win for everyone!

Correctional officers must have the ability to recognize the behaviors of psychologically impaired ill inmates, whatever the cause, and have best practice communication strategies to effectively and safely deal with them. Correctional Officers are the eyes and ears of the facility. It is often their reporting and documentation that sustains the housing and treatment of mentally ill offenders.

To be sure, there are times that the only appropriate response is to initiate a use of force response so that a dangerous mentally ill inmate can be subdued, restrained, and removed to a crisis unit for stabilization. Such actions are not taken to punish the inmate, but rather as a concerted effort to improve the safety and well-being of themselves and others. Most tactical responses are implemented in an extremely controlled manner, and are video-taped as well. This is to minimize the possibility that either the inmate or officers are harmed. In many such cases, the mentally ill inmate will not even understand the exact nature and circumstances of their actions. It is only in retrospect that they will have realized how out of control and dangerous they were.

A Collaborative Process

One of the more important innovations in the supervision of incarcerated mentally ill inmates is the development of a *clinical treatment team* consisting of one or more supervising correctional officers (usually from the classification division), a clinical caseworker, and other clinical or medical staff as necessary. In any correctional setting, a successful collaboration between correctional officers and treatment team members requires a foundation of mutual respect, shared information, on-going training regarding the care, management and treatment of mentally ill inmates, and ongoing communication and cooperation of all treatment team members.

Weekly meetings with all involved divisions ensure that the appropriate information is shared. The Classification Officer is often the key person that consolidates information and disseminates it as needed. Officers on the floor, in most instances, usually do not need to have access to an inmate's protected health information. For instance, the floor officer does not need to know that an inmate has, for example, hepatitis or MERSA: only that the inmate is isolated due to medical reasons (All correctional officers should be using gloves and other personal protective equipment when responding to critical events, so in most cases, it shouldn't matter what the inmate's symptoms are). However, some diagnoses—whether they are mental health or physical health—must be shared with staff. Tuberculosis is one disease that is rampant in correctional facilities, and extreme precautions must be taken to ensure that it does not spread. The same holds true for mental health diagnoses. Classification officers need to know an inmate's diagnosis in order to schedule services and treatment as well as housing for the inmate, but the floor officer does not need these specifics in order to complete most of their duties. The key is to disseminate information that is pertinent to key people while protecting the inmate's right to privacy. As will be discussed in the latter sections of the book, floor officers need to be familiar with general patterns of behavior, regardless of diagnosis, in order to engage in best practice interventions as needed.

Correctional officers and mental health staff each have distinct professional cultures and missions that must be mutually respected among the members of the multi-disciplinary treatment team. Officers, by definition, must remain detached and set themselves to resolving issues, not building a therapeutic relationship. The focus of mental health professionals, in contrast, is characterized by individualized treatment, informed consent, and to some degree in a jail setting, negotiated compliance.

Compared to the daily contact by correctional officers, clinicians generally have brief contact periods with the inmates under their care. Therefore, officers are usually the first to notice substantive changes in an inmate's attitude, appearance, and routine, as well as deterioration in hygiene, or an increase in irritability or aggression. Pertinent timely information from officers contributes to effective diagnostic assessment by clinical staff and ongoing monitoring of mentally ill inmates. Beyond reporting to clinical staff, officers are first responders to inmate issues or misbehavior and as such have significant role in suicide prevention and crisis intervention.

The division in perspective between officers and clinicians can be narrowed through cross training across both disciplines; in other words, exposing clinicians to matters of security and correctional officers to matters of clinical interest. Ideally, cross training should begin in new employee orientation for both groups where clinicians are educated about security policy, staff safety, and the need to follow established procedures. Correctional officers learn to recognize behaviors associated with mental illness and suicidality, as well as the role(s) of the officer in promoting sound mental health policy while enhancing safety and security, intervention tactics, de-escalation methodologies, etc. This training should be repeated by both groups at least yearly and should be mandatory. In some states, yearly suicide intervention training for corrections officers is mandated by law. Other more specialized training for both disciplines should be scheduled and conducted as program needs dictate or as new laws and policies are promulgated.

Training should also encourage strong and consistent documentation of inmate issues and incidents for both disciplines. At least one part of the training should focus on teamwork—when it is appropriate to include another division and when it is not. If your cell extraction team is called out, the time for negotiation by mental health professionals is over (although there are times that the cell extraction team, itself, may engage in negotiation to elicit inmate compliance before higher uses of force are initiated). However, your mental health team could definitely respond to an inmate who is despondent, especially if the officers on duty feel this is a major change in the inmate's behavior. Every division needs to be clear about what part they play in any given incident. This ensures there will be no offended feelings or confusion, the inmate receives the best care, and everyone stays as safe as is possible.

Communication between custody and mental health staff creates an atmosphere of trust. Cooperation and flexibility allow for a quick, timely, coordinated response to minimize potentially dangerous inmate misbehavior or responses. Our overarching goal is that everyone goes home unharmed (including the inmate!) and everyone feels respected and valued.

CHAPTER 6

What Should Happen at Intake?

Classification

An effective jail program will have a system to classify all inmates at intake. This involves the use of a program tool that allows staff to determine the security level, special needs and/or program placement most appropriate to the inmate in question.

Effective classification systems, a part of the inmate's permanent record, also include reclassification or review of the inmate's status. Reclassification, through both face-to-face contacts and monthly general assessments, is an important tool to staff to identify if the inmate is displaying a change in attitude, mental status or situation may have an impact on the facility, staff, and other inmates. An effective classification system rewards positive behavior by reducing the inmate's custody level, increasing his or her ability to participate in programs and work details. In some instances a reduction in custody level allows an inmate to participate in programs such as jail drug-treatment that could result in an early release, even though most inmates are not in custody in local jails long enough to complete such programs. Even in brief stays, inmates can benefit from the ability to participate in bible study or Alcoholics Anonymous meetings. Another positive incentive is that reduced custody levels result in being housed in units that allow more variety in commissary purchases. They can also benefit from more social contact with other inmates, something often essential for mental health and wellness.

Effective programming also provides a disincentive for negative behavior by the imposition of more restrictive custodial conditions, reduced commissary, or other privileges, segregation from the general population, decreased time outside of their cell, or transfer to a higher custody level. Ultimately, classification can serve as a predictor of the inmate's propensity to re-offend once they are either released or sent to a state facility to complete their sentence. Thus, parole and probation officers are very interested in how an inmate conforms to both initial assessments as well as whether they are maintained at a lower or higher level of restriction.[5]

Intake: Gathering Critical Information

Initial intake is to establish the acceptability of the inmate into the facility—medically and mentally. A second interview during the actual booking process helps to define an initial classification level. If a jail has a formal classification division, a third, more in-depth, face-to-face interview is scheduled twenty-four hours after incarceration.

Inmates are most often assigned an initial risk value during the intake process, a basic triage that will determine the inmate's initial placement in a minimum, medium, or a maximum custody level. This value is based on the inmate's age and available data regarding their criminal history, specifically their types of arrests (felonies or misdemeanors), as well as any prior incarceration history, gang affiliations, drug and alcohol use, medical, psychiatric and dental needs, work history and skills, educational/vocational skills, prior military services, history of adjustment or failure on parole or probation. *Some inmates, at booking are in obvious medical or mental distress and this supersedes all other classification criteria.*

Most inmates do not have further interaction with classification officers after the face-to-face interview unless they are placed in some type of special housing. If an inmate requires special housing, their status should be reviewed every thirty days in order to keep track of any changes (both bad and good) that have happened in the last month. Information needed to change an inmate's housing or classification does not need to originate with the classification team; more often than not, the information comes from the floor officers.

Different Layers in the Intake Process

Gathering information is the key to appropriate inmate placement. Ideally, the correctional facility's Jail Management System (JMS) should allow staff to add to the inmate's record at any time. Most systems allow for minor disciplinary problems or case management notes to be added in a narrative.

At intake, officers must check to ensure the appropriate charging documents are being brought in with the inmate—a citation, warrant, order of arrest and detention, etc. Incarcerating a person is a major violation of their rights unless you have the appropriate charging documents. <u>Wise officers initially focus on the documents (while of course fully attending to safety issues) before their focus changes to the inmate.</u> There are tactical considerations in how this is accomplished — people made to wait in a state of uncertainty, not knowing how long this will continue, are more volatile than those who are apprised by the officer that he or she will first review the inmates documents, which will take approximately "x" minutes, and then the interview will start.

Once the intake officer is clear that the inmate has been properly charged, they will then ask medical and mental health questions to ensure that the inmate is healthy enough to be incarcerated. They should also ask if they have brought any medications or if they need them. If an inmate has just been in a car accident after eluding police in a high-speed chase, they may need to go to the hospital! Inmates that have open weeping wounds should be cleared at a hospital before admittance, due to the rampant spread of MERSA—antibiotic-resistant strains of staph infection. Inmates that have recently had a major surgery or have injured themselves also need to be medically cleared at a hospital.

Officers will then ask if they have any injuries or if they have tried suicide in the past twenty-four hours. If an inmate states they are currently suicidal (a common occurrence at arrest) they are not necessarily rejected at the booking window. Instead, the facility's suicide protocol would be immediately initiated. In this event, activities such as fingerprinting and booking photos will be postponed until after the inmate has been seen by a mental health professional. If an inmate is still suicidal after seeing a mental health professional—the suicide protocol still takes precedence over any jail processes.

Booking Process

Every inmate who makes it through the intake screening will now go through a second classification step. Officers will ask about gang affiliations, sexual orientation, whether the inmate has been previously victimized in jail, and whether they need protective custody. Along with this information the Booking Officer will run a criminal history check to see if the inmate has a past history of violent behavior or if the inmate is a registered sex offender (RSOF).

In most states, inmates who are known to be violent, to be carrying guns or other weapons or inmates who are suspected terrorists will have alerts entered into their criminal history, so the arresting officer is warned before encountering the person.

Inmates who commit crimes against children are usually segregated from general population inmates. Not every registered sex offender has committed crimes against children, but many inmates are absolutely unforgiving of another inmate who comes in with this moniker. Gangs live by iron-clad codes, and some have rules regarding the harm of children. Any gang member with this in their code of conduct is required to assault any other inmate who is a sex offender (if they find out about it). Other inmates, intending to check for informants, sex offenders, and rival gang members often demand to see another inmate's paperwork. Many jails, therefore, will place an inmate's court paperwork in their property rather that give it to the inmate in the unit if the paperwork mentions something that would put them at risk.

The Booking Officer will also check to see if the inmate has a history of disruptive behavior. Most officers recognize problem inmates ("frequent fliers") at the booking window and already have precautionary officers armed with less-than lethal-tools (pepper foam or Taser™) in place before the inmate even enters the facility.

If the agency is fortunate enough to have a classification division, one of the classification officers should complete a third screening, building upon what the intake officer and booking officer have documented, which should include a face-to-face interview, ideally after the first twenty-four hours of incarceration, but certainly within seventy-two hours. After twenty-four hours, an inmate has usually detoxed enough (if needed) to be able to give coherent answers.

Inmates can be placed in special housing for a myriad of reasons ranging from simple medical needs to a security threat to the facility. These are often our most fragile inmates needing a great deal of interaction from staff of all different divisions.

If an inmate must be placed in a segregation unit, the classification division should review their classification every thirty days. This ensures that any deterioration or improvement of the inmate's condition can be evaluated for possible reclassification to a different level of security.

Threat Assessment

Subsequent to booking, an inmate may be moved up or down the custodial risk scale from their initial classification. This secondary assessment process is where officers' experience and intuition can play a valuable role in assessing the inmates risk level. The officer may override the inmate's manifest risk value, and recommend a more intensive level of custodial supervision. This is especially true for inmates suffering from mental illness, as their illness alone may dictate more intensive case management. Inmates who have, for instance, a known history of suicide attempts will not be placed in a room alone. Inmates who are brought in on heavy charges (killing a child or a well-known member of the community, or any other particularly heinous crime) will inevitably be moved up in security level if for no reason other than their own safety.

Intake officers should attempt to undertake a detailed threat assessment. All information has a context. For example, you may become aware that an inmate used to own several knives. That fact, in itself, tells you little. You need to know why he owned them: for cooking, for a collection, or as part of his rape kit. You need to know if he has ever used them and in what context, and what the weapons mean to him. Another inmate, a woman, is depressed. Any information about her personal history of victimization, suicidal behavior, or violence may prove vital in determining proper housing and programs (such as a chaplain visit) that would help to keep her stable during incarceration.

Remember that mentally ill inmates are sometimes too decompensated or overwhelmed to undertake a comprehensive interview. However, whenever possible, ask each inmate direct questions about their previous history of assaults and their potential for violence. Correctional officers can review each inmate's official criminal history rather easily, and this information can be used to ascertain the inmate's truthfulness in response to questioning.

Essential items in threat assessment:
1. **A Past History of Violence.** This is perhaps the most reliable predictor of future violence. A capacity for violence is both innate and learned: the more it is used, the easier it is to use again, and the more likely it will be chosen as a preferred "problem-solving" activity. It is also rewarding: power over others often is the best experience of some inmates' lives. If the inmate is local, most officers know who the "fighters" are and will request extra officers to meet them at the booking window.
2. **History of Bullying or Intimidation**. This is the psychological counterpart of physical violence. Several different types of inmates tend to "strong arm" other inmates when placed in a general population unit. Any inmate who is high up in a gang hierarchy will inevitably end up either running a unit, or coming into direct conflict with other "alpha" inmates, particularly those from other gangs. Some inmates don't need to be in a gang to be natural bullies. The best way for an officer to ascertain out is to ask good questions on the front end of an incarceration, as well as observe how the inmate behaves when under the pressure of the interview.
3. **Prior Incarceration**. Any arrest is a heightened risk factor, even if it was for a non-violent crime. The inmate may be terrified or outraged at the idea of being incarcerated again. Furthermore,

with the prevalence of physical and sexual assault within correctional institutions, the non-violent arrestee may have come out a very different person than they went in.[6]

4. **Possession of Weapons, Fascination With Weapons, Past History of Using Weapons.** A fascination with weaponry, or fantasizing about them in a pathological manner, is very definitely a heightened risk factor. These inmates, if known, usually have an alert code associated with their name.

5. **History of Physical Abuse or the Witnessing of Physical Abuse and Violence.** Beyond a history of personal victimization, it is particularly traumatic to have witnessed abuse of a family member. The victim of abuse often hates his own weakness, and begins hating weakness in others as well. Once this occurs, it is a natural move for some people to begin victimizing that which they hate—the weak.[7] The vast majority of women in jail are victims of sexual or physical violence and enormous numbers show symptoms of post-traumatic stress disorder. Many become violent at any sign of aggression from another inmate or even an officer.

6. **Head Injuries.** These are associated with impulse control problems. A history of closed head injuries is endemic among violent felons.[8] Many of our returning military veterans, some of whom may be incarcerated, also suffer from Traumatic Brain Injuries (TBI), the signal injury of the wars in the Middle East. Some proportion of those with TBI may have hair-trigger tempers and difficulty controlling negative emotions. Information that an inmate has suffered a TBI offers advanced warning that an inmate may be very explosive. Furthermore, if the inmate does inform you that he or she has a history of closed head injury, medical staff should be made aware of this fact. They may be in an emergent state or still be in a condition where treatment is needed to alleviate a condition that continues to damage their brain.

7. **A History of Mental Illness**. Chronic patterns or symptoms of mental illness may exacerbate an inmate's ability to follow rules and regulations and in some cases precipitate violent outbursts or violence. On the other hand, the illness may leave the inmate vulnerable to predation by his or her peers in jail.

8. **Fear of Attack or Invasion of Personal Space**. Paranoid and fearful inmates may lash out in defensive violence. If you are properly "tracking" the inmate, you should be aware if they become increasingly stressed when in close physical proximity to you during the interview process. The street officers may have already experienced this, so whenever possible, get information from the arresting officer about their behavior on arrest

9. **Low Frustration Tolerance and Inability or Unwillingness to Tolerate Limit Setting**—"I want what I want and I want it now—and you'd better not keep me from it." Such an individual may explode from sudden calm: for example, if there is a delay in the lunch line. Officers often observe this during the intake process, with an inmate quickly becoming impatient, physically agitated, snappish, and giving a sense that they are "wired tight." Some inmates are already known by officers for low frustration tolerance, for which they should be flagged in their record.

10. **Recent Stressors and Losses**. Bereavement, separation, divorce, job loss, and, of course, incarceration can make an inmate more willing to become violent, feeling that they have nothing left to lose. This is something you will not usually find out during intake, but threat assessment is an ongoing process, and if the inmate has a lover or spouse break up with them, if they get more

time unexpectedly stacked on, if they are fired from their job while in jail, or any other such stressor, the risk they present to others increases, sometimes exponentially.

11. **A Feeling of Victimization and Grievance**. Certain inmates may feel victimized by society in general, or hold a grudge with "the system," in which their current predicament is always someone else's fault. In many instances the correctional officer becomes the "face" of the system for the inmate, and then the target of their grievance. This is often revealed during the intake in an unending litany of complaints, blaming, and verbal aggression. This can often be a sign of paranoia, where the inmate feels under almost perpetual attack from all directions. They store up grievances, and "appoint" others as their designated enemies.

12. **Almost All Intoxicating Substances Can Be Disinhibiting.** Intoxicants tend to "dissolve" the internal barriers that hold us back from our primitive desires, among them aggression. Intoxicants include alcohol, drugs, industrial chemicals and prescription medications. If inmates are addicted, they usually come in high so the only information needed is what, how much, and how often.

13. **Physical Pain or Discomfort (Particularly Chronic).** Aside from illness or injury, this also includes withdrawal from drugs and alcohol. Unfortunately, many medications that help mentally ill people can have very nasty side-effects, particularly when the inmate is inadequately monitored, and this, too, can be maddening. Inmates with any medical condition should have a separate interview and intake process with medical staff.

14. **The Inmate Has Already Given Up.** Some inmates expect every interaction to be difficult or negative. Their response can be, "What the hell. Nothing will help. If I'm aggressive, at least I can make my mark on the world—or on you."

15. **Severe Pathological Behaviors.**
    - Rapid mood swings—such inmates are unpredictable, and can escalate into a rage unexpectedly.
    - Boisterousness—a loud, almost aggressive happiness, in which there is no attempt to "include" others in the laughter or entertainment.
    - Hallucinations—particularly auditory command hallucinations that may be telling the inmate to do something terrible.
    - Mania—this is a state of excitement, typified by rapid speech, grandiose thinking, very poor judgment, and impulsive behavior. It is a behavior we see in people with bipolar disorder (manic-depression), intoxication on stimulants such as methamphetamine or cocaine, and not infrequently, alcohol.
    - History of predatory or manipulative behaviors.

16. **Interactional Factors Between the Aggressor and Victim.** The aggressor paradoxically views their target as having power over them, views them as being inflexible or controlling, or denying the aggressor his due. In short, the aggressor usually believes himself to be the victim. This dynamic is so obvious that it seems almost unnecessary to include here, but we have all seen officers who forget, with one inmate or another, that you are always the enemy. Any officer who ever believes that he or she has a friendly relationship with any inmate will soon find themselves in profoundly dangerous situations. On the other hand, officers who are regarded as tough but

fair are actually far less likely to elicit personal hatred from an inmate (never forgetting, however, there are some inmates who regard all correctional officers as enemies or prey).

17. **Religious and Cultural Clashes.** Culture is any set of rules and customs that organizes relationships between people.[9] Officers should avoid any religious, political, or cultural debates with inmates. However, correctional officers should make an attempt to be aware of the cultural mores and religious practices of their inmates, so they won't *inadvertently* insult them (as long as this caution does not compromise their authority). Be aware that some cultures sanction violence and these cultural rules may be different from one's own mainstream culture.[10]

18. **Tattoos and Gang Affiliation.** Gang membership and interaction with other gangs is complex and the best way to handle the intricacies of their interactions is to have a person on staff dedicated to gang management. Inmates may not admit to gang affiliation, but their tattoos will often tell you a different story. They may keep this information to themselves if they want to get close to a rival gang member in jail in order to carry out a "hit" on them. Many gangs have fight-on-sight orders, meaning that if they see a rival gang member, they must fight or be disciplined by their own gang.

Ongoing Threat Assessment to Reduce Risk

Following the face to face interview, the classification officer may find that they need to release an officer alert or update to the officers working in the facility. Alerts contain details of how the officers should deal with a certain inmate, particularly with those who are mentally ill. In the latter case, it is not always due to deliberate resistance to authority. They may simply be unable to retain or comprehend complex information. Alerts will specify both procedural matters, such as the requirement to always handcuff an inmate while he or she is being moved, as well as suggestions for the most effective way to communicate with the mentally ill inmate to elicit compliance (for example, "Inmate Hathaway is very paranoid, but it has been observed that if one of the transporting officers talks with him about music, he is less likely to be assaultive"). Alerts should not be posted where other inmates can see them.

The supervising classification officer must remain in regular contact with the other members of the inmate's treatment team to discuss the inmate's compliance, or recommend changes to the program.

Figure 6.1 Stay in Your Own Lane

If you are having a multi-disciplinary meeting, report what you observe—behaviors, incidents, and compliance events. Do not usurp other professional's role or responsibilities. For example, you may recognize behaviors that lead you to believe the inmate is schizophrenic, but leave the diagnoses to the professionals. Instead, use the descriptors in the latter part of this book. Be a good witness, take copious notes, and stay in your own lane.

CHAPTER 7

Taking into Account an Inmate's Mental Illness During Write-Ups and Disciplinary Hearings

Officers are responsible for maintaining order and when necessary, charging inmates with rules violation reports or infractions. Mentally ill prisoners frequently receive discipline reports and are punished for behavioral problems that are manifestations of their illness rather than malevolence or an intention to make trouble. Consider that it is regarded as "destruction of property" when such items as sheets, towels, shirts, etc. are used in attempted suicide by hanging. Even acts of self- mutilation are a destruction of property because, in this case, the state's property is the inmate's body. This presents the correctional officer with quite a dilemma, given that a custodial institution generally functions best when the rules are "fair, firm, and consistent."

One of the most effective approaches in this area is to ensure that correctional officers receive ongoing training that will assist them in determining when inappropriate behavior might be a symptom of a deeper underlying mental illness, signaling the need to not only record the rule violation but to also immediately refer the inmate to a mental health practitioner.

Change from baseline behavior is one of the most significant warnings that the individual may be decompensating. Among these warning signs:

- **Changes in Hygiene.** Not bathing (strong overpowering body odor), not brushing their teeth, combing their hair, or wearing rumpled dirty clothing.
- **Inappropriate Clothing or Clothing that Is Inconsistent With Temperature or Season**. This would include sweatshirts and/or jackets during the summer. Refusing to wear clothing at all or wearing clothes inappropriately—for example, shirts as pants.

Figure 7.1 Caution Regarding Clothing: It's Always More than One Thing

Security rules should never be suspended because an officer believes an inmate to be suffering from a mental illness. Inappropriate clothing is also indicative of an inmate carrying contraband such as weapons and/or drugs; therefore, appropriate caution must always be exercised in detaining and/or searching the inmate.

- **Significant Changes in Diet.** This includes not eating or missing meals that are normally eaten by the inmate.

- **Change in Mood.** Such inmates may be withdrawn, depressed, and lethargic or may be irritable or uncharacteristically defiant
- **Manic Excitement.** Rapid speech, gesture and movements, over-exuberance, and boisterousness **(Chapter 43)**.
- **Psychotic Behaviors.** The expression of delusional ideas, talking to oneself, or interaction with visual hallucinations **(Chapters 41 & 42)**.

If an inmate evinces any of these "red flags," they must hopefully be calmed, and at minimum, safely controlled. The correctional officer then needs to ensure that the inmate is seen as soon as possible by trained clinicians to further assess the inmate's needs. The inmate should not be left alone until there is a clinical order to do so, following assessment. This may be immediately or within the next hour, but should not be prolonged beyond the current shift unless there are unavoidable circumstances. For facilities that do not have twenty-four hour mental health care, this inmate will have to be housed in a place that is safe for them and others until they can be assessed. Aside from the treatment issues of concern, this immediate response will help staff ascertain if the inmates actions were driven by their mental illness or volitional (by choice), information that is essential for the disciplinary hearing.

Disciplinary Hearings

With mentally ill inmates, jail disciplinary hearings, which are set up in a quasi-judicial manner, should judge whether an inmate is competent to participate in the proceedings, and whether the prisoner's conduct reflected cognitive mental health impairments or was volitional. Correctional officers share information at disciplinary hearings through their description of the inmate's actions during the rule violation as documented on the rules violation report (RVR) or on a supplemental document such as an incident "chrono." The officer might be called as a witness by the senior hearing officer, by the inmate, or the inmate's clinician (who should also be a member of the disciplinary committee). Due to their mental health problems, the inmate should always be assigned a staff assistant who will aid the inmate to understand the disciplinary process as well as ensuring that he or she receives full due process.

Whether found guilty or not of an infraction, the hearing may decide to require placement in a specific therapy or psycho-education/counseling group and/or placement into an intensive behavioral therapy unit. Sanctions can also be reduced to a lesser rule violation in order to implement a punishment that is more instruction/learning oriented as opposed to a punitive sanction that may lead to more degeneration in an inmate's mental state.

The preceding information does not negate in the slightest the fact that all inmates must be accountable for their actions and behavior. It simply requires that mental health staff and correctional staff assess how best to manage the inmate's behavior while ensuring that any relevant clinical and medical needs that are revealed by the infraction are addressed.

Figure 7.2 Fair, Firm, and Consistent Does Not Mean Rigid

Correctional officers have considerable latitude in effectively enforcing rules and ensuring safety. Consider the following example of three inmates, each of whom refuses to leave his cell:

Inmate #1 is a hard-core fighter, who is simply bored, and considers a fight with officers to be a kind of contact sport. After he is instructed to leave his cell, he laughs and kicks his cell-door, howling, "Bring it on, screws!" The officers quickly and expeditiously remove him from his cell, using powerful, controlled methods of physical force. He is put in restraints.

Inmate #2 is angry because officers inadvertently damaged a picture of his daughter during a mail check. A lead officer uses tactical paraphrasing to "line up" with the inmate (**Chapter 57**). Without compromising staff authority in the slightest, the officer validates that the inmate is understandably upset. The inmate calms down and leaves his cell voluntarily.

Inmate #3 is having a psychotic break and is terrified that if he leaves his cell, rats will invade his mattress and devour him while he is asleep. He needs to go to the infirmary to get a blood-draw to assess if his medications are at the right level. An officer takes the extra time to calm him down, and eventually, places a lit flashlight on the inmate's bed, the cell being locked behind them. The inmate has told the officer that rats attack in the dark. He is reassured that the rats will not invade his room because of the extra light on the bed.

The officers are fair in each case, they are firm in each case, and they are consistent—they determine the most effective tactic to elicit compliance.

CHAPTER 8

Drug Use by Mentally Ill Inmates

Law enforcement and correctional officers are required to protect and serve, not perform as medical personnel. The inmate's mental illness or drug use may not have been recognized during their arrest, and once incarcerated, it may be days before they are properly diagnosed and treated. Given that drug intoxication could be termed, a "time-limited, externally-imposed mental illness," it is very possible that the drug-affected inmate may be funneled into the wrong housing unit, the wrong programming, and may experience delays in getting effective treatment. The same could happen in reverse with a mentally ill inmate, especially one who also uses drugs or alcohol. Without a proper "triage" of the inmate when they come in the door, it may take days or a week to get the inmate into the proper cell and into proper programs so that they benefit from their surroundings instead of being damaged by them. Therefore, inmates that are under the influence of substances are commonly housed separately and placed under more consistent observation that inmates that are not intoxicated.

The level of illegal drug availability and inmate drug and alcohol abuse has been constant and high over the past decades in almost all jails, despite concerted efforts toward reduction. Drugs reach inmates in many ways—through visitors, by mail (letters, post cards, etc.), through inmate food and clothing packages sent by approved relatives and friends, through the complicity of corrupt staff, by inmates with clearances that allow them to work off jail worksites, by civilians who throw or launch objects that have been filled with contraband over jail walls and fences. A recent phenomenon in contraband in jails, cellular telephone smuggling, has only exacerbated the problem of substances abuse in jails.

Inmates who receive prescribed medications, will on occasion, circumvent jail policies and hoard these medications and sell them to other inmates as part of the illicit black market within the jail.

Most jail drug trade and trafficking is controlled by jail gangs, and sold at exorbitant prices, with the going price often ten times that of street value. Gang-related drug activity is a primary cause of jail violence.

The use of alcohol in jail presents as great or greater problem regarding inmate behavior and officer safety. Though the incidence of violent crimes committed by mentally ill prisoners is no greater than that of the general jail population, the incidence of violent crime by the mentally ill who at the same time abuse drugs and alcohol is far greater.[11] Therefore, any steps to interdict the use of drugs and alcohol within the jail will be of profound benefit to the mentally ill inmate, above and beyond all the other reasons it is necessary.

Policies to Mitigate Drug Availability

It is, unfortunately, impossible to eradicate illicit drugs and alcohol in jails, yet there is much that administration can do. The following jail drug and alcohol reduction strategies, while not necessarily complete, provide a framework whereby safety for correctional officers, other correctional staff, and inmates is enhanced.

- **Zero-Tolerance.** Although it may be impossible in practice, policy must dictate zero-tolerance of smuggling, possession of, production, use and trafficking of drugs for all staff, inmates, and visitors.

- **Training.** All correctional officers and other correctional personnel should be trained regarding substance abuse relevant to the core task of zero-tolerance.

- **Direct and Random Testing.** Direct and random testing of inmates for drug and alcohol is ideal. However, unless an inmate is on state supervision or signs a work contract, they cannot be tested for drugs unless they consent. That still leaves many inmates that we can test.

- **Sanctions.** Ensure the appropriate application of sanctions and penalties for inmates involved in the possession, use, and trafficking of illicit drugs and alcohol, including criminal charges for introducing contraband to a correctional facility—usually a felony.

- **Random Searches.** Ensure correctional officers engage in both routine and random searches of inmates, personal property and cells, dorms, and bed areas. Ensure complete body as well as property searches of all inmates received into or transferred out of the facility. Any and all inmates who work off jail grounds must be adequately supervised by assigned correctional officers and subject to routine and random searches.

- **Searches of Visitors.** Ensure correctional officers search all visitors and visitors' property during visiting periods. Implementing off-site "video-visiting" facilities has helped to reduce this avenue of influx for drugs.

- **Searches of Staff.** A truly secure unit will include random searches of staff and their property. (Policy in this area should be thoroughly reviewed by competent jail administrative staff as well as a legal advisor before implementation.)

- **Monitoring of Correspondence.** Ensure all outgoing mail (non-confidential) is monitored and scanned by correctional officers for possible inmate drug transactions. All inmate packages and non-confidential mail must be monitored and scanned for possible attempts to smuggle drugs into jails through letters, cards, or packages, or correspondence concerning a future buy or other drug related matter.

- **Secure Storage of Medical Supplies.** Ensure that all drugs/hypodermic needles contained within the jail's clinic and/or hospital are completely secured from inmate hands, and that all medications, needles, etc. are routinely monitored, audited, and counted at least once per shift.

- **Monitoring of Medications Distributed to Inmates.** Controlled substances including narcotics, anti-depressants, psychotropic drugs, etc. should, if possible, only be administered in a jail clinic area under strict scrutiny by staff that ensure that the inmate swallows the medication, whether liquid or pill (direct observation method).

- **Monitoring of Over-the-Counter (OTC) Medications.** All such medication sold through the jail's inmate canteen or commissary must be reviewed by jail administration and medical staff and pharmacists to ensure that the OTC medications are neither intoxicants nor can be a component in the manufacture of same.

- **Proper Equipment.** Ensure that correctional officers are properly equipped with tools to facilitate the prevention of contraband into the facility, such as flashlights, search kits, Kevlar gloves, mirrors, narcotic/drug detection devices, metal detectors (both stationary and scanning devices), cell phone detection devices, etc.
- **Drug Detection Dogs.** Establish and/or utilize an available canine drug detecting dog team to routinely and randomly search the facility.
- **Inmate Clothing.** Ensure inmate clothing is controlled, issued only by the facility and designed to facilitate staff searches, not the concealment of contraband.
- **Yard Scheduling.** Ensure that inmate yard schedules as well as outer perimeter patrols are scheduled and designed to minimize outside introduction of contraband.
- **Control of Foodstuffs.** Ensure all products such as spices, sugar, bread, condiments, juices, fruits, etc. are strictly controlled and accounted for. (These products and many others can be used by inmate to produce jail wine (*pruno*).
- **Control of Material Used to Fabricate Pruno.** Ensure that plastic bags, containers, etc. are controlled and minimized to reduce the incidence of inmate producing pruno.
- **The Opportunity for Spiritual Support.** Provide spiritual opportunities within jail and encourage inmate participation as deterrents to the use of drugs and alcohol.
- **Education.** Encourage inmate participation in literacy, educational, and training programs.
- **Substance Abuse Groups.** Provide inmates with the opportunity to participate in substance abuse treatment programs as budgets permit, including self-help groups such as Narcotic Anonymous (NA) and Alcohol Anonymous (AA).
- **Treatment.** Encourage open and frank discussion of substance abuse among all inmates through small and large group counseling, Interdisciplinary Treatment Team (ITT), etc.
- **Support Services.** Provide a range of support services including medical and mental health services, prevention services, HIV testing, etc.
- **Specialized Unit.** If budgetary process allows, develop a unit of correctional officers specifically trained in intelligence gathering, contraband prevention, gang prevention, drug interdiction processes, and direct liaison with local courts and other law enforcement agencies.

CHAPTER 9

Specialized Units

Segregated Housing

Inmates are placed in segregation for several reasons: as a consequence for rules infractions, to keep them safe from other inmates at their request (protective custody), because they are too dangerous to be kept in general population (administrative segregation), or for medical reasons. Mentally ill inmates should ideally be housed in locked wing reserved for the mentally ill, if such a unit is available. Mentally ill inmates should not be housed in the same unit as inmates under disciplinary lock down, if separate units are available.

Inmates in segregation units spend the bulk of their time in their cells with a couple of hours out of their units each day for showers, telephone calls, and exercise. Inmates are generally allowed fewer possessions than they would were they in general population, and visiting is behind-glass, non-contact visiting, or video visits. Video machines are installed either in the unit or on the floor for the inmate; their visitors are in another building. As mentioned earlier, although this is a huge improvement for security, it is yet another layer of isolation for the inmate and the visitor.

Prisoners with pre-existing psychiatric disorders are of greater risk of suffering further psychological deterioration when placed in isolation, or segregation/security housing units. Of course, there are some mentally ill prisoners who are so dangerous and volatile that they may not be able to interact with other inmates in a general population setting and require a more segregated, higher custody setting; however, even with these inmates, mental health treatment must strive to ensure that they do not become even more ill. Making this difficult is the rule that inmates in segregation units are prohibited from all programs, including religious ones. These programs take place in a group setting and inmates in segregation often do not have the social skills or willingness to comply with rules so that they can participate in a productive manner. It is always a give and take between security and treatment, scaling back one in order to make room for the other.

It is difficult for clinicians to maintain adequate continuity of care, including medication monitoring, caseload review, etc., in segregated housing. Without extraordinary steps by staff, isolation also decreases the likelihood that the mentally ill inmate will improve his or her condition. Isolation breeds more isolation. This is apparent when inmates would rather spend their "out time" in their cell talking through the glass to officers rather than showering or making phone calls. Many officers try to take time during walk-throughs to chat with these inmates in order to decrease acting out behaviors. Bilingual officers can be invaluable here—bilingual or non-English speaking inmates often want to speak with someone in their native language.

Isolated inmates have a very high suicide rate, far more than the suicide rate of inmates in general population. Therefore, suicide risk assessment must occur either prior to or within a short period of time following an inmate's placement in a segregation unit. Correctional officers need to have a higher level of vigilance when dealing with this population of inmates, and welfare checks must take place with greater frequency than in non-lockdown units.

Qualified mental health practitioners must regularly assess segregated inmates who are known to have serious mental health needs. This facilitates the early detection of psychological deterioration and may even ward off decompensation into psychotic states, depression, or anxiety. During these rounds, each inmate should be briefly visited to assess whether there are any emerging problems. The clinician should establish a dialogue with the officers assigned to the unit as well as review the corresponding segregation unit watch log in order to identify any inmate who appears to be showing signs of mental deterioration or other problems. Classification officers should also complete thirty day reviews in which they meet with each inmate. It would be preferable, with the availability of escort officers, and adequate clinical room or office space in the segregated housing unit, for the clinician to conduct the assessment in a setting that offers sound and visual privacy. However, this is not always possible, and in many cases, the clinician must conduct all mental health assessments at the cell door.

Classification backs up the mental health team by making sure the inmate is in the proper physical environment. As inmates become more mentally stable, their classification should loosen up.

Effective communication among staff, whether it is through the jail's internal mail service, word-of-mouth, or intranet, is of upmost importance. Floor officers are the first line of defense for an inmate whose mental health is deteriorating. Informing the clinical team that an inmate is doing worse (or better) helps the mental health professionals provide appropriate mental health care. Officers get repaid by having to deal with a stabilized inmate instead of one in crisis.

In an ideal situation, a segregated mental health correctional program should offer ten to fifteen hours per week of out-of-cell structured therapeutic activities in addition to unstructured exercise or recreation time. With limited resources and funds, this is often not possible in local jails, where the best they can manage is stabilization.

Protective Custody Units

Protective custody refers to the non-punitive segregation of inmates from the general population both to protect a prisoner from harm by other inmates, and to protect other prisoners and/or staff from harm. Frequently mentally ill, such inmates also may be:

- Pedophiles, child murderers, and child abusers.
- Gang members, particularly "de-briefers (those inmates providing information to the authorities).
- Gay, transsexual, or transgender inmates, and others at risk of sexual assault.
- Inmates who achieve notoriety on the outside who may be subjected to pressure by other inmates.

- Inmates who are themselves witnesses to a crime, either on the outside or in jail, or have provided testimony and states evidence on other inmates, gangs, and criminal entrepreneurs.
- Inmates nearing the expiration of their sentences may "manufacture" a protective housing need in an attempt to avoid disciplinary infractions or to otherwise be isolated from prisoner general population politics prior to their release. Such inmates truly hope to never return to custody, because if they were ever incarcerated again, they would have a "Protective Custody" label. Other inmates, assuming they were any one of the other categories listed here, might consider them "fair game."
- Corrupt or criminal public servants including, law enforcement personnel, civil servants, legislators.
- Juveniles who have been certified as adults by the court, usually because they have committed a particularly heinous crime, are nonetheless, often at risk for victimization.

Figure 9.1 Author's Experience: A Juvenile in the Adult Facility

A juvenile was charged as an adult for a sex crime against a child. This meant he was to be housed in the adult facility as opposed to the juvenile facility. Obviously, a sixteen year old could not be housed with adults so this necessitated segregation housing for him. He immediately went through our suicide protocol after he made statements of intent to harm. After several days of observation, it became apparent that, not only did this juvenile lack the ability to understand or speak English, he barely spoke his native language (which was a mix of Native and Hispanic languages). He could barely read and evidenced significant mental delays. He was rapidly deteriorating in an isolated cell, unable to communicate with anyone. Unable to adequately address this juvenile's needs, the officers brought the special needs of this juvenile to the attention of the administration. The administration worked with the courts and Mental Health Services to expedite the juvenile's court case and move him to a specialized psychiatric hospital for juveniles for diagnosis and stabilization.

Despite good intentions—attempting to ensure inmate safety—the absence of normal social interactions and purposeful, rewarding activities can be emotionally, physically, and psychologically devastating. Inmates can lapse into states of despair and rage, endangering the safety of both correctional officers and other inmates.

Mentally ill inmates in protective custody need to be managed in much the same manner as those in other segregated housing facilities. The cause of their sequestration may different, but their psychological needs are much the same.

Psychiatric Units

A number of jails throughout the United States have developed specialized housing units[12] separate from the general population to treat mentally ill inmates. These highly structured units, mostly available at state level institutions or particularly large and well-funded county jails, incorporate a low ratio of inmates to clinicians; group and individual therapy; and a multi-disciplinary approach.

Correctional officers assigned to such a unit have an important and unique role. The officers' ability and authority to provide discipline with applied sanctions is an important tool in managing and curbing maladaptive, recalcitrant behaviors of inmates assigned to the unit. At the same time, although not licensed therapists, officers provide therapeutic intervention for inmates by clearly defining boundaries and consequences, particularly in regards to manipulative and splitting behaviors **(Section V)**.

CHAPTER 10

The Role of Medical Staff
Within the Jail

Medical/Psychiatric Services

Inmate Medical Services must include the care and treatment of the mentally ill with specific services contingent on the core mission of the institution (local jails focus on stabilization and referral, for the most part, rather than long-term treatment). Medical staff should include Licensed Vocational Nurses (LVNs), Registered Nurses (RNs), physicians, clinicians, case managers, and other mental health specialists.

Major federal cases have been successfully litigated by prisoner advocate groups throughout the nation concerning prisoner rights in receiving constitutionally mandated levels of psychiatric and medical care while in jail.[13] Less than adequate care leads to costly litigation that may profoundly impact necessary custodial resources, impacting the availability of money for hiring of new officers, maintenance of the officers, and training and safety issues. On both a practical and moral level, the prompt identification of serious psychiatric and medical issues and their subsequent prompt resolution leads inmates towards a view of staff actually concerned for their well-being.

Mental Health Assessments

As discussed above, it is necessary that any inmate manifesting what appears or is known to be mental illness, undergoing a disciplinary proceeding, must receive a mental health assessment to determine if their current mental state is a barrier to the inmate's understanding of the disciplinary proceedings (**Chapter 7**). Generally, a licensed clinical psychologist is charged with the responsibility to conduct an informal mental health assessment prior to any adjudication of in-house charges against the inmate in question. Full mental health assessments for competency for criminal charges must be court ordered.

The Jail Pharmacy

Adequate resources with trained and licensed staff are necessary to maintain the medication regime the large numbers of mentally ill individuals in custody. An appropriate formulary, adequate for all inmates' pharmacological needs, should be available as well as an effective, timely method for distribution to affected inmates. Correctional officers are usually not qualified to hand out medications to inmates and should not be involved in this process, beyond the security and safety required for all involved participants.

A pharmacy inmate management system allows for timeliness in the filling and refilling of orders as well as identifying individual inmate medication type and dosage needs. Reports should be available for transferring and paroling inmates to enable the inmate's continuum of care, as well as providing medications to inmates released from custody into specialized programs (**Chapter 12**). It should also be possible to transfer such records between community mental health facilities and correctional facilities (with the appropriate signed releases) for the same reasons.

Records/Filing

Effective correctional mental health programs have an organized records operation that provides an up-to-date compendium of every inmate who has accessed mental health care in the facility. The filing of mental health and/or medical orders must be timely, and records must be secure and accurate, while preserving patient confidentiality and HIPPA mandates. There should be a way to add-in reports from officers regarding an inmate's behavior without allowing unwarranted access to records by non-medical personnel.

Medication

While correctional officers are not in any position to dispense medications, officers should be present during medication passes to ensure the inmates are actually taking their medications and not "cheeking" them (pretending to swallow the medications but actually hiding them in their mouths to save for later, to trade or to store up medications to overdose). Special note should be made when inmates refuse medications as this may negatively affect inmate behavior or be a sign that they are decompensating.

What such information is not confidential, correctional officers should know:
- Name of medication(s) that an inmate is taking, and what particularly dangerous side-effects they may cause
- Inmate's history of discontinuing medication(s), and behavioral warning signs when this occurs.

The authors recommend that every unit in every correctional facility be supplied with **Mosby's Drug Guide for Nurses** [14] or a similar guide, or have a direct link to a reliable online source, approved by the jail medical staff, in order to help familiarize officers with the various medications available, and to help identify any pills that may be taken from an inmate during a search or an arrest.

Figure 10.1 Why Do They Stop Taking Their Medication?

There are many reasons inmates resist taking their medications, discontinue them, or take them intermittently. Among them are:

- **Unwelcome Side Effects.** Among possible side-effects are muscle spasms, intolerable itching/crawling sensations in the limbs, tongue thrusting, tremors, impairment of sexual functioning, dry mouth, weight gain, weight loss, skin disorders, even life-threatening disorders that must be monitored through such invasive procedures as regular blood-draws, to name but a few.

- **No Effect (or so it seems).** Many psychiatric medications are not "felt" beyond their side-effects. They don't make the inmate "high," or even "better." Apart from the side-effects, the inmate simply feels like "him/herself." Feeling good, therefore, one draws the natural conclusion that the drug has done its job, or in other cases, does not work, and therefore can be discontinued.

- **No Effect (in truth).** Many of the medications simply don't work for a specific inmate. They may have had high hopes that the medications would have helped, even cured them. All that they got, instead, were the sides-effects.

- **The Illness Is Better Than the Cure.** Sometimes, even apart from noxious side-effects, the illness can feel better than the "cure." Many psychotic individuals find that the medications muffle or suppress delusions and/or hallucinations, but they don't make them disappear. Furthermore, the medications often do not touch the belief system around the delusions. Life on medications, for such people, is like living under a sodden blanket. What is reality to them may be muffled, tranquilized, and constricted, but not otherwise changed. For such people, the medications may help them live a more stable, uneventful life, but just as we shake off constricting bedding when we are too hot and constricted, psychotic individuals may discontinue medications, simply to have, in their view, air to breathe.

- **Mania, the "Up-Side" of Manic-Depression.** This can be a state of high-energy and ecstasy. Medicated life, on the other hand, can be flat and boring. **(Chapter 43)**

- **Intoxicants Preferred to Medication.** The inmate's use of illicit drugs and/or alcohol leads them to discontinue their prescribed medications.

- **Taking Own Medication Is Impossible.** The inmate is simply incapable of taking medications by themselves every day.

SECTION II

The Mentally Ill Inmate:
"Outside"—The Other System

CHAPTER 11

In Between: Continuity of Care
Requires Restoration of Benefits

Most social services cease when an individual is incarcerated. The government does not like to provide money or services to inmates whether they are mentally ill or not, given that their housing, food, laundry and medical needs are now being covered by another entity. What we end up with is the shifting of payment from one budget to another.

<u>It is imperative that a specific individual within your jail is responsible for helping mentally ill inmates get their benefits re-instated before they leave incarceration!</u> Any lag time in the resumption of benefits only leaves the inmate open to victimization and decompensation. Jails must begin to work in concert with outside social service agencies to coordinate benefits for inmates leaving custody in order to ensure timely re-instatement of needed medications and housing.

We are increasingly seeing a need for veterans' services inside our correctional facilities along with the "regular" assortment of social services. Our recent military activities abroad have left some warfighters severely affected by Post Traumatic Stress Disorder. Homelessness is epidemic among our veterans. There are a number of resources that are available to our veteran population, but it is imperative that our services coordinators in the jail assist our veterans in getting the services they are entitled to receive.

CHAPTER 12

Mental Health Court and Diversion

As we continue to empty the state hospitals, and tighten the admission requirements for outpatient services, many people with mental illness find themselves incarcerated, maintained in a system that is ill equipped to provide services and support. This chapter will address options for working with the misdemeanant mentally ill which focuses on jail diversion.[15]

The Sequential Model for Jail Diversion

Suppose you are a patrol officer, and you spot a man urinating in the alley. The man appears disheveled and confused, and states that he is both homeless and a veteran. As you talk to him, the more you realize he needs treatment rather than an arrest. In the sequential model, you call your local community mental health agency and refer him for diversion. If you can secure his compliance, you drop the individual off at an evaluation center, and inform him that if he follows up with this referral, he will not be cited for "urinating in public," and may have an opportunity to get treatment and housing. You complete the paperwork and are on the road again within fifteen minutes. By facilitating appropriate treatment you also achieved a secondary but equally important goal—getting the law enforcement officer back on the streets as quickly as possible.

For another example, let's suppose that this individual has a warrant for a failure to appear (FTA). He is booked into the jail and the jail staff is made aware of his history. A second diversion point can occur here as the jail staff and the court chooses to review his case, and refer him to diversion rather than wait for another hearing date. **Intercept and treat versus adjudicate and house.** Given that research has shown that mentally ill offenders will be incarcerated eight times longer than the average inmate in jail or prison and at seven times the cost, this is obviously a very expensive "revolving door." It can also be both labor intensive and frustrating for jail staff required to deal with these high intensity, special needs inmates.

An ideal system would provide many opportunities for diversion. Munetz and Griffin (2006)[16] conceptualize the diversion process as a system of multiple entry points with filters that would "catch" or contain people with severe mental illness (SMI) in ever-narrowing groups. With this concept, the largest portion of people would be served through an active mental health system utilizing "best practice standards." Further on in the system, individuals on probation would be caught in the filter and referred for treatment.

Illustrations: The Sequential Model[17]

One example of an attempt to create a diversion program was that of Washington State, in 2007, with the implementation of Senate Bill 5533. The background of the bill states:

> In September 2006, the Washington Association of Sheriffs and Police Chiefs (WASPC) and the Washington affiliate of the National Alliance on Mental Illness (NAMI) held a summit to address the increasing numbers, recidivism rates, and longer jail terms of offenders who suffer from mental illness....
>
> This bill attempts to address that problem by creating a partnership between mental health service providers and the criminal justice system. There are many components to the bill, all of which are aimed at getting individuals into services that are appropriate for their needs. In the long run, this approach should save the counties and the state money. The bill does not mandate any one approach, but rather it develops options to enhance currently available resources. The three main options are: (1) the development of crisis stabilization units that are law enforcement and patient friendly; (2) authorization for police detentions directly to treatment; and (3) authorization for prosecutor initiated treatment alternatives.
>
> This is a situation that we all know intuitively should be better; however, it must be balanced to assist individuals without violating their liberty interests. The purpose of the bill is to address the causes of the revolving door cycle and, hopefully, intervene in a manner that will prevent people from getting into the cycle." (SB 5533, 2007)

This bill provides a number of changes to the system in Washington State. It decreases the demand on the number of psychiatric beds, provides guidelines to officers about diverting mentally ill individuals, creates options for multiple entry points and creates opportunities to invest in crisis triage systems.

From a police officer's perspective the legislative intent was good. If you can decrease the time it takes to make a referral, the more likely you are to use the system. One example from Yakima County stands out. In the past police would take mentally ill suspects into custody and would transport them to the local hospital. Officers complained that they would stand by for hours as the individual waited in the lobby, was eventually seen by the doctor and then, still later a crisis worker. This was an inefficient use of time, and the sheriff and officers wanted a quicker response. The local mental health provider and law enforcement worked together to create a behavioral health diversion program that takes less than fifteen minutes for an officer to make a referral. This reduced the officer's time off-line and increased the likelihood that they would use the program. The benefit to correctional officers was to limit the time involved with a destabilized inmate, if they had to incarcerate them at all.

To summarize, the use of behavioral health diversion provides time-saving to law enforcement (return to patrol), decreases the number of event related injuries, and improves access to crisis triage systems. It decreases the amount of potentially harmful time spent incarcerated keeping both inmates and officers safe from injurious events. This has been supported by research in New York, Florida, Ohio, Oregon, and Texas. Kent State University Department of Sociology[18] completed a review of behavioral health diversion programs and found that people completing the program had a reduced rate of re-incarceration, those individuals treated for depression had a lower rate of re-incarceration, those participating in outpatient commitment services had a reduced rate of hospitalization than prior to their involvement and those who were unsuccessful in completing the mental health program had a higher rate of incarceration following discharge from the program.

Figure 12.1 The Forensic Mental Health Team: An Enhancement of the Sequential Intercept Model
By Executive Lieutenant Adam Hopkins of Washoe County Nevada Sheriff's Office

Given our primary mission, the "Care and Custody" of those in our facilities, our burning question has been if we are we doing enough to provide the necessary mental health treatment for mentally ill inmates, and how can we bypass the revolving door this group invariably finds itself in? Our county currently uses the *Sequential Intercept Model*. After evaluation of the specific needs in our community, we have enhanced this program with our *Forensic Mental Health Team* (FMHT).

One of the most crucial problems we faced was a lack of *acute* bed space at the state mental health facility for admissions from the street, hospitals or from our detention center. Whatever progress we had made within our in-custody programs was lost once the inmate was released from custody, and returned to the same environment that caused their deterioration in the first place. Ironically, there was no lack of hospital beds, but this abundance was in the chronic program. Through consultation among the FMHT, the state shifted bed classification, without, therefore, any need to change current staffing levels. Now, not only are mentally ill inmates placed in acute beds when they need it, this has had an added benefit of opening up bed space for local hospitals as well. This change was crucial for other aspects of the program to be accomplished.

The FMHT is comprised of Nevada state mental health workers and Sheriff's Office employees, both civilian and commissioned. The state has provided, at no cost to the county, a full-time discharge planner, who works directly with our full-time social worker to enhance placement and follow-up of mentally ill inmates. Once released, one of three full time case managers provided by the state, takes over and arranges housing, medications and general living assistance, all in an attempt to break the recidivism cycle for these inmates. A core of 100 recidivist mental health inmates was originally identified through data sharing agreements. To date (March, 2013), forty two are enrolled in the program, and another twenty are on a wait list.

Upon release from jail, the state now provides each participant with fourteen days of medication, which gives ample time to set up care upon release. Program Coordinators ensure participants take their medications and assist them in daily tasks such as attending doctor appointments, shopping, etc. County Social Services, which was already collaborating with the Sheriff's Office on a serial-inebriant program, was invited to our team meetings and became involved by volunteering to partner with the state to locate additional housing.

The cost, per inmate, is between $2,000 and $4,000 per month. Although more than initially anticipated, it is still far less than the costs of long-term or repeated incarceration and hospitalization. The primary expense is housing. The program has begun utilizing housing provided by non-profit organizations. Recently, a local non-profit committed to renovating a current property in an effort to provide additional housing for our participants and renovation is underway. The State of Nevada is also in the planning phase of utilizing current space within the state system for additional housing. The state provided space in an unused building that will be used specifically for our type of participant. It is due to open in April 2013.

The model created through this collaborative effort is now being used across the State of Nevada. We are now receiving calls from the state prison system asking if the team could assist their population as well.

The FMHT is now a monthly addition to a group of elected officials both local and state, court personnel, county management, county social services and various law enforcement agencies with the focus being the streamlining of court and detention services. The feedback from this group is positive and validates that the goal of curbing recidivism within the mental health prisoner population is being achieved.

NOTE: An expanded discussion on the FMHT is in my article, publication pending, entitled "*A Country in Crisis: Launching a County/State Collaborative Forensic Mental Health Team, an Enhancement of the Sequential Intercept Model,*" which will be accessible at NICIC.gov/nationaljailexchange

CHAPTER 13

The Role of Probation and Parole as Part of an Overarching System of Both Custody and Care

The number of people on probation in the United States has increased remarkably—an estimated 6.7 million people in 2010, a two-fold increase in the last twenty-five years, from one in seventy-seven people to one in thirty-one. The PEW Center (2012)[19] released the following statistics.

- In Fiscal Year (FY) 2008, the thirty-four states for which data are available spent $18.65 billion on prisons, but only $2.52 billion on probation and parole.
- For eight states where twenty-five years of data were available, spending on prisons grew by $4.74 billion from FY 1983 to FY 2008, while probation and parole spending increased by only $652 million. This means that while prisons accounted for one-third of the population growth, they consumed eighty-eight percent of the new corrections expenditures.
- The thirty-three states that were able to provide data reported spending as much as twenty-two times more per day to manage prison inmates than to supervise offenders in the community. The reported average inmate cost was $79 per day, or nearly $29,000 per year. The average cost of managing an offender in the community ranged from $3.42 per day for probationers to $7.47 per day for parolees, or about $1,250 to $2,750 a year.

There are multiple opportunities for intervention (sequential intercept) from pre-arrest through post-adjudication **(Chapter 12)**. Probation and parole services, then, is one of the filters for developing interventions. This chapter will address some of the challenges facing probation services, and options for working with mentally ill individuals that may decrease re-offending and re-incarceration.[20]

Service Access in the Community

With limited access to social services, as well as limited funding, meeting requirements for standards of care and dealing with the co-occurring disorders limits the number of available services that probation/parole officers (PO) have access to. There are a number of key features required to address the essential needs of mentally ill probationers. One of those elements is a unique case management style that requires an active integration of internal (in-house) and external resources to meet probationers' needs. When supervising the mentally ill offender, the PO must not merely act as a referral source or monitor.[21] Instead, the specialty PO actively maintains a close working relationship with treatment providers, and actively strives to secure social resources (e.g., SSI, housing, transportation) for the offender.

Pre-arrest and post release planning are imperative for any client a PO believes will naturally fall back into the arrest cycle. Case management planning for these offenders should include bi-weekly or monthly meetings with local correctional personnel to ensure there is a continuity of care for at-risk offenders. Client decompensation poses a risk of harm (violence, suicide or medical emergencies) to all parties involved.

PO generally have an idea what clients are going to "fall off the grid" and into an arrest cycle. They can alert the local facilities and provide pertinent information (case manager's names, protective payee contact numbers, and support information) so that the client continues to receive needed medications and to ensure their bills are paid so they do not lose their housing. Upon release, clients will need to be picked up by someone other than:
- Their pimp.
- Their drug dealer.
- The relative that is taking their SSI checks to fund their own drug problem.

Getting the mentally ill offender into a stable environment that is drug, alcohol, and crime free is vital to helping them to a successful probationary period and hopefully a productive lifestyle afterwards. It is essential that they are picked up by a case manager, and that the person helping them with their finances—if they are not able to do this on their own—is not taking their money for other purposes. Sometimes this involves making a mental health case manager their protective payee—anything to make sure the client keeps their housing while they are incarcerated and after release.

Referring a person for treatment does not remove their liability for criminal behaviour, but it does provide additional options or tools for reducing re-incarceration. The use of civil commitment laws, access to mental health courts, and specialized probation services can reduce the number of mentally ill individuals that enter our legal system. Examples of this can be seen in New York and forty-four other states that have implemented some type of "Assisted Outpatient Treatment" (AOT).[22] The odds of arrest in any given month for participants who were currently receiving AOT were significantly lower than the odds for participants in the pre–AOT and pre-voluntary agreement group (the reference group). The odds of arrest were nearly two thirds lower for participants receiving AOT, compared with the odds of arrest for a reference group, who were not currently receiving such services.[23]

When we ensure a continuity of care, we work with the offender to give them the best opportunity to escape the arrest cycle. This is a benefit to all agencies involved and has been shown to have a measurable positive effect on budgets. The wonderful by-product of the agency co-operation in planning is optimal care for the offender.

CHAPTER 14

Mental Health and Psychiatric Services on the "Outside"

It is imperative that all of the care that the inmate receives during incarceration is coordinated with all the other agencies that are involved or will be involved with the inmate after release. Medical, mental health and care, and probation and parole services all play a role in the treatment of a mentally ill inmate once they have returned to the community. The nature of inmate's illness as well as what kind of crises they find themselves will dictate which agency will take the lead in the care of the inmate. If an inmate is out of control, care and custody would take the lead in restraining the inmate: they may be required to return to mental health court, or parole/probation may revoke their community custody and they may be returned to jail. If an inmate were suicidal, mental health would take the lead in establishing a treatment plan and safety contracts. If an inmate were in a health crisis, then medical services would take the lead. Taking the lead however, does not eliminate the need or the participation of the other parts of what would otherwise be a treatment team. Services must be "wrap-around," not one-at-a-time.

Mental Health Services

In ideal circumstances, an in-house mental health team in the jail achieves stabilization of the inmate. In fact, this may only last for a couple of weeks after release, where, once re-incarcerated, the in-house mental health team has to start all over again. Ensuring continuity of care from incarceration to release and beyond is the key to keeping the inmate healthy and the community safe. It is not enough, however, to simply refer inmates to local mental health agencies. Although they may be mandated to serve any clients with specific diagnoses and funding, many agencies are ill-equipped to serve aggressive, sometimes jail or street-hardened, mentally ill individuals. Therefore, it should be the responsibility of jail social services to:

- Find out what services the agency actually has, and what type of client they are able to offer treatment. It makes little sense, for example, to send a stimulant-abusing individual, with no mental disorder beyond his or her drug abuse, to a facility that offers no drug treatment.
- Ensure that the inmate is correctly diagnosed. Far too many anti-social, even psychopathic, inmates are referred to social services agencies, simply because they are "weird" or "disorderly," or have a substance-abuse problem that affects their mental status. Once in the mental health agency in the community, they may be non-compliant, threatening, or worst of all, victimize vulnerable non-criminal mentally ill patients at the community agency. Send individuals whom the agency can actually treat.
- Ensure that parole/probation is aware of the inmate's mental health needs, and what barriers to treatment the inmate presented while in custody. Some inmates cannot be safely managed at a

mental health agency itself, they still truly needs medication or case management. Community corrections should go the extra mile, so to speak, to facilitate treatment and to assist the mental health agency with any problems that arise. For example, one of the writers consulted with some agencies that now provide treatment to dangerous mentally-ill individuals *in the lobby of the local police station.* Another option might be the parole/probation office itself.

- Particularly when there is leverage through ordinary courts, through the mental health or drug court, or through parole/probation, release should include both trip-wires and sanctions to encourage or even enforce compliance with treatment requirements.

Figure 14.1 Caution: It's not the mandate, it's the enforcement

All too often, trip-wires and sanctions are mandated by court-order or conditions of release, and then they are either ignored, or those on the team, for any one of a number of reasons, minimize it when the offender violates a rule or sets off a trip-wire. One of the writers has consulted on a horrific case, in which a dangerous, mentally ill individual was on a very strict court order regarding supervision and treatment, and he was neither adequately supervised nor treated. He later murdered an individual, the focus of his rage and paranoia.

The Emergency Room

Because access to primary care has diminished and emergency departments are ever-increasingly used by the homeless, aged, and undocumented as their primary source of medical care, emergency rooms must see far more people than what would be assumed, based on a consideration of pure per capita medical emergencies. Mentally ill individuals in crisis take up more time than most ordinary patients. The majority of emergency room physicians believe the increase in ER visits by individuals with mental illnesses is having a negative impact upon access to emergency medical care for all patients—causing longer wait times, increasing patient frustration, and diminishing the capacity of hospital staff. Many hospital emergency rooms would truly prefer that no mentally ill individuals be taken to their facility. There is considerable pressure to discharge and to decrease hospital admissions to the small number of available psychiatric beds.

Hospitals, as well as the system(s) that fund them, should accept that they bear responsibility for this problem as well. Under healthcare reform, hospitals that readmit patients within thirty days of discharge are to be fined for readmissions. On the positive side, this has created incentives for hospitals and managed care to reduce the over-utilization of hospital stays and to create a system where follow-up, "care management," and treatment coordination is mandated. On the other hand, this can result in people being released before they are psychiatrically stabilized, once again a potential danger to themselves and the community.

As our readers surely know, this lack of hospital beds has resulted in the misdemeanant mentally ill being sent to jail, over and over again. Sometimes it takes someone to say, "No" before the system changes.

Take the example of Summit County Sheriff Drew Alexander. On February 13, 2012 he announced that the county jail would no longer accept violent mentally ill and mentally disabled people arrested by area police—perhaps becoming the first facility in the country with such a policy.

> "We're not going to be a dumping ground anymore for these people," he said. The sheriff had long complained that housing the mentally ill and disabled in jail is inhumane, and they belong in a mental hospital where they can be better treated. For years, he has threatened to stop taking such people if they are violent and until they have been treated first. He is following through now after a federally funded review of mental health programming at the jail recommended, *"that those people be referred to the hospital emergency room or the psychiatric crisis center for evaluation prior to being accepted into the jail."* [24]

We are not suggesting or encouraging you to refuse mentally ill people in your jail or correction facility. It should not come to that. Nonetheless, systems need to change and adapt. Hospitals, community mental health, and jail systems need to work together. Doing this shares the costs and creates opportunities for new alliances and funding opportunities. [25]

Adopt the following goals in your hospital referrals:
1. Communicate and build a relationship with the treating physicians and medical staff in the local hospitals. Speaking to a designated liaison will give you a clear picture of your wait time and determine the flow for patients receiving treatment.
2. Time for a mental health admission to the emergency room should not exceed the time it takes for a standard medical patient to clear.
3. Use of a drug screen for a medically stable patient may be unnecessary and delay discharge or referral.

Establishing a system in which the jail supervisor can call the emergency room before the inmate is transported to share vital health and security information keeps everyone safe and allows the emergency room personnel to set up what they need in advance. Emergency rooms are not equipped to deal with violent mentally ill inmates for long periods of time. They are; however, vital in stabilizing and/or medicating an inmate. Inmates that are violent or out of control could be mentally ill, in kidney failure, have an enclosed bleeding head wound, or even be on the brink of death. <u>Never, ever should one of these inmates be left alone with hospital personnel!</u> Just as it is not the correctional officer's job to administer medications to a violent inmate, it is not emergency personnel's job to engage in combat with them.

The goals of emergent psychiatric services are rapid stabilization and brief treatment. After an inmate/patient has been admitted and stabilized, all efforts should be made to establish an effective treatment plan once they return to jail. Collaboration between jail medical and mental health staff) and the psychiatric hospital treatment team is essential.

In addition to modification of treatment and case management strategies, an important concern is jail formularies. Many facilities try to decrease costs by controlling medication, shifting, for example, to a once every two weeks or once a month injectable psychiatric medication, saving thousands of dollars monthly for a chronically mentally ill patient. It is essential that jail staff discuss recommended medication and treatment options while the inmate is still in the hospital, including a clear discussion of different formularies that may serve the same clinical need, sometimes at vastly different cost.[26]

SECTION III

Core Requirements for De-escalation and Control of Agitated, Aggressive, and/or Mentally Ill Individuals

CHAPTER 15

The Development of a Safety Mindset

Correctional work is always dangerous. Officers should never be "comfortable" in a unit, on a tier, in the recreation yard, or with an inmate. It doesn't matter who or what they are or did—they are a danger to you. Whenever you are in the units or interacting with inmates, be present in the moment. Recognize your body positioning, be aware of your physical environment, and pay attention to the signals your body gives you **(Chapters 16 and 17)** that might indicate that a dangerous situation is developing.

Although this book centers on verbal de-escalation skills, we must start at a more basic level, because the contributing causes of many critical incidents can be attributed to a lack of attention to basic safety precautions. This must begin *before* you start your workday. If your mind is unfocused, your ability to notice early warnings signs of potentially dangerous situations will be impaired. For example, officers cannot allow personal or familial issues to intrude upon their ability to focus on the job at hand.

The development of correctional awareness is based upon the following three fundamental assumptions:

1. Being pro-active about safety issues must be a primary concern of all correctional staff: managers, supervisors, line officers, and support staff.
2. There needs to be consistency and a common understanding in the application of safety procedures and emergency protocols at all levels of the institution.
3. Adequate staff safety preparedness and correctional awareness is not a once-and-done training event: ongoing communication is required between all levels of staff, and a regular review of safety protocols, operational policies, crisis response processes, physical site safety issues, and ongoing training for all staff is crucial. A variety of issues, including overcrowding of cell and dormitory areas, the custody level of the inmates supervised, gang affiliations, physical plant problems, design flaws such as blind spots as well as ever-shrinking correctional budgets impact upon the level of risk.

Beyond those systemic issues just mentioned, attendance to a number of factors will definitely make a safer worksite.

1. **Solid Boundaries.** A predictable and fair set of rules concerning the relationships between inmates and staff, staff and other staff, and among the inmates themselves must be established and enforced. Inmates and staff need absolute clarity regarding what behaviors are permissible and which are not. Inmates (and staff) need assurance that relationships will be professional. Staff members must not act in any way amongst each other that will negatively affect the supervision of inmates.

2. **Adaptability**. Notwithstanding the necessity for a predictable environment and standardized procedures, correctional staff must on occasion also be flexible. Staffing constraints, logistical problems, and disruptive inmates require immense creativity. Standardization must never become inflexible and dogmatic, but rather, adaptable to the changes routinely occurring in a correctional setting. Blind adherence to standardization can particularly impinge on the well-being of mentally ill inmates. Notwithstanding, officers and staff must never lose sight of their overarching goals: institutional safety and fair, but strict enforcement of the rules must take precedence over anything else.

3. **Presence and Accessibility**. The safest agencies are ones where correctional officers and staff have contact with inmates. Boundaries and security concerns must be maintained at a hundred percent levels, but correctional officers can only ensure safety when they are an *active* presence in the lives of the inmates they supervise. Positive interactions with officers offer mentally-ill inmates a pro-social role model to follow, and an opportunity to practice new social interaction skills. This also can promote a modicum of professional trust between inmates and officers, making a volatile environment a little more stable with every positive interaction.

4. **Good Training and Regular Practice**. Correctional officers have a professional and moral responsibility to be well-versed and skilled in de-escalation methods, both verbal and physical. While this certainly requires an effort on the part of the individual officer, departmental policy must ensure that de-escalation training is made available and mandatory, and that times are set aside on a *regular* basis to practice these skills. One of the best ways to maintain and enhance skills is to have one defensive tactic/verbal de-escalation drill, taking no more than five-ten minutes at every staff meeting or the beginning of every shift change.[27]

5. **Integrity**. Beyond all else, officers must be persons of integrity, who are rightly held to the highest moral and ethical standards. Inmates must be aware that officers are vigilant in maintaining ethical and moral relationships towards the inmates they supervise. Without this, all the de-escalation methods in the world are just empty words.

Staff Meetings Should Always Include a Focus on Safety Concerns

Supervisors and administrators should conduct regular staff meetings to promote, discuss, and build upon existing procedures as well as share information critical to the tasks of the day. This will strengthen the professional bonds necessary for the safe operation of the agency, increase officer morale, and foster staff cohesion throughout the watches. While thoughtful preparation may not prevent a critical incident from occurring, an alert, informed and well-trained staff can reduce the impact of such events through a coordinated planned response.

After Action Reviews (AARs) are particularly important in the wake of a critical incident, in the review of planned actions such as a search of a cell, block of cells, or dormitories, or post incident reports resolving an inmate/staff hostage situation. AARs aren't to be used as finger-pointing exercises, where some look to lay blame for problems or difficulties during an operation. Some things are likely to not go as planned or anticipated in even the most successful operation, and improvement begins with a thoughtful discussion among those involved. Therefore, AAR's must focus solely on what can be done to improve the process and enhance everyone's safety for future operations.

After Action Review Focusing on the Inmate's Actions

Correctional staff must make an effort to learn more about the patterns of behavior that might have preceded a prisoner's aggression, as well as any actions on the officers' part that were either unhelpful or contributory towards an inmate becoming violent. Correctional officers need to note the following:

1. What were the circumstances that led to an aggressive encounter?

2. What was the *first* sign that indicated that the situation was getting volatile or dangerous?

3. Remember what the inmate(s) said and did in the moments just before the aggressive incident.

4. Generally, people are able to control their verbal signals better than their non-verbal signals, so recall the inmate's body language prior to the incident. Tension can also create a change in the quality of the voice such as rate of speech, pitch, and/or volume.

5. What do you believe you should have done differently?

6. What planning did you do in regard to that inmate subsequent to the aggression? How happy are you with that plan?

7. Did you report the encounter, and to what degree do you believe the institution backed you up? Officers are encouraged to report any incident in which they felt threatened in any fashion. Over time, these reports will provide the data for a general representation of the more common threats that officers face when performing their duties. Safety protocols can then be fine-tuned to concentrate on the most common threat.

Figure 15.1 Record Keeping Is Crucial to Safety

Good record keeping, be it departmental forms or chronos, is crucial to safe and effective supervision. In fact, poor record keeping or illegible notes in the inmate's file should be considered professional malpractice. Clear and concise documentation is essential to the safety of fellow officers and staff. Critical information should be highlighted, or underline printed in ink, in the case of hand written records, so that anyone opening the file is immediately aware of the risk factors involved.

Washoe County, Nevada, uses a method entitled "Confidential Custody Bulletins (CCB). These bulletins highlight individuals about whom staff need to be aware for both safety issues or litigious reasons. Mental health status can also be noted in a CCB, if it poses an unusually high safety risk to staff.

Crisis Response and Intervention

Correctional officers in institutional/jail settings are typically first responders whenever a mentally ill inmate requires assistance up to and including crisis situations such as attempted suicide. As soon as it is reasonably possible, the first responding correctional officer should utilize the institution's radio and designated code call system, and call for back-up assisting staff. When responding to an apparent suicide/suicide attempt in a cell or when an inmate, mentally ill or not, is assaulting or being assaulted in a cell, the officer shall follow institutional policy regarding the number of staff necessary before a cell door may be opened. Staff safety is paramount in all situations.

Physical Site Safety

A physically secure and well-designed facility will enhance security, while simultaneously leaving the inmate with fewer opportunities to act aggressively. Remember, staff may not only interact with inmates in their cells or in the exercise yard. Spaces such as personal offices and dedicated interview rooms should have a minimum of furniture and no clutter. If possible, you should also position yourself closest to the door in case you need to exit quickly. Although privacy issues may be of concern to the inmate, the authors recommend that officers never close their office door when conducting an interview by themselves. Not only will a closed door prevent others from detecting an escalating situation, closing your office doors will simply present a barrier to anyone helping you.

If a closed door cannot be avoided, then the officer (s) should ensure that the area immediate to the office is cleared of other inmates and that any office windows remain unobstructed by blinds or curtains. Finally, the officer (s) should notify other officers and/or supervisors of their intent to conduct an inmate office interview. These practices will minimize the possibility of staff harm due to inmate violence in the office setting and also minimize or make unlikely inmate claims of inappropriate or misconduct on the part of the officer(s).

Establishing a secure office may be compromised due to architectural design and/or physical plant limitations, as well as the financial constraints of your institution. For example, the installation of modern security and video surveillance equipment can be prohibitively expensive. However, there are many ways of enhancing security that are relatively free of cost, requiring only that officers and staff be alert to safety issues and communicate with one another. Listed below are just a few of the issues to consider regarding physical site security:

1. Control ingress and egress to the office proper. As many offices utilized by correctional officers are in the inmate housing or program areas, the control of inmate egress and ingress can be challenging. One way to control the flow of inmates to a staff office is through the use of office schedules for inmate interviews, and adherence to an inmate pass system for non-routine inmate movement (such as office visits). Officers must escort each inmate into and out of the office. Never allow an inmate to wander unescorted through the office. The use of "out-of-bounds" lines around the office will deter inmates from loitering without a valid pass. Finally, constant communication with other staff about one's whereabouts either through a radio, phone or face-to-face should always be used.

2. Security doors must remain locked if they are to be effective. Propping a security door open, or leaving the door unlocked to facilitate staff movement negates its intended purpose.

3. Dedicated interview rooms should be established and used to conduct all inmate interviews.

Such rooms can remain free from any extraneous clutter, office equipment, and furniture, leaving the room free of many potential weapons.

- Any object can become a weapon. Keep desks free from pencils, staplers, paper hole-punches, and other office equipment.

- Are picture frames or corkboards secured to the walls? Any item that can be removed from the walls or picked up easily is a potential weapon.

- All necessary office furniture and equipment must be in good condition and in proper working order. Loose chair parts and light furniture can be used as weapons as well. When designing an office, or acquiring new furniture, safety must be considered in addition to comfort and aesthetics.

- Personal photographs of family members and loved ones or any other personal items have no place within a correctional setting where inmates might view them. Photographs and/or personal items may provide sufficient information to identify your home, address, lifestyle, and that of your family members, and may therefore compromise your family's safety. Finally, personal items also encourage the inmate to talk about *your* family, hobbies, or other interests.

- Outside your personal office space, give consideration to all hallways, stairwells, staff and public elevators, parking and storage areas, and the reception area if present. Are there adequate sight lines to see who is entering the area? Is the lighting adequate in hallways, stairwells, and parking areas?

- If your department authorizes the use of weapons of any kind, make sure that they are in a locked metal cabinet, lock-box or drawer when not in use.

- In certain settings, it is necessary to use wands to screen for weapons, and requiring inmates to remove bulky overcoats, "hoodies," and outerwear and headgear that can easily conceal weapons. Ensure that long, matted or braided hair be scrutinized as a possible location to secure a weapon. Razor blades are often "cheeked;" be aware that an inmate may be casually speaking with you, but at any moment, they can spit a blade into their hand.[28]

- Emergency numbers should be programmed into the office phone system or posted nearby each telephone extension in the office. Off-hook alarm system should be a part of your telephones' features. An off-hook alarm will notify a central control point of your emergency and location. The *installation* of off-hook alarms or panic buttons is not enough, however. Drills should be conducted regularly to ensure that they actually work, and that designated officers actually respond when an emergency button is pressed.

- Mobile radio units must be compatible with an all-call emergency call system, and the radio should contain site specific and/or incident level specific emergency response calling codes.

- Correctional officers should also enter all emergency contact information into their cell phones, including numbers for local police departments, treatment centers, and their home office.

- Finally, if you are interviewing high custody, violent inmates such as those found in supermax, maximum security jails or within administrative segregation, the use of an expanded metal secured holding cage should be utilized to maintain staff and other inmates' safety.

Tactical Response Planning

Even the most secure office site may not prevent an inmate from becoming aggressive. No matter how confident you may be in your skills at verbal de-escalation, violence is best handled by a team. Officers should enlist the help of others whenever possible, rather than trying to resolve a dangerous situation on their own. However, the willingness to assist a fellow officer is not enough. Officers and support staff must know *how* to help if things do go wrong. Therefore, officers and staff <u>together</u> must have a workable tactical response plan. Appropriate responses range from verbal control to actual physical restraint/use of force. Officers and staff must *practice* the requisite techniques so that they can make proper decisions in order to act effectively, with minimal delay. Each officer and staff member must be fully aware of their designated role, and possess the skills and training necessary to carry out their assigned duties.

Correctional facilities should also develop an emergency staff response protocol that identifies on a watch-by-watch, post-by-post basis, response requirements at the levels of first responders, secondary responders and third responders, and radio coded appropriately. This will ensure that staff response levels are sufficient and timely to meet the emergent situation, that <u>only</u> those designated as responders will do so, leaving to other posts the responsibility to maintain control over non-affected areas of the facility. Tactical response will, thereby, not strip staff from other vital areas, given that such incidents can be a diversion from another situation in a different part of the jail.

Individual limitations must be taken into account when preparing a safety plan, and responsibilities should be assigned accordingly. For instance, some officers should be designated as communications officer, responsible for establishing and maintaining effective communications with emergency responders or other staff. Others may be better suited toward the tactical aspects of the response plan, such as the physical control of aggressive inmates, or the establishment of physical site security.

An effective safety plan must include consistent preparation for violence *before* it occurs. Officers have a professional responsibility to inform fellow officers and staff members that a confrontation may occur when a particular inmate reports to an office, or program/housing area. Not all potential emergencies can be foretold, but many can be anticipated, and an appropriate response can be planned. Failure to do this is a guaranteed formula for escalating an otherwise manageable encounter into a critical event. Therefore, never "surprise" other officers or staff with a last minute request for assistance *after* the inmate has already been admitted into an unsecure area. Even the best laid plans will not prevent an emergency from arising, which is why regular practice of the safety plan is a requirement for the safety of all concerned. Regular practice will also highlight areas of the response plan that need to be modified and improved, *before* a true emergency occurs.

Figure 15.2 Don't Let the Abnormal Become Normal

We can't underscore how important it is to check out your concerns and intuitions with fellow officers, and sometimes with professionals outside your office. Don't only consult others when you are concerned about an individual. **Sometimes, you should consult when you *should* be concerned and aren't.** Some correctional officers become so familiar with pathology that the abnormal becomes normal. The officer no longer reacts in a natural way, tolerating or not noticing covert aggression, boundary trespass, or grooming behavior. Officers can easily become complacent when dealing with familiar inmates. Note that just because you have not been hurt (yet) does not mean you are doing a good job of keeping yourself safe.

Tactical Concerns

Inmates must be effectively pat searched and pass through metal detectors as they move from one secure area to another. Some officers become far too dependent on the metal detectors and become inefficient or lazy when pat searching inmates. Inmates have access to many heavy-duty plastics items: spoons, mops, mop buckets and other items. Many of these can be broken and whittled down to make excellent shanks—none of which will register on a metal detector or wand—but are just as deadly when slipped in between your ribs or lodged in your eye socket. Conduct pat search thoroughly and often, conduct frequent safety and security checks of each unit and conduct cell inspections on every shift.

Another foundation of safety on the tiers and yards is knowing your population. Much of your "intel" of an inmate population is acquired when the line officer just observes:

- Which inmates associate with each other?
- Are the inmates separating themselves by race or gang in an open area?
- Are there one or two inmates moving from group to group?
- Are there inmates that don't move around without an entourage of other inmates?
- Are there one or two inmates that appear to be keeping watch for other inmates?

All of these situations could be predictors of an upcoming crisis event (inmates suddenly separating by race or gang can be indicative of an upcoming group altercation) or they could be just an anomaly. Sometimes the only advanced warning is knowledge of your population.

Figure 15.3 Individualized Safety Planning—Beyond Institutional Rules

As officers move throughout their duty stations, they should be acutely aware of their surroundings, while simultaneously, almost automatically, running through every different scenario that could possibly happen as well as what they would do to best handle that situation. Do you want to be the person wondering what to do when a mob of inmates is running toward you during a riot scenario? Do you want to be the person trying to figure out where to hide and ditch your keys when the inmates have taken over the jail? In New Mexico, inmates flayed the inmates in protective custody. Do you have a plan to protect such inmates—the job you took an oath to do when you accepted your badge? Every officer should have a plan about where they would go and what they would do if there were a riot, if they were hurt, or if they were taken hostage, in each and every area they work. Make sure you have a plan for every situation you can imagine, because inmates imagine a lot of situations in which you are naked or dead.

CHAPTER 16

Training Your Intuition (Correctional Awareness)
to Pick Up Danger

Correctional Awareness

A sense of spatial awareness, of potential escape routes, likely weapons, and access to help should become a natural part of the correctional officer's personal and professional life. This routine attentiveness is often referred to as "correctional awareness." Some folks (correctional officers and inmates alike) are naturally good at this and others are not. This section offers a method to teach correctional officers and staff to pick up danger on an intuitive level.

Enter a room with a predator's mind and a predator's movements: slowly, gracefully, with calculation. Imagine that you are going to hurt the next person who comes into that room. How would you cut off their escape routes? What could you use as a weapon? Where would you position yourself to attack? How could your victim best escape?

Do the above exercise on an occasional basis. Consider it a refresher course on the mind of a predator. Done over time, you will start to develop the ability to automatically scan any location to see if there is anything there which makes it a place of danger, as well as switching your mind on to picking up predatory or other dangerous behaviors on the part of inmates.

Figure 16.1 Author's Experience: Scanning Saves Lives

A correctional officer entered the cell of an elderly inmate, somewhat demented. She had no history of assault in over twenty years of incarceration in various institutions. People took her for granted.

She began screaming at the officer to get out. The cell was not messy, but it was filled with all sorts of small objects, the collection of decades in the prison system. The officer's eyes picked up something on the back of the woman's toothbrush. She'd fixed a razor blade to the back of the brush, but kept the bristles intact, so it might pass a cursory inspection.

As it turned out, she was acutely psychotic. She believed that Satan would come in the cell door to steal her soul, so she planned to back up, grab her shank, and slash the throat of the "Lord of Darkness." The correctional officer's habit of scanning, trained through the above exercise, very likely saved him from a very difficult situation.

Intuition: That Small Voice to Which Officers Must Listen

Intuitions, "gut feelings" are sometimes vague, but they are often the *first* signs that one is in a dangerous situation. Not only should experienced officers be sure to voice their intuitions at staff meetings, but newer officers, too, must not be hesitant to relate their concerns and ask questions:

1. Officers should not minimize their gut feelings and intuitions when exchanging information. Don't begin by stating "I know it's nothing, but...." In doing so, the officer may lead others to minimize the situation as well.

2. Officers should not be hesitant because they don't have "hard evidence" to support their concern.

3. Veteran officers or senior staff members must not belittle other officers or support staff that are intuitive. Even the most senior officer has not experienced every possible contingency.

4. Differences among officers and staff must be discussed respectfully, particularly in regard to questions of safety. If one person's intuition is discounted or dismissed, he or she may cease to speak up, and vital information regarding everyone's security will be lost.

Figure 16.2 Author's Experience: Life-Saving Intuition

Once, on a mental health outreach requested by a landlord, some internal sense commanded me not to knock on the resident's door and to retreat to my car. I literally backed down the steps, not taking my eyes from the house. Returning to the office, I wrote in the person's new chart in huge red letters "Something is wrong. Don't go to this house without police back-up."

Thankfully, a co-worker heeded my "irrational" advice, and several days later, she and the police found a floridly psychotic woman waiting with a gun behind the door. In a previous psychotic episode, she had been attacked by two men intent on raping and murdering her. She held them off with a firearm and was eventually rescued by police. Now, some years later and again in a psychotic state, she was waiting with her gun as I approached the house.

It is probable that only my not knocking on the door saved my life. When my co-worker went to the house with the police, whom the woman viewed as rescuers, she open the door and willingly turned over the gun. What did I perceive? Was it a stirring of the curtains, a soft click of the bolt of a semi-automatic weapon being pulled back, or was it ESP? To be honest, I do not care. What matters is that we, and anyone we work with, respect such intuitive commands.

CHAPTER 17

Honing Intuition Through Awareness
of Personal Spacing

Communicating with mentally ill inmates is often difficult, particularly when they are becoming agitated. Suppression of all anger should not be our goal. While always remaining ready to respond to any assault, correctional officers must develop the ability to differentiate between true aggression, with the very real possibility of physical attack, as opposed to the inmate who angrily tries to communicate frustration: expressing their upset with the court system, their personal difficulties, or treatment issues.

The manifest behaviors of aggressive inmates will be discussed in detail in subsequent chapters. This chapter will focus on developing the ability to *sense* when a potential aggressor is beginning to escalate.

Comfort Zones and Physical Spacing

Agitated people lose the ability to accurately listen to what you are saying, much less maintain a coherent train of thought in their own right. Instead, they track other aspects of communication: your muscular tension, the amount of physical space between you, the positioning of your hands, and the quality of your voice. You should be doing the same.

As the inmate becomes more agitated, the correctional officer must take care to remain calm and prepare for the possibility of a physical confrontation, while simultaneously maintaining focus on verbally de-escalating the situation. **Most importantly, the correctional officer should not feed the anger, particularly by losing his or her own temper. Most people can't sustain anger for more than a couple of minutes, so if you can keep your composure, many inmates will calm down on their own.**

It is not enough to learn a list of the typical behaviors that aggressive people are likely to display. Although the *basic* emotions are physically expressed in pretty definitive ways, irrespective of culture, non-verbal behaviors can be idiosyncratic: not only do people often have their own ways of physically expressing their emotions, but they also have their own ways of interpreting (or misinterpreting) yours.

Correctional officers must hone their intuition to detect subtle warning signs that a dangerous situation is developing. The leading edge of intuition is a sense of personal space. This is not just a matter of feet and inches. Simply asserting that you keep an arm's length and a half, or two arms' length apart between you and a subject is not enough. How much space would you want if the person has a blade, or is twice your size and half your age?

Our attitude can also affect our sense of space. For example, the more relaxed you are in the company of someone you trust, the less personal space you require (something that manipulative aggressors try to take advantage of). When you are uncertain or suspicious of someone, you instinctively move to get more distance from them. If you are having a bad day, you need more space to tolerate anyone's proximity.

Figure 17.1 Two Cautions Concerning Personal Space
- DON'T step inside someone's personal space, unless you are doing so to establish a clear tactical advantage.
- DON'T accommodate anyone by allowing them to stand too close to you.

You MUST be aware of the physical sensations engendered within you when someone enters your "zone." When you set such a limit as "Inmate Tran, I would like to hear what you have to say, but you are standing too close. Move back five feet, and then we will continue to talk."

Whatever reply you get will be excellent threat assessment information. You are dealing with very different individuals when one, told to step back, responds with profuse apologies compared to someone who smirks and says, "What's the matter, are you nervous around men?"

The Brain Wants to Survive

There are parts of the brain that are solely concerned with survival. These parts of the brain don't care about being polite, politically correct, or intellectualizing why someone is the way they are. These parts of the brain don't even use words. They perceive by recognizing significant patterns, and signal their recognition through physical sensations and reactions. The survival section of the brain is fast, about half a second faster than the thinking brain. About to step on a squiggly shape, you jerk back your foot even before the rest of your brain thinks, "SNAKE!"

Inter-personal space has a kind of "texture" that we perceive through both physical and emotional reactions. You train intuition through becoming more aware of the signals your body sends to you. Paradoxically, many of us get "skilled" at tuning out those signals, treating them as a kind of unwanted "noise." Being mindful of the space between you and others, and the physical sensations it evokes, can give you an early warning system that a situation is becoming potentially explosive. Thus, if someone is aggressive, psychotic, excited, depressed, menacing, hateful, or is trying to con you, the survival brain recognizes a pattern and reacts with physical reactions. For example, when in proximity to the scared person, perhaps you feel warmth in your chest, but with the con-man, your lips compress and neck tightens. With psychotic people, you feel a sensation of cold in your stomach and your hands and jaw clench with aggressive people. There are no rules to these physical reactions: they are individual to you.

Some of your physical reactions may be unpleasant or unflattering to your own self-image. For example, let us imagine that you get somewhat sick to your stomach when facing an aggressive person, or experience a subtle, but real sense of disgust when dealing with someone who is depressed. You don't need to change this reaction—it's a warning system, not a mark of character. For example, you are talking with an inmate and you notice that previously mentioned sense of disgust. Although he is smiling, perhaps talking fast, you know that this physical sensation happens to you very often when dealing with depressed and despairing individuals. So you shift the conversation to assess that, because a sense of hopelessness and helplessness, the hallmarks of that state of mind, can lead to either suicidal or homicidal thoughts.

If you continue to hone your awareness in this matter, you will develop a form of conscious intuition called **MINDFULNESS**. Mindfulness is the ability to be consciously aware of what is going on in your interactions with another person.

Where these reactions really come in handy is when someone is trying to hide their intentions: smiling, for example, while trying to get close to you to stab you. Let's imagine, in this case, it is an inmate whom you helped when he was at risk of rape from a jail gang. Your thinking mind tells you, "He wouldn't want to hurt me! I saved his life!" But your eyes are tightening and you are getting the same tension in your lower back that you have had on every occasion when someone assaulted you in the past. Don't talk yourself out of it! A very sharp blade is about to hit you right in the gut.

By taking notes later on your physical reactions, one type of "after-action review," you are training yourself to recognize the patterns, consciously, that your survival brain notices unconsciously. Instead of surmising "I was having a lucky day. Something told me not to go to that section of the yard," you say, "I had that feeling in my hands I always get right before a fight. I knew something was going to happen, so I moved to the side and saw him standing behind a screen of inmates with that five pound weight."

Figure 17.2 Don't Label the Message, Associate It With the Situation

It is very easy to train yourself to become more mindful. Carry a small notebook in your pocket. If you encounter an individual who interacts with you in a significant way (aggressive, manipulative, depressed, etc.), note down (later) how your body reacted.

We should be far more concerned with physical sensations than what we normally refer to as "feelings," our *description* of emotional states. For example, you have a sensation of high energy, with tension in your stomach. Some would call this "anxiety," while others would call this "anticipation." If you think that a sense of anxiety does not "fit" the situation you are in, you will tend to ignore the physical sensation, or talk yourself out of it, saying such phrases to yourself as—"I'm being silly. There's no reason to be 'nervous' here."

If, on the other hand, you merely associate a physical sensation with a situation, i.e., "Every time someone tries to con me, I get a little smile and tension in my neck," you will notice your physical reactions without biasing them based on what you *think* you should feel.

Figure 17.3 Author's Experience: When Intuition Was Not Heeded

An individual once thanked me profusely at the end of our meeting. Instead of the warm pride I get when I've helped someone (and I HAD helped him), I had a very strong reaction that I always have when someone overtly threatens me. I mentally brushed it aside, thinking, "I'm being an idiot. The man just complimented me." Sometime later, he poisoned me. I am only alive today because he chose to degrade me by contaminating my food rather than putting something lethal in it. I learned in the ugliest way possible to always pay attention to what my body "tells" me. The body is linked to structures in the brain that serve to protect us from danger through pattern recognition rather than verbal cognitions. To treat our bodily reactions with disrespect is to disavow that which has kept humanity alive for millennia.

SECTION IV

Centering: Standing With Strength in Crisis Situations

CHAPTER 18

Introduction to Centering

Supervising inmates who may be mentally ill, drug dependent, victims of traumatic events, struggling with developmental disabilities, brain injuries, poverty, or a lack of education is an honorable calling. You will be in a position to help, sometimes, some of the most unfortunate members of society. At the same time, some are among the most violent and criminal members of humanity.

Such work can also be terribly demanding. Being enraged, frightened, confused, or intimidated by an inmate can be debilitating and can result in poor decision-making. Even more troubling is when you realize that your reactions to the inmate made things worse. Internalizing feelings of frustration can lead to burnout, a state of being which could be summed up in the phrase, "I don't want to see any more of this," something that could get you or a fellow officer killed, when you do not pay attention at moments when awareness is most necessary.

Stress Is a Safety Issue

This is surely one of the most stressful jobs in the world. It is a different kind of stress from a war zone, where one tries to survive in the midst of enemy fire. Rather, the correctional officer, by choice, is locked in an environment where hostility is endemic and violent assault by inmates occur at any time. In other words, it is a world of constant *potential* violence. Such high levels of stress can lead to impaired judgment, substance abuse problems for correctional officers as well as a myriad of medical problems including hypertension, diabetes, etc. Stress can fuel cynicism or anxiety, as well as eliciting feelings of contempt or hatred towards inmates. When the officer's expectations of immediate inmate obedience are unintentionally brought home, it can lead to devastating problems in one's family, leading to high rates of divorce and dysfunctional relationships with one's children. Extreme stress also leads to high rates of turnover at correctional facilities, and the constant loss of veteran officers negatively impacts safety issues for remaining staff and inmates.

Opportunities to mitigate stress among correctional officers include structured peer support programs, employee assistance programs (EAP), and supervisor assistance in identifying employees who are overwhelmed and getting them the assistance they require.

There is no doubt that good leadership has a profound effect on staff morale and institutional safety. Good leadership supports secure settings by creating a culture of safety, dignity, respect, and accountability. There is a certain level, however, that nothing from "outside" can help. Stress must be addressed from within.

The strategies in the following chapters of this section revolve around maintaining self-control, even in extreme crisis situations. Mastering methods of self-control is a way for you to model proper behavior to others. This is the ability to adapt to circumstances. Not only will this make you more able to roll with the problems that any inmate presents, but also, it will make you more effective in crisis situations.

Figure 18.1 Author's Experience: Centering Is for Survival

When preparing this chapter, we had a concern that some officers would consider these chapters on centering, particularly on tactical breathing, as "touchy-feely." Here's an example from the front lines.

We were called for back-up in our sally-port entrance where a soon-to-be-incarcerated inmate was fighting with the law enforcement officer who had transported him. Correctional officer Number One was already on scene, and Officer Two and I were shoulder-to-shoulder hitting the double security doors to the sally port.

Most law enforcement officers secure their guns in security lockers or the trunk of their vehicle before taking an inmate out of their cruiser. This one didn't. Through the open back seat doors of the cruiser, I saw the police officer and one of our own on the ground, actively fighting with the inmate. In a millisecond, though, my vision narrowed into tunnel vision. All I could see was the officer's gun, sitting on the front seat of the cruiser, easily within reach of the inmate if he could just break free for a second. Officer Two and I didn't need to say a word. I broke right and he broke left, and we started locking and slamming cruiser doors to **secure that gun**! I do not remember clearing the front end of the car after we accomplished that. My next memory is hitting the cement on my knees to pull the inmate's head back, before he could bite my officer. On impact, I automatically drew in a long breath and suddenly, no more tunnel vision. My world opened to the big picture again. I started tactical breathing, as we got the inmate in a restraint chair. I *maintained* tactical breathing when the inmate started seizing, and we (Officer Two and me again) started unlocking and chucking restraints, to get him prone. The Nurse was behind us yelling, 'Hurry! Hurry!" Officer Two and I were talking quietly "Left arm free, you grab that, etc." Our hands were going fast, but my breathing wasn't.

Coincidentally, the Internal Affairs Investigator (I. A.) for our agency, a sergeant, was standing behind us. He had responded to the radio traffic, and had witnessed the entire event. After the crisis event was over I asked him how long it had taken us to get the restraints off the inmate and get him to the floor. I was concerned because the leg irons had been put on the inmate when he was fighting with us, and one key hole was up and the other was down. It had been very difficult to get access, and it took a couple of tries to get that leg iron off. I asked the I.A. Sergeant if it was three minutes or four before we got the inmate to the floor. He said he had timed it. It was only sixteen seconds.

Because I have both trained for this, and been in frequent crisis events, I was able to push through the natural stress reactions would otherwise happen in my body when it is under duress. Tactical breathing allowed me to mitigate those effects and provide the assistance needed to my fellow officers and to the inmate.

CHAPTER 19

A Fair Witness—Peer Support is a Survival Tactic

There may be nothing worse than feeling helpless or shamed after experiencing a physical or emotional assault. This is especially so on our jobs, because if an inmate is verbally or physically violent toward us, our professional pride is also attacked. One often feels isolated when under assault, even with others present. This sense of isolation gets far worse if there is no one with whom we can discuss the event. Some of the things that most powerfully affect correctional officers are so ugly or appalling that officers are reluctant to discuss them with their spouses or other family members. To do so would be inviting violence or obscenity into their home, and correctional officers don't wish to pass that kind of burden on to a loved one.

In such circumstances, you need *fair witnesses*, people who know you, who respect you, and who are willing to hear you out. Such peer support can include strategizing sessions, (debriefings) or tactical review, but we must underscore that there are times that this is the last thing you need, because the problem is not one of tactics—it is how the incident affected you. The presence of a fair witness informs you, often simply by being there, that you are still a part of the team, and that your negative, even traumatic experience, is not unique to you, but something that any one of your teammates might experience.

Figure 19.1 Safety Works Both Ways

To some of our readers, this chapter may seem far from a discussion on safety, but when we talk about someone "getting our back," it does not only mean that they are with us while going through the door. If we don't have an assurance that someone will be there after we come back out, it's a lot harder to go through the doorway in the first place.

Many jails and correctional agencies have formalized the fair witness process through a system of peer support, commonly referred to as Critical Incident Stress Management (CISM), or Critical Incident Stress Debriefing (CISD). A critical incident is an extraordinary event that forces a correctional officer to face vulnerability and mortality during the course of their official duties. These incidents typically occur without warning, and jeopardize one's physical safety and/or emotional well-being. Incidents such as being victimized in an assault or engaging an inmate in a lethal force encounter can overwhelm the correctional officer's stress capacity. A prompt and structured departmental response can reduce the negative consequences of such incidents and help restore the affected officer's physical and mental health.

CISD members are fellow officers who are trained to respond to critical events, and provide the affected correctional officer with assistance. In the event of an emergency, CISD members report to the scene as soon as possible where they will assess the correctional officer's physical and mental well-being, request that emergency medical services be dispatched to the scene if necessary, or serve as a liaison to other first responders already present. The CISD member will also accompany the affected correctional officer to the hospital, if necessary, and attend to any number of related duties, such as contacting his or her family. A prime responsibility is to hear out the officer so that he or she can safely talk through the incident with an assurance of absolute confidentiality, if they feel the need to speak about their experience. Please note that some individuals do far better by working things out on their own, at least for a time: not everyone needs, and no one should be required, to speak.

Following the incident, the CISD member will consult regularly with the affected officer's immediate supervisor and recommend services (counseling, for example) for the individual as deemed necessary and appropriate. They will also assist with any necessary paperwork that must be completed by the affected officer. Typically, the CISD member will contact the affected officer once a week for at least one month following the incident, and remain in contact with them until they are confident that the affected officer's physical and emotional needs have been addressed.

Figure 19.2 The Debate Concerning Documentation in CISD

Some CISD protocols recommend submitting a critical incident report to the administrative unit for the purpose of collecting information necessary to provide short and long-term assistance to the affected officer and to document activities, services, and progress.

There is a legitimate concern that, although this report is not intended to be used as an investigative tool, there is the potential that it can be. As an official record, it may also be subpoenaed in a lawsuit or other legal proceeding. Therefore, many CISD protocols recommend, and we concur, that nothing should be put in writing. This helps the affected officer feel like he or she can talk more freely. Written records should be confined to formal after-action reviews.

In many states, the right of the privacy for the peer support system is upheld by state law. The law is written similarly to the privacy protections afforded to clients of therapists—unless there is a crime reported or a harm threatened to another, the peer support client and provider cannot be compelled to reveal what is talked about during the peer support interactions.

CHAPTER 20

It's Not Personal
Unless You Make It So

Responding to an inmate, perhaps mentally ill, on a personal or emotional level, no matter what the provocation, will cloud an officer's judgment, while distracting him or her from legitimate safety concerns.

At any rate, although their attacks on you might *seem* personal, that is only true if you make them so. If the attack is invalid, what is there to be upset about? And if what the inmate said is valid, you knew it anyway, so what are you upset about?

- They call you fat? Well, you knew that already, didn't you?
- They called you a Nazi? Well, you aren't, so why are you taking it personally?

Correctional officers must also remember that personal feelings of revenge, of "getting even," are unacceptable in the true professional, and your actions must be the result of unbiased decision-making, based on the facts at hand. Inmates must not be violated simply because of a personal vendetta or hurt feelings. Consider obscenity:

- Some inmates use obscenity and verbal violation to get you focused on what they are saying rather than what they are doing.
- Others are just spewing verbal garbage, and suddenly realize that you have lost focus, upset at what they just said, and are open to attack.
- Still others suddenly perceive, in your response to what they said, that *you* are infuriated, and they "attack you back first," because they believe you are about to react.
- Others challenge you by trying to offend you or by making you explain yourself. In this case, provocative challenges are for the purpose of getting psychological leverage on you.
- Lastly, your reaction is a form of information gathering for the inmate. If, for example, you react when an inmate calls you fat—he now knows what sets you off, and he and probably every other inmate in the institution will use this at every opportunity.

Figure 20.1 Author's Experience: Creating a Win-Win Situation in Response to Those Trying to Push Your Buttons

It is a given that in a crisis situation, your protocols must be followed. In non-crisis situations, however, creating win-win situations with inmates allows the officer to meet whatever objective is at hand (making the inmate lock down for instance) and allows the inmate to feel alright about how the situation ended for them.

For example, a mentally ill inmate was housed in a single cell in a segregation unit. A movie was being played for the inmates. They could watch by standing at their door and looking through the window. During my segregation check, I noticed that this particular inmate was naked below the waist. Although she was housed alone, this is a violation of facility rules, and it is a rule we enforce to impose a sense of normality for the inmates. By the "book," I could have closed the cover on her window and denied her the movie. Instead, I asked why she did not have her pants on. She told me that the underwear "bite." We compromised that she did not have to wear the underwear, but the pants were required. I waited until she put her pants on (to ensure that she actually followed through), and let her continue to watch the movie. Perhaps some may find this a trivial example, but these small win-win situations, with the rules still enforced, accumulate as positive interactions that create the possibility of the inmate gradually becoming more compliant in future interactions.

No One Will Own Me

The verbal aggressor is trying to "push your buttons," often in an attempt to elicit an unprofessional or off-centered reaction. As previously described, the brain is organized to respond to danger through pattern-recognition. A large object moving rapidly towards us, a sudden pain, or a violent grab initiates a cascade of responses—fight/flight/freeze/faint—that are geared to keep us alive in the worst of circumstances. At lower levels of danger, particularly that presented by another human being, we are provoked into posturing—dominance/submission displays—that serve to maintain or enhance our position in a social structure.

The curse of being human, however, is that these survival responses are precipitated by any noxious stimuli, particularly those that shock or surprise us. When someone unexpectedly violates our sense of right and wrong or verbally assaults us, we often respond by automatically shifting into those responses, even when survival is not truly an issue. **When our buttons are pushed, we react as if we are threatened with bodily harm.**

Taking Inventory

Anything that pushes our buttons, and sets us off-balance, puts us at risk. A technique called *bracketing* makes it harder if not impossible for others to even get to our buttons. Bracketing is a technique that entails facing your vulnerabilities head on, and making them "bulletproof."

Not surprisingly, we are most likely to lose our temper (our flexibility, our edge and our strength) when we are blind-sided. Sudden emotional shock elicits the same responses in the nervous system as a physical attack. For example, if someone suddenly insults your race, religion, or gender, it is very likely that you will shift into a response using those parts of your brain that express raw emotions. The limbic system is not concerned about the truth, about negotiation, or how to make peace. Instead, it views the world as one at war, with the other person trying to destroy one's position of strength.

Here is a worksheet that can help you name and bracket your own hot buttons. (You may photocopy it to work on.) Once you work it through, keep those hot buttons conscious in your head. Keep or throw away the worksheet as you choose.

Some example statements may include:
1. I can't stand it when someone attacks or demeans <   >, because that's something I love and treasure.
2. I feel outraged when someone demeans <   > because it is something I believe to be unquestionably right and good.
3. People get me defensive when they say or point out <   >, because, to tell the truth, I hate it in myself (or, it is a flaw….).
4. When people say or do <   >, I lose it because it's as if they are taking control of me, or disrespecting me.
5. They better not say <   >. That's the one word I won't take from anyone.

Statement	Why Does this Get to Me?
EXAMPLE: When people say or do < >, I lose it because it's as if they are taking control of me, or disrespecting me.	

Taking inventory is the equivalent of checking your kit before going out into the unit. Every morning, upon waking, and maybe a few times during the day, you run a mental inventory, as if flipping through a set of cards, and call to mind each of your emotional triggers. By bringing them to consciousness, you prepare yourself for the possibility that someone may try to set you off. This is merely the equivalent of checking your mirrors before backing out of your driveway. When (not "if"), an inmate tries to push one of your buttons, you are not surprised or caught off guard. If you take inventory, you center yourself for another day, ready for the worst without it tearing you down.

If you are able to accurately take this inventory and implement it into your day-to-day mental activities, then you have a good handle on who you are and what is important to you. Before walking into the jail, before putting on your ballistics vest or your side-arm, before you load your custom assault rifle, you had better know yourself to the core, and that core needs to be rock-solid. If it isn't, inmates will see right through you. You can't carry any issues on your sleeve, even good issues such as military service. The moment they catch on, they already know too much about you. Once you are aware of your buttons, you should have responses already prepared in case they try to blindside you. Those responses should roll off your tongue as if they were the most natural response in the world.

You must establish a steady infallible core, both for yourself and for the people around you. You are obligated to the other members of your team to refrain from escalating a situation, even when the inmate pins you with some sudden insight or "tell" that they read in you. You must present yourself as the embodiment of strength and calm, both for yourself and your team, when you are involved in crisis events, especially when your teammates are scared or otherwise off-balance.

Figure 20.2 Author's Experience: On not being "owned"

Our correctional facility was host to a somewhat notorious serial killer. The inmate was infamous for escape attempts, manipulative behavior (above the norm) and rapid escalation into violence. Staff were directed to observe this inmate continuously when he was out of his hardened cell (in the dayroom) during his out-time. We were also directed to limit conversation with him, because he had a history of getting information about staff and using it to his advantage. I often sat watch on him when he was out of his cell. Although uneducated, he was both very intelligent and a fabulous storyteller. Just as leopards are beautiful, human predators can be very charming.

Even though I observed him from outside the unit, my body was on high alert. The inmate tried to get information from me (*I call this a 'bump.' Sharks bump objects or people with their nose or take a small sample bite before going into an all-out kill. Some inmates do the same thing.*) He tried to find out if I was ex-military. When I told him that was personal information and therefore none of his business, he first tried to convince me that being in the military was not personal. When I told him that I was the one that got to decide what was personal for me, he exploded, going from laughing and affable to screaming and throwing objects in the room. I remained quiet with a blank expression. When he did not get the reaction he wanted he started calling me obscenities, starting with "bitch." The only response I gave him was to quietly say, "Lock down." As I expected, the next word out of his mouth was that which usually sends female officers into outer-space (starts with a 'c'). All he got for the effort was a monotone, "lockdown." Officers were piling up behind me—nothing angers officers more than an inmate calling their boss foul names. I wouldn't let them in the unit.

This inmate expected and craved the fight. All he kept getting was that same word: "lockdown." He sort of "popped a mental clutch" because he didn't get the outcome he wanted. He finally went into his room and slammed the door shut—lockdown. I looked at my teammates, told them thanks for the support, but their safety was much more important than me being called a few ugly names. I felt the assault coming long before it started—while he was still friendly. With such advanced warning, I stayed calm and non-reactive, giving him literally "nothing," and kept my staff away from a useless bout of violence from a killer who desired only that.

CHAPTER 21

Circular Breathing:
Be the Eye in the Center of the Hurricane

Aggression and violence can smash through a previously peaceful day with the suddenness and force of a hurricane. Chaos doesn't only take over the day; it may also overtake you. However, when you can respond by stepping coolly into the worst of situations, you embody the eye of the hurricane, with all the chaos coalescing and revolving around you. The root of this skill lies in breath control. Using a method called "circular breathing," you regain control of your physical self. When you control your body, you control your life. Then you are in a position to take control of the crisis as well as the person causing it.

Figure 21.1 A Clarification From One of the Authors

Lest there be any confusion—This is NOT a "time-out" where you take a few deep breaths and then return to the subject, refreshed. Rather, you are training your body and mind to immediately go into this breathing as a *response* to danger and stress. It is a trained response that should be instantaneous. And remember—you can still be moving very fast while breathing very slowly.

As someone who has practiced the following technique for over thirty years, I can assert that it has become automatic. Unlike my younger days when the adrenalin would hit and I'd start breathing fast and high in the chest, my breathing usually slows down in emergency situations. You develop a "pseudo-instinct"—trained response so bone-deep that you don't even have to think about it, any more than you have to tell yourself to yank your hand from a hot stove.

Two Variations

Circular breathing is derived from East Asian martial traditions and was used to keep warriors calm on the battlefield. There are two variations. Try both, alternating between them, until you know which one works best for you. From that point on, exclusively practice the one you prefer. *If you train regularly, it will kick in automatically, rather than being something you must think about.*

Circular Breathing Method #1: Initial Practice Method

- Sit comfortably, feet on the floor, hands in your lap.
- Sit relaxed, but upright. Don't slump or twist your posture.
- Keep your eyes open. (**As you practice, so you will do.** If you practice with your eyes closed, your newly trained nervous system will send an impulse to close your eyes in emergency situations. If you want to use a breathing method for closed-eye guided imagery or relaxation, to get *away* from your problems, use another method altogether.)
- Breathe in through the nose.
- Imagine the air traveling in a line down the front of your body to a point two inches below the navel.
- Momentarily pause, letting the breath remain in a dynamic equilibrium.
- As you exhale, imagine the air looping around your lower body, between your legs and up through the base of your spine.
- Continue to exhale, imagine the air going up your spine and around your head and then out of your nose.

Circular Breathing Method #2: Initial Practice Method

- Sit comfortably, feet on the floor, hands in your lap.
- Sit relaxed, but upright. Don't slump or twist your posture.
- Keep your eyes open. (**As you practice, so you will do.** If you practice with your eyes closed, your newly trained nervous system will send an impulse to close your eyes in emergency situations. If you want to use a breathing method for closed-eye guided imagery or relaxation, to get *away* from your problems, use another method altogether.)
- Breathe in through the nose.
- Imagine the air going up around your head, looping down the back, falling down each vertebra, continuing down past the base of the spine to the perineum, and looping again, this time up the front of the body to a point two inches below the navel.
- Momentarily pause, letting the breath remain in a dynamic equilibrium.
- As you exhale, imagine the air ascending up the centerline of your body and out your nose.

How to Practice Circular Breathing

Some people find that imagining their breath has light or color is helpful. Others take a finger or object to trace a line down and around the centerline of the body to help focus their attention. Again, choose which of the variations works better for you.

First practice this method while seated. Once you develop some skill, try circular breathing standing, leaning, or even while driving. Most people find that after a short period of time they don't need to visualize the circulation of the breath. You literally will feel it, a ring of energy running through your body. You begin to feel balanced and ready for anything.

Once you are comfortable with your chosen pattern of breathing, experiment with it in slightly stressful circumstances, like being caught in traffic, or sitting through a meeting as a supervisor drones on about new paperwork requirements. When this becomes an automatic response, you will also naturally shift to this type of breathing in emergency situations. If you have practiced enough, it kicks in by itself. There will no longer be a need to tell yourself to "do" circular breathing. It will become automatic, replacing old patterns of breathing that actually increased anxiety or anger within you.

Remember, this is a skill to be used during emergencies. You are enhancing your ability to do whatever is needed: to fight, to dodge, to leave, to think strategically—whatever is required for the situation at hand.

When to Use Circular Breathing

The way you organize physically affects your thinking. For example, if you let your body slump, breathe shallowly, and start sighing, after a while, you will actually start to feel depressed. If you clenched your fists, and start glaring around you with a lot of tension in your body, you will start to feel angry. (You have probably observed a number of inmates working themselves up from anger through rage into an attack in just this way.) Similarly, circular breathing creates its own mindset; one adaptable and ready for anything, equally prepared for an easy conversation and for a fight, yet fixed on neither.

This method of breathing is very helpful when you are anticipating a potentially dangerous situation, anything from walking down the tiers towards a disturbance, or preparing for a parole hearing with an often-volatile inmate. This breathing activates the entire nervous system in a way that enhances both creativity and the ability to survive.

Even in the middle of a confrontation, particularly a verbal one, there are many times when this breathing will have a very powerful effect, on both yourself and others. People tend to template their mood to the most powerful individual close by. Not only do we get more stressed or upset in the presence of an upset person, but also we become more peaceful in the presence of a calm one. We are sure that you know officers who, when they walk onto a scene, often calm it down before they have said a word. You have probably seen the opposite as well, officers who just flame everyone up without saying a word. Using this breathing method is a vital tool in making you the former type, a correctional officer of quiet power.

Use this method of breathing after the crisis as well. You need to regroup to go on with the rest of your shift. Circular breathing will bring you back to a calm and relaxed state, prepared to handle the next crisis, should one occur.

If we bring feelings from a crisis situation back home, we carry violence back to our family. Therefore, before entering your home, sit quietly in your car or even in the yard, and practice this breathing for a moment or two. The only thing that should come home is "you," not the crises you have weathered.

Circular Breathing to Ward Off or Even Heal From Trauma

Figure 21.2 A Note on Circular Breathing to Ward Off Trauma
Although the material in this section may seem a little to "therapy" oriented, it is invaluable if you ever find yourself having difficulty dealing with a traumatic reaction and, for one reason or another, help is either not available, or you can't or should not (due to legal repercussions or concerns regarding "fitness for duty" evaluations) take advantage of the help that is offered. Keep this in reserve for those times when you need it.

Post-Traumatic Stress Disorder (PTSD) is not defined by how horrible the event sounds in description. It is defined by the victim's response to the event. PTSD is not exactly a problem of memory; it is a problem because the event has not fully *become* a memory, and rather, is still experienced as if it is happening in present time. When an event is fully a memory, it is experienced as something in the past, over and done with. Another way to think of it is a scar, it may not be pretty, and it certainly is a sign that something significant happened, but it no longer hurts. A trauma, on the other hand, is an open-wound. It is an *experience*. It is not in the past, and in fact, may be affecting every moment of the person's life, or emerge suddenly, when evoked by something that elicits a sense that the event is happening again.

Figure 21.3 Author's Experience: Flash Images Versus Traumatic Images
It is very common for correctional officers to walk past a room in their facility and see a flash image of an event that happened in that particular area. The most common of these images seems to be the re-occurring image of an inmate hanging in a room when an officer had to either cut the inmate down or helped during the event. The first time this happens can be very startling. It is important in our high-stress field to distinguish what is a common bi-product of an event (seeing a momentary image of a previous crisis/traumatic event) and what is more severe, such as seeing that image everywhere and feeling imprisoned by it.

In PTSD the person's nervous system is set to react as if there is an emergency whenever the trauma is recalled. This can be anything from an explicit memory to a small reminder. For example, although he does not consciously know why, a correctional officer gets anxious every time someone coughs. This is because one of his team coughed right before a riot went off. Image-associated breathing techniques, which affect the brain as a whole, can assist people in realizing that the event is over, no longer part of one's current life. The following should be helpful in handing PTSD:

1. Imagine that something very upsetting has happened to you, either recently or in the past.

2. Whenever you think about it (or it forcibly intrudes into your consciousness), your body tenses or twists in various ways. Your breathing pattern often changes. If you physically organize (with your breath, muscular tension, posture, etc.) *as if* something is happening, the brain believes that it truly is occurring right now. That is PTSD.

3. If this is your situation, go someplace where you won't be disturbed for a while. Make the mental image of that trauma as vivid as you can tolerate. This takes some courage, because most of us simultaneously "avoid-as-we-remember." If only for a moment or two, meet it head on. Notice, in fine detail, how you physically and emotionally react. As difficult as this may be, it is important to establish for yourself what your baseline response is to the trauma. You must clearly experience what it "does" to you when you recollect it.

4. Now take a couple of deep sighs. Sighing breaks up patterns of muscular tension and respiration. This is like rebooting your computer when the program is corrupt.

5. Mentally say to the ugly experience: "Move right over there to my right (or left). I'll get to you in a minute." For some people, it is even helpful to make a physical gesture, "pushing" the experience off to the side. You won't be able to *force* yourself to stop thinking about an experience if it has psychological power. Instead, move it aside, as if you are guiding a wounded person to a waiting room, while you organize yourself to properly deal with it.

6. Now initiate your preferred method of circular breathing.

7. As the memory creeps back in (and it will), just breathe and center yourself, again placing the memory off to the side. Once again say, "I'll get to you in a minute." You can't fight it, so don't try. Just ease it aside until you are ready.

8. When your breathing is smooth and your body is centered, you will be relaxed like an athlete, ready to move but with no wasted effort.

9. Now, deliberately bring that ugly memory or trauma into your thoughts and imagination. As you again find yourself reacting, continue circular breathing, trying to bring yourself back to physical balance as you focus on the traumatic memory.

10. Bit by bit, in either one session or a few, you will notice that you are increasingly able to hold the image with a relaxed body and a balanced posture. You are now able to re-experience the memory without the same painful, tense, or distorted response you had in the past. You are, metaphorically speaking, turning the open wound into scar tissue. You are not wiping the slate of memory clean. Rather, you are placing it in a proper context—something that happened to you, but does not define you.

Figure 21.4 The Value of Circular Breathing Imagery

What is particularly valuable to many correctional officers who use circular breathing imagery is that it allows one to take power back on one's own. There is no doubt that counseling, sometimes, is invaluable. However, it is sometimes hard to find a good counselor who understands a correctional officer's situation.

Furthermore, ongoing litigation, in which confidentiality can be threatened by subpoena or court order, can sometimes force correctional officers to forego counseling that they might really need. This particular breathing method offers an option when counseling is either not an option, or something that the correctional officer does not want.

Furthermore, if you can, on a daily basis, "inoculate" yourself against stressful, even potentially traumatic experiences, life will continue to be enjoyable, or will become enjoyable once again, even as you continue to work in a highly stressful environment. You will begin to develop something author David Grossman calls a "bulletproof mind." The goal is not trying to restore some kind of mythic "innocence," that one had "pre-trauma." The goal is to relegate the experience to its proper place—something ugly that happened sometime in the past.

CHAPTER 22

The Intoxication and Joy
of Righteous Anger

Most people consider anger to be a harmful emotion, one that upsets the angry person as well as the recipient. This is not true for everyone. Some people, certainly including some correctional officers, don't mind fighting, particularly when they believe their cause is just. These individuals go off-center in an interesting way, becoming calm, even happy, when someone offends them. As a boxer once stated in regards to an opponent, "When he gets hurt, he wants the round to be over. When I get hurt, I get happy." Such people, when functioning in a professional capacity, have an especially difficult task, because when they feel *good*, they are in danger of becoming part of the problem. Instead of imposing calm, they escalate the situation—not minding it in the least.

Circular breathing **(Chapter 21)**, for those who are anxious, stressed, or frightened provides a real sense of peace and relief. However, if confrontation feels good to you, such calming breathing feels like the last thing you would like to do. You think, "Center myself? Hell, no. I'm right where I want to be." The righteously angry correctional officer may be known among his or her peers for this type of reaction, but he or she is the one most likely to *not* recognize this, and *not* believe they need to do anything to rectify it. If this description fits, your task is to recognize the special joy that comes with righteous anger, and act to center yourself to a calm state of mind, even though in the heat of the moment, it feels like a loss rather than a gain.

This is not about becoming some sort of sage: never angered, never off-balance. There are times when you should be angry—it may even help keep you alive. However, the real issue here is the correctional officer who reacts angrily to even the slightest provocation, or worse, one who treats every inmate, in every situation, with anger. Such officers simply serve to escalate minor situations into serious ones, heightening the chances for a physical altercation with the inmate, placing everyone involved in danger unnecessarily.

Protecting Your Family From What You Otherwise Would Bring Home

Another type of righteous anger is that evoked when someone does something so clearly evil that one feels annihilation of the perpetrator is the only justifiable response. Returning to the subject of the last chapter, this is a particularly important example of how such breathing can protect your family. For example, all three of us (authors) have had the experience of feeling utterly contaminated by being in the presence of the perpetrators of child abuse or sexual assault. Having done our job well, so that, for example, we have gotten a confession, evidence to make a case, or have helped ensure that an inmate never had access to the child again, we each have left the room feeling a failure because we did not take their throat between our hands and squeeze the life out of them.

All of us made sure that we never brought this feeling home. We would sit in our car, running the breath around our body, maybe going to a quiet place in the house or yard and working through the images in our brains so that when we walked into the presence of our spouse and children, the only thing each of us ever brought home was ourselves. No child molester or other evildoer will ever walk into the house with us.

SECTION V

Dealing With Those Who Have
Unusual, Intense, and Eccentric
Communication Styles

CHAPTER 23

Overview of Section V

What is a mental illness anyway? Is it any odd or eccentric behavior, or should we not confine the term for more serious disturbances of behavior and thought. It sometimes seems that we lump together mental phenomena that are as disparate as a common cold and lung cancer. Yes, both may make breathing difficult, but they are very different disorders.

This book focuses on behavior, not on illness. Correctional officers should not feel it incumbent upon themselves to diagnose what an inmate may be suffering from, even in the most general way. If someone behaves in a way that makes it difficult to communicate with them, or even more problematically, enacts disruptive behaviors, then the correctional officer (you) should be prepared with several skills, among those are the following:

1. The ability to recognize said behavior as showing a pattern.
2. The knowledge of best practice communication strategies to respond to a person who is displaying said pattern, whatever the cause of the behavior may be.

Not everyone who needs to be calmed or de-escalated is aggressive. However, those who display unusual or eccentric patterns of behavior are more difficult to communicate with, and when the ability of people to communicate breaks down, the risk of aggression increases.

IMPORTANT NOTE: a mentally ill or eccentric inmate may display more than one of the behaviors described in subsequent sections. Deal with whatever behavior is most prominent.

Figure 23.1 Don't Get Stuck in the "Everlasting Why"

It is easy to get frustrated in dealing with the same problematic behaviors day in and day out, especially if those behaviors deviate from to what most human beings finds comforting or normative, As a correctional professional, it is easy to fall into the trap of the "Everlasting Why." The Everlasting Why is what correctional officers try to answer when inmates do unexplainable and often harmful things. When an inmate smears his own feces all over his room or body, or even eats it, or acts in disruptive or violent ways when they would accumulate enough "good time" and actually get released, with a little calmer attitude, it is easy to fall into the trap of trying to understand these behaviors. It is the normal human condition to try to make sense of things, to place things in order—even on a basic level, our brains seek to find the patterns in wallpaper or shapes within the clouds.

If you fall into the trap of trying to answer the Everlasting Why when it comes to mentally ill inmates, you will find yourself in a constant state of frustration and anger. At best, you may be lucky enough to figure out that certain things you say or do evoke certain behaviors from an inmate. Sometimes, the inmate gives a warning sign before he or she act outs. There will be, however, an entire host of inmates that have behaviors that are not even comprehensible to themselves.

Don't try to figure out the "Why." Instead try to figure out the best ways to manage the behaviors. Any other approach is a hard lesson in futility.

CHAPTER 24

Rigid Personality: Asperger's Syndrome and Other Similar Disorders

Despite what can be formidable intellectual abilities, often sectored in one area of knowledge, inmates with rigid personalities often have tremendous difficulty in negotiating social interactions. They find other people to be confusing and/or threatening, and to make matters worse for them, they find it very difficult to know from facial expressions, body posture, and vocal tone, what others are feeling or thinking.

People with Asperger's syndrome are frequently socially withdrawn, often very intelligent outcasts, who may live their lives mostly in an online environment. Such individuals are becoming more involved in computer crimes, particularly hacking. They are not suited for life within the confines of jail, and therefore, are often placed in protective custody. Other inmates, particularly some schizophrenics, often show a similar combination of "cluelessness" and rigidity in communicating with others.

Such rigid personalities become fixated on their own preoccupations, and may imagine that everyone else shares them too. As one inmate with Asperger's syndrome said, when asked what the other inmate who beat him up was thinking, "Oh, he was thinking of high energy physics." When asked with astonishment why he would be thinking of that, the inmate replied, "What else could he be thinking about? Quantum mechanics is the greatest scientific discovery…" It was a good ten minutes before the correctional officer could get him off the subject. Such rigid individuals can also be very literal (concrete), and can get "stuck" on certain thoughts and behaviors (obsessive). Others are simply not interested in or aware of other people's feelings, which can lead them to be very blunt or brutally honest.

Figure 24.1 Two Examples of Socially Clueless Statements by an Inmate Displaying Rigid Personality Traits

- "What is the bump on your face? It's quite ugly. You know, it could be a melanoma, which could cause your face to simply rot away, or it could infect your brain and then you'd die. I've seen photos of tumors that have actually eaten right through a person's cheek and you can see their teeth and tongue out the side of their face."
- "You've gained a lot of weight in the last year. I don't mind, but many men don't think that is attractive."

There is no malevolent intent here. Other people's feelings—unimaginable and incomprehensible—are simply not a relevant bit of data for such a person. Instead, they see themselves as giving you the equivalent of a public service announcement.

Such a person usually seems stiff and socially awkward. Their voice may be too loud, and they may sound odd. Their eye contact may be "off," or non-existent, and they are sometimes physically uncoordinated. They do not pay attention to the effect that their actions or appearance might have on others. They are frequently insensitive to body spacing. Because they find people unpredictable and unreadable, they frequently experience high anxiety. As a result, they use self-soothing movements like flapping their hands or rhythmically tapping an object and/or body part to help distract them from what stresses them out. Although these inmates do not normally pose a threat to other inmates (other than giving offense in one way or another), they may be victimized due to their odd behaviors and blunt responses. Inmates in general population have little tolerance for oddities. If you are fortunate, one of the inmates will tell you to, "Get this guy outta here before he gets hurt."

If you are dealing with an inmate with a rigid personality, stating or reiterating the rules is the first method of intervention. If an inmate had difficulty figuring out what an officer wants him to do, and the officer's body language, tone of voice, and facial expression are incomprehensible, the rules, clearly stated, will be very reassuring. On the other hand, "tactical paraphrasing," (**Chapter 57**) which is so often recommended as the best tactic to deal with upset inmates, will often result in the inmate becoming increasingly confused or upset. State each rule in a matter-of-fact way, as if simply providing information. State the obvious. Follow this up with a logical sequence of steps to resolve their problem:

- In a matter of fact tone, explain the rules. She says, "Why should I lower my voice? I am angry!" The reply should be, "Because it is the rule to speak about grievances with a quiet voice." "That's a stupid rule," she replies. "Nonetheless," you say, "it is the rule."
- Give them a logical alternative way to follow-up on their grievance.
- Even more than with other individuals, try to avoid physical contact unless it is tactically required. Many folks with rigid personality traits detest touch, and can react violently. Only touch them when you are taking physical control (defensive tactics).
- If they continue to be non-compliant, you may have to physically require them to comply with your order, but take the extra time in the manner we suggest whenever possible.
- Another trait that you will sometimes observe with the rigid personality is *echolalia*. What this means is echoing what you say, usually word for word. You must be able to distinguish between the provocative inmate who mocks, trying to aggravate or distract you (that should be obvious from the smirk on their face or other manifestation of attitude), from the individual with the rigid personality who simply repeats what you say in a flat tone of voice, usually with no eye contact. In the latter case, the individual is probably so overwhelmed that they cannot organize their mind to verbally respond to what you are requesting or ordering. Seeking to somehow

stay out of trouble in what is, to them, a chaotic situation, they simply repeat your words—it *must* be important because, after all, you said it. In many such circumstances, you may have to "physically guide" them to where you want them to go. Often, the inmate will remain passive. Hold their limbs firmly, but not forcibly or harshly, if they are not combative. Nonetheless, such individuals, if they are startled or fearful, may start flailing their arms or lash out in trying to defend themselves. Be ready for that—whatever the motivation, it is still a violent act—and that flailing limb can knock you out.

- If they are displaying a physically repetitive movement, such as flapping their hands, understand that it is for the purpose of calming themselves down. Nonetheless, if the movement (hand flapping near the waist or chest) could resemble a move towards a weapon, order them to stop, by telling them that it is, for example, "against the rules to wave your hands near your waist while standing near a correctional officer." When they ask why, simply repeat that it is against the rules. When they ask if it's alright while speaking on the phone or alone in their cell, say that it is alright in that circumstance, but not face-to-face. Understand that their incessant questions are an attempt to try to figure out just what they can and cannot do. It is not game-playing. However, they often feel the need to cover all possibilities. ("What happens if a giant Asiatic hornet somehow flies between us? Can I flap my hands then?") Sometimes, after a few too many questions, you should take over and give a general policy that, hopefully, will cover all variations.

Figure 24.2 Example: De-escalation of Someone With Rigid Personality Traits

Pavel. "I can't go to my disciplinary hearing tomorrow. I saw seven spiders in my cell, and that is bad destiny."

CORRECTIONAL OFFICER. "Pavel, you are required to go to the hearing, no matter the number of spiders you have seen."

Pavel. But this could mean a disaster for someone. Seven spiders are terrible.

CORRECTIONAL OFFICER. "The rule is that inmates must appear in such hearings when ordered, and this applies even when the inmate believes that there are unlucky signs."

Pavel. "Destiny, officer, not bad luck."

CORRECTIONAL OFFICER. "It is still the rule, destiny or not. The rule has no deviation."

Pavel. "How about if a meteor hits the jail?"

CORRECTIONAL OFFICER. "Pavel, the rule is ironclad. If you are scheduled to appear at the hearing, you must appear, unless I call you and inform you that court is cancelled.

Pavel. Something bad will happen—it's destiny."

CORRECTIONAL OFFICER. "Nonetheless, you will be there at 10:00 A.M. It is the rule."

Figure 24.3 Review: Dealing With Rigid Personality

You will recognize the inmate with a rigid personality because they get stuck on subjects that seem rather odd in the circumstances. They seem unaware of their effect on others. Their emotions, if they are even displaying any, are not those you would expect in the given situation. Recalling your school days, they often act like the kind of person who was, unkindly, called a "nerd." To deal with this type of individual do the following:

1. State the rules in a matter-of-fact way, as if simply providing information.
2. Follow this up with a logical sequence of steps to solve their problem.
3. Discussion about their feelings will be counter-production. Tactical paraphrasing (**Chapter 57**) or other ordinary tactics to deal with an angry person tend to make things worse.
4. No physical contact unless it is part of defensive tactics or physical control.
5. Don't get deflected from your task. Like a parody of a lawyer, they may bring up possible exceptions to your order. "Step through" the objections and simply state that they are required to follow the rule.
6. When the rigid person repeats what you say (echolalia), they are not giving you attitude or mocking you. They truly cannot think of anything else to do. Yelling at them or ordering them to stop will most likely not succeed. They will simply repeat your order in a flat tone of voice.
7. Use this type of strategy only when it is clear that this is the type of inmate you are trying to interact with: rigid, stiff, concrete, and socially out-of-sync. They will be either coldly logical (like Spock or Data, from Star Trek), or frustrated, and out of control. In the latter case, as always, control based on the mode of rage (**Section XII**) they are displaying.

CHAPTER 25

Tell It Like It Is:
Communication With
Concrete Thinkers

Concrete thinkers have a lot of difficulty, or even a complete inability, to understand metaphors, slang, or imagery. Instead, they take everything you say literally.

Figure 25.1 Example: How Concrete Thinking Causes Problems for an Inmate

We had a minimum security inmate working in our laundry room. Inmates manufactured the jeans worn by all the other inmates, and it was the laundry room worker's job to wash, dry, and fold them into organized piles for distribution. Our laundry worker was doing a fantastic job until he encountered jeans that were not previously labeled as to their size. He was given a permanent marker, and told to label the jeans clearly so they were easily identifiable. Most any other person would have written the size on the inside of the back waistband. Our intrepid worker took the "easily identifiable" part to heart and labeled the jeans small medium and large accordingly. However, since he had already folded the jeans, the part that was at the front (and therefore 'easily identifiable') was the seam down the front of the jeans from the waistband to the groin, it was here that he wrote "small," "medium, " or "large" in large block letters in permanent ink. For about six months after this, none of the male inmates would wear small or medium pants for fear that the label bore some sort of personal reflection on their anatomy, rather than their pants size.

When communicating with concrete thinkers, correctional officers should use short, clear sentences, using simple language that is easy to understand. Remember, they only understand what you say in a very literal manner, complying with the specific, while not even understanding the general principal. Speak in a firm manner, and refrain from showing too much emotion. It's not personal. If you become angry or frustrated the inmate will react to your emotions, not your instructions.

Figure 25.2 Example: A Non-emergent Dialogue Between a Correctional Officer and an Inmate Showing Concrete Thinking

CORRECTIONAL OFFICER. "Okay. So you don't have to worry anymore."

Concrete Person. "I wasn't worried. I was upset."

CORRECTIONAL OFFICER. "Oh, okay, you were upset. Anyway, the nurse is coming, and will be here shortly. I want you to sit tight."

Concrete Person. "How do I sit tight? Should I wrap myself in a blanket?"

CORRECTIONAL OFFICER. <Sigh> "No, you don't have to wrap yourself up. I meant you should sit quietly and…."

Concrete Person. "You mean I shouldn't talk?"

CORRECTIONAL OFFICER. "<Aghhhhhh> No, you can talk! I want you to talk! It's a figure of speech!"

You get the idea. In the last example, what might be a better way to accomplish the task? Imagine this just from the CORRECTIONAL OFFICER'S side:

- The nurse is coming.
- Sit in the chair right here.
- Yes, sit where you are right now and keep talking to me.

Figure 25.3 Review: Concrete Thinkers

You will recognize **Concrete Thinkers** because they take what you say literally. Therefore:

- Use clear, short sentences, with a firm, calm voice.
- Give directions using simple words that are easy to understand.
- Show a minimum of emotion. Don't get irritated when the inmate does not immediately understand you. They respond much more to your tone of voice than to what you say.

CHAPTER 26

Information Processing and Retention: Consolidating Gains

Many mentally ill inmates develop the ability to "fake normal." People around them may do frightening things, but they don't show their fear. Other people may anger them, but they smile and pretend everything is all right. Conversations and ideas may be too complex, too fast, or irrelevant to what is going on inside them, but they have learned to pick up the rhythm of other people's speech, nod at the right moments, and smile or laugh when needed.[29] Never assume that a mentally ill inmate understands what you have told them just because they nod their head at the right moment. You need to verify that they understood you.

In dealings with the mentally ill the following points have been proven helpful:

1. **Least Effective Method.** The least effective method is to repeat using other words. If they have either tuned you out or did not understand you the first time, they may fake understanding again. This is different from the repetition you must do with the disorganized inmate (**Chapter 38**), when you DO repeat yourself when giving instructions, as a form of behavioral management. In that instance, your repetition is to "get through" the confusion. Repeating yourself and assuming the inmate understood what you said often fails.

2. **Repetition by Inmate**. Have the inmate repeat your instructions. However, some mentally ill inmates may echo what you say, so this, too, does not prove that they actually understand or will follow through.

3. **Open Sentences.** A better method is open sentences. For example, "So, Inmate Hussain, if I've got it right, I will call the doctor tomorrow and explain the problem. And you will…" Of course, you expect (hope) that the inmate will complete the sentence.

4. **Write Down Important Points.** Write down the most important points. Many mentally ill inmates don't assimilate a lot of information that they hear, no matter how hard they listen. The correctional officer may find that writing the most important points of the conversation or agreement on a 3 x 5 card is quite helpful. Remind the inmate to check the card if they have any difficulty remembering what they are supposed to do. (We are aware that there are many circumstances where this strategy would be out of the question, but all of us have used it on occasion.)

CHAPTER 27

Coping With Stubborn Refusals

There are many occasions when inmates refuse to comply with directives, sanctions notwithstanding. Of course, if you have been bossing them around, patronizing them, or treating them with disrespect (beyond, of course, your professional responsibility to maintain order and control, which will, of course, be primarily in the form of direct orders), it should not be surprising if they resist you. All people, mentally ill or not, have pride, and no one likes another person talking down to them or controlling their lives. If it is not your approach that is creating the problem, what, if anything, can correctional officers do to elicit compliance, without having to resort to the violation process?

1. **Focus on the Task.** Correctional officers should never take a mentally ill inmate's non-compliance personally.

2. **Clarify the Message.** Correctional officers must be clear on what the inmate is required to do regarding their immediate supervision plan. Don't bring up previous examples of their non-compliance, such as "the last time this happened," or "you always," or "remember when you." Stay here-and-now.

3. **Control the Interview.** Stay on topic and don't allow the person to divert your attention to unrelated issues, as mentally ill inmates will naturally do.

4. **Use a Strong and Calm Voice.** Keep your tone of voice strong, but not demanding or aggressive.

5. **De-personalize Your Role.** Remind the inmate that you are enforcing the policies of the correctional facility, and that any sanctions are the result of the inmate's behavior, not anything personal.

6. **State the Consequences.** Correctional officers should be very clear in explaining to the inmate the consequences and possible sanctions that may be imposed for non-compliance. This should be provided as "information," rather than threat, the same way you tell your kid on a cold winter day, "If you stick your tongue on that metal pole, you are going to get stuck." Such consequences include placement in a treatment facility, loss of various privileges, being placed on confined to quarters (CRA) status or housed in a temporary segregated unit for non-compliance with established rule and policies.

7. **Place the Power in the Inmate's Hands.** Without handing over one iota of your authority, allow the inmate to be the decision maker, and clarify their role in complying, or not complying with an order. Say something along the lines of "It looks like you've got something to decide. You have a couple of choices. You CAN comply with my order. Or, you can refuse, and be taken before the classification committee and tell them why you don't feel like complying with the facility's programs. And we will place you in administration segregation pending that meeting." Correctional officers must never threaten anything that cannot be backed up with action. Simply state the facts of the consequences for non-compliance. Based on their response, follow through with the appropriate action.

You can also point out the benefits of following through with what you are directing them to do. You needn't offer any rewards or promise anything, but you can point out the obvious, such as, "You know classification does their interviews on Mondays, and that it sure would help with your request to get moved if they came in and saw how clean your room was...." In this instance you are not offering anything more to this inmate than any other inmate: just helping them realize how they can help themselves.

Figure 27.1 Author's Experience: The Tactic of Deflection

In dealing with one very large and aggressive mentally ill female inmate who would rarely keep her pants on, I found out that she could sing fairly well. When medical, classification or our mental health team would come to see her, I would ask her to get dressed and she would refuse, often charging the door. Her use of profanity was legendary. Usually (not always) I could get her to keep her pants on if I asked her to perform a song for whoever was there to see her. She would sing (surprisingly well!) and dance a bit. The outcome was that she was happier and, at times, would comply with the interview process. The unexpected outcome was that the other divisions that dealt with her got to see her in an entirely different light, and they began to interact more with her. With less of a sense of social isolation, her dysfunctional behaviors decreased.

CHAPTER 28

Stuck: Coping With Repetitive Demands, Questions, and Obsessions

Sometimes inmates will make repetitive demands for information, for permission to deviate from their supervision and treatment plans, or to impose their own conditions for their supervision, such as, "program hopping" in order to find something that is to their liking, or "shopping" for the right officer to get what they want after being told "no" by several others

1. Some inmates become "stuck" with an obsessive thought or idea. No matter how many times you answer their question, they have to ask it again. This is often a sign of Obsessive-Compulsive Disorder (OCD), which is frequently missed by evaluators, because people become skilled in covering up such a humiliating problem. Those with Rigid Personalities **(Chapter 24)** also show this trait. Such people experience unbearable anxiety when they don't give in to the obsession or compulsion. The correctional officer may be the first to really notice OCD behaviors when an inmate gets stuck on things and can't "let go." The officer should refer the inmate to psychiatric services for further evaluation and/or treatment of this specific disorder.[30]

2. An inmate may obsess as part of another disorder like schizophrenia, developmental disability, or other serious impairments. Their repetitive questions or obsessing on a single point may be due to information processing errors **(Chapter 26)**.

3. Sometimes an inmate repeats a question *intending* to be irritating or challenging. In a bland tone of voice, simply say, "You already know the answer to that," or otherwise calmly point out that they already have the information, and *move on*. By disengaging, you are saying, "I'm not participating in the game."

4. Mentally ill inmates sometimes *perseverate*, meaning they are stuck on a subject and feel like they have to talk about it, often at length. This behavior is slightly different from the almost automatic kind of locked-in quality of the OCD inmate. These inmates simply get stuck. This is often a particular problem with inmates in mental health units. In this case, the correctional officer may say something like, "I know this is very important to you, and you want to talk about this and ask me questions. But you also know I have a lot of work to do, so I will make you a deal. Sometime between the hour of ten and eleven in the morning, we can talk about this for three minutes and thirty seconds, and no longer. It's your job to think carefully about what you need me to know about the subject each day, because when the time limit is reached, that is it. Any further information will have to wait until our next contact." Note that the reason for the "odd" number of minutes is that it sounds important, as if you have calculated it down to the second.

Figure 28.1 Coping With Obsessive Questions and Demands

1. If the problem seems to be OCD (a mental disorder that is involuntary) refer to psychiatric services.

2. If it is due to information processing errors (usually because of a serious mental disorder), refer to the information in **Chapter 26**.

3. If it is game-playing, disengage.

4. For the inmate who just gets stuck on things, give them a brief, time-limited interaction, once a day, to voice their concerns.

CHAPTER 29

The Need for Reassurance

Some people are quite anxious by nature or circumstances. For others, intolerable anxiety is either their primary illness, or one of the most troublesome symptoms of their mental disorder. Anxiety is living as if something that you are afraid might happen, **is happening right now**.

Imagine an inmate who has been traumatized, either before they were incarcerated, or as too often happens, during their period of imprisonment. Despite what sympathy that you may have, don't treat them like they are weak: that will support the weakest aspect of their personality. They may think that something awful is going to happen and that is why you are talking in such careful tones. At the same time, don't affect a cheerful, "ain't no big thing" tone of voice. This kind of falsity will make the person either uneasy or irritated. Instead, speak in a matter-of-fact tone. Take their unease into account, but speak with an expectation that they are strong enough to manage their anxiety.

> **Figure 29.1 Author's Experience: The Power of Reassurance in Inmate Management**
> One inmate was terrified that he was going to be transferred to a Supermax facility, even though there were no grounds for that occurring. While such a pattern of behavior was, at times, quite frustrating to the correctional officer, the few moments she spent talking to the inmate, reiterating that such transfers were based on infractions of behavior, not at random, were met with extreme gratitude, and this inmate was otherwise compliant with the rules of the jail.

CHAPTER 30

Dealing With Mood Swings

Such inmates can be very difficult to communicate with, much less de-escalate, because just as progress is made with their current mood, they shift into another. They can be verbally abusive, provocative, complaining, passive-aggressive, blaming, apologetic, ingratiating, and friendly all in the space of an hour or less. They often try to get control of others even when they have no control over themselves.

Coping With Mood Swings

Rather than getting frustrated by the inmate's mood swings, something that will be reflected in your own body language or words, remain balanced and emotionally non-reactive. **A correctional officer can influence them by being exactly what they are not.** The more the correctional officer is unaffected by an inmate's emotional storms, the more likely that the inmate will calm down **(Section IV)**.

Figure 30.1 Review: Mood Swings

Inmates with mood swings shift emotions rapidly with no relationship to the situation they are in. Remember:

- Don't mirror the individual's emotional state or lose control of your own emotions.
- Control them through controlling your own emotions. Remain powerfully calm.
- Speak in a firm, yet calm and controlled manner.
- Because they display any emotion you can imagine, use general de-escalation tactics, as described throughout this book, as needed.

CHAPTER 31

They Aren't Moving:
What to Do?

Sometimes you tell the mentally ill inmate to do something and all they do is stare at you vacantly, voice a million questions, express misgivings or anxiety, or drift off into mumbling about something completely different.

Other mentally ill inmates seem to lack motivation; they just won't do what we think is good for them. We are referring here to the inmate whose mental illness impedes their ability to accomplish the things they are required to do, not the defiant inmate.

The correctional officer must assess the inmate's actual ability to comply, and use their discretion when determining what constitutes an acceptable level of compliance, or at least a concerted effort at compliance on the inmate's part.

If the inmate is actually defiant, the correctional officer should initiate the official violation process and bring the inmate back before the classification or treatment committee for a violation hearing, or possible modification to program. The violation process may be incredibly motivating for some inmates. Correctional officers should not be reluctant to document a violation report against a mentally ill inmate or overlook their non-compliance because of their illness. On the other hand, this may serve as the evidence to establish that a modification of their treatment plan is necessary.

Figure 31.1 Using One's Genuine Mental Illness as Manipulation

Some inmates have learned to use their mental illness as an excuse for their failure to comply with even the most basic rules and regulations. Mental illness becomes their "fallback" position for their non–compliance, so that they never accept any personal responsibility. If correctional officers are assisting a mentally ill inmate, they should never do things for the inmate that they could do for themselves, other than perhaps scheduling certain appointments (and this is done primarily so the correctional officer knows the appointment was indeed scheduled), or helping them navigate some institutional bureaucracy.

Mentally ill inmates must be held accountable for their actions, and safety concerns certainly outweigh any exigent circumstances related to the inmate's mental capacities. Beyond the issue of basic accountability, correctional officers, as part of an interdisciplinary team, have a responsibility to document facets of inmate behavior indicative of treatment program compliance or non-compliance.

Correctional officers should also be mindful of how they attempt to motivate the inmate. Do you like the sound of your voice? Are you overly threatening? Or conversely, are you pleading with them? Correctional officers must retain their dignity when trying to motivate inmates. Give directions in a firm tone of voice. When you are dignified, the inmate will respect you more, sometimes in spite of himself. Inmates are far more likely to be compliant for correctional officers who are perceived as fair and equitable in their approaches, and who maintain a high level of integrity and professionalism when interacting with inmates.

Figure 31.2 They Aren't Moving—What to Do?

- Don't do for them what they can do for themselves.
- Don't require them to do things that they are incapable of doing.
- If they are truly non-compliant, use the violation process for motivation (or sanction if they continue to refuse).
- Act with dignity. Don't try to "cheerlead" them into compliance, berate them, complain, or any one of a number of actions that compromise your integrity in the interests of getting them moving.

CHAPTER 32

Should a Correctional Officer
Ever Apologize?

Some inmates store up grievances, allowing feelings of persecution and perceived personal slights to affect their entire worldview. With mentally ill inmates, these feelings can be more problematic, because their memories may be distorted or even delusional. Frequent complaints about old history can become a significant barrier to an inmate's compliance with their supervision and treatment plans, not to mention being extremely aggravating to the correctional officer who must continually turn the inmate's attention to immediate issues.

As a correctional officer, you represent the last stop along the inmate's journey through the criminal justice system. Feelings of animosity toward the arresting police officer(s) and other correctional officers, perceptions of civil rights infractions, dissatisfaction with their legal representation, and bitterness toward the sentencing judge—all of these resentments are now directed toward you, one more authority figure who is intruding into their life, and telling them what they can and can't do.

As already described, correctional officers must refrain from reacting emotionally to the inmate's inability to move beyond the past, even as you try to redirect their attention to the present situation. Above all, don't personalize the inmate's complaints or their feelings of prior injustices. Correctional officers can hardly be expected to bear the emotional burden for the entire criminal justice system, nor should they feel responsible for any actual mistreatment or improprieties surrounding an inmate's case that occurred previous to their incarceration, or in another institution.

1. **Acknowledge Their Concerns.** Quite often inmates merely need to express their frustrations or feelings of helplessness regarding their case, and they view the correctional officer as the only available outlet to do so. Sometimes, permitting the inmate to express their feelings (as long as they do so in a brief and appropriate manner) may be enough to alleviate their anger. Don't agree or disagree with them, or otherwise reinforce their feelings of persecution, just recognize their complaints and then move forward. **Do not, however, allow the inmate to revisit the issue at every encounter.**

2. **Apologize.** If the inmate's complaints do, in fact, concern your actions, think about it quickly, but carefully. Perhaps, in this instance, you were wrong. If so, apologize. In some situations, this is enough. However, the authors can't stress strongly enough that officers should be wary of apologizing to an inmate as a means of moving them off of a specific subject or grievance. An apology may lead the inmate to believe they are now in control of the relationship, and that the correctional officer will act cautiously so as not to upset them in the future. By acting ethically

and professionally at all times, and staying calm and in control, a correctional officer is much less likely to say or do anything for which they would ever need to apologize.

3. **If an Apology Is Not Enough.** Correctional officers may say to the inmate, "You are still upset about this. You want to talk about it again, don't you?" Notice that you don't ask the inmate; you merely state your understanding. This gives them the opportunity to correct or adjust your understanding so that if their complaint is legitimate, you are able to effectively put it to rest.

4. **Complaints as Their Own Reward.** Certain inmates are never satisfied, because the complaint becomes a "rewarding" activity in itself. Others bear a pervasive resentment toward their correctional officers, an institution, or even life itself. For them, complaints are merely a way to express hostility or an attempt to control you by insisting on talking about things on their agenda. In these cases, simply take the issue off the table, forever. Remind the inmate that you have already addressed their complaint, so that there is nothing more to discuss. Terminate the contact if they continue.

Figure 32.1 Review: Should a Correctional Officer Ever Apologize?

- If they have a general grievance towards their situation and the criminal justice system, acknowledge their complaints in a "one-and-done" manner, as long as you neither apologize for things that are not your fault or responsibility and you don't compromise your authority.

- If you have wronged the inmate, <u>if it does not put you in danger and if it, thereby, **enhances** your authority</u>, then you should apologize.

- If the inmate is stuck on the issue, say, "You are still upset about that," or something similar, giving them an opportunity to clarify why it is still a problem for them.

- If the inmate is using the grievance or complaint to get control of the exchange, distract you, or simply complain for the sake of complaining, shut it down. Call them on their game and don't allow it to continue.

CHAPTER 33

Useful Tactics for Dealing With Symptoms
of Paranoia and Persecution

Figure 33.1 This Chapter Focuses on the Paranoid Attitude

This chapter focuses on tactics specific to paranoia. Rather than the delusional state (**Chapters 41/42**), we are here discussing an attitude, with the following characteristics: a sense of being persecuted, blame of others for any problem, and a hair-trigger sensitivity to being vulnerable. We are here talking about something much more common than the fixed false beliefs and hallucinations of the psychotic paranoid inmate. It is, in this case, a character trait, one that, by the way, is held by the vast majority of inmates in any correctional institution. If they did not have this attitude going into the penitentiary, the majority develops it once they are institutionalized.

The paranoid inmate has a motto of life: "If there is a problem here, that would be your fault." The paranoid world is one of dominance and submission: they try to dominate the people in their life, and arc terrified or enraged at being forced to submit.

We are not only referring to a psychotic or delusional state, but also the far more common paranoid character, in which the inmate (without delusions) has a consistent *attitude* of blame, resentment of authority, fear of vulnerability, and an expectation of being betrayed by people he or she trust. Stimulant users, notably those using methamphetamine, cocaine, and cathinones ("bath salts"), frequently display these behaviors. It is also a very common "solution" that criminals arrive at to

excuse any failure. Many paranoid inmates are essentially terrified that they will be made vulnerable, but they cover it up through aggression towards whomever they are afraid. One helpful image is an angry porcupine, all quills, with a soft underbelly, hunched over, ready to strike in hair-trigger reaction. Character traits and behavior patterns of paranoid inmates include:

- **Paranoid Inmates Interpret Relaxation as Vulnerability.** Therefore, they become *more* paranoid when you, their correctional officer, begin to establish rapport with them. Friendship means letting your guard down. Don't be surprised if paranoid inmates suddenly flare up with suspicion or accusations during times that are uneventful or even, within professional limits, friendly.

- **Being Mistaken Or Wrong Is Another Form of Vulnerability.** Rather than admitting wrong-doing or mistakes, paranoid individuals reflexively ***project*** negative feelings on the other person. If they feel hate, they believe, "You hate me." If they neglected to leave the yard for a medical appointment, they will claim, "You set me up. You knew I couldn't get there on that day."
- **Paranoid Inmates Live Like Detectives.** They continually search for evidence to prove what they already know is true. They have ***ideas of reference***, in which they believe that other conversations, glances, or actions are directed at them. They assume that others are conspiring about them, talking about them, laughing at them. Ironically, their reactions, in response to their own paranoia, frequently cause others to act in exactly the way the paranoid person expects.
- **Paranoid Inmates Make Others Uncomfortable Or Afraid.** Because of their aggressive, brooding" or standoffish behavior, they can make other people uncomfortable or afraid. If they sense fear in you, they expect you to attack, and they "attack you back first," fear driving their own aggression.

Try to Let Them Know What Is Going On

Because paranoid inmates are so suspicious, they will often question your actions and instructions. Clearly and explicitly explain the rules and regulations of their supervision plan. Correctional officers should also make clear their expectations of compliance, and explain the violation process, as well as the potential consequences of non–compliance. Even if you must perform a cell extraction, put them in solitary confinement or protective custody, explain what you are doing and why, once they are secure. If they have a sense that you treated them in good faith, despite requisite severity, things are more likely to go well next time. However, you should not accept being quizzed incessantly. You are not required to explain every action. It might be a tactic to throw you off guard or distract you, or simply control a few moments of your day.

Personal Space: Physical and Psychological With the Paranoid Inmate

Many paranoid inmates are preoccupied, even obsessed, with fears that they will be invaded, violated, or controlled in some fashion. The more severely psychotic may be afraid that they will be sexually violated, even in situations where that is not a possibility. Some of the following are, of course, relevant when dealing with any inmate, but they are doubly important when an inmate is paranoid.

- **Maintain the Angle.** Whether standing or sitting, turn your body at a slight angle (blade stance), so that physical "confrontation" is a choice on their part rather than a requirement. If you directly face a paranoid inmate ("square up"), you *force* them to turn away if they do not want to face you. Paradoxically, the stance that is safer for you makes them feel safer in turn.
- **Mindfulness.** Never let your own guard. You are in an avalanche zone, and anything could set off another slide.
- **Differentiate.** Paranoid inmates feel safest when you differentiate yourself from them, so that they don't feel—emotionally—that you got under their guard. It is better to be somewhat emotionally distant rather than too warm and friendly.

- **Too Friendly.** Be aware when things are getting too relaxed. It is not only about you maintaining awareness. If the paranoid inmate relaxes, they may suddenly startle, realizing that for a brief moment, they let their guard down. They may respond by exploding to make sure you do not "take them over."
- **Cover Your Triggers.** Paranoid inmates will try to provoke you. If you lose your temper, they will feel justified in whatever they do to you, and it may just as well key into their terror-based aggression. A slang expression for this is "fear biters." They bark and snarl and when you react, they attack as if you attacked first.

Is There a Specific Paranoid Rage or Violence?

There is no specific "paranoid rage." Instead, paranoia is an "engine" that drives rage in all its various forms. De-escalate the inmate using tactics specific to the mode of rage they are exhibiting (**Section XII**) rather than de-escalating "paranoia" itself. Paranoid inmates can exhibit traits of fear, frustration, intimidation, and manipulation. With their focus, however, they are rarely disorganized. Even so, some disorganized inmates can experience an "omni-directional dread," a pervasive terror that is inescapable. Unlike paranoia, however, this pervasive sense of terror has no target.

Figure 33.2 Review: Paranoia and Persecution

The paranoid inmate has an attitude that if anything is wrong it is another person's fault. Whether delusional or not, they see others as conspiring against them or persecuting them.

- De-escalate based on the behavior, not the paranoia.
- Let them know what's going on.
- Speak in formal tones. Do not be too friendly.
- They will try to provoke you so they can "hit you back first."
- Be aware of both physical and emotional spacing. Maintain a correct distancing, neither too close nor too far.
- Differentiate by not being too friendly, and if they are delusional, clearly separate yourself from their paranoid ideas without arguing (**Chapters 41/42**).
- Maintain your calm: the paranoid inmate is usually assaultive when they feel under attack, when they perceive you as controlling, or when they perceive that you are afraid.
- If you do place them in custody or otherwise control them, let them know what is going on and why. Paranoid inmates are most likely to become dangerous when they base their actions on their imagination rather than on reality.

SECTION VI

Recognizing the Strategies of
Opportunistic and Manipulative Inmates

CHAPTER 34

Divide and Confuse:
Borderline Personality Disorder
and Splitting

Figure 34.1 Author's Note

Individuals with borderline traits frequently display suicidal and para-suicidal behaviors, which will be discussed in detail in **Section VIII**.

Personality disorders are habitual patterns of behavior that sometimes cause an inmate, and almost always, others associated with them, considerable problems. Most types of personality disorders, however, do not cause behaviors that significantly affect safety. Several, however, are often associated with dangerous behavior: paranoid personality **(Chapter 33)**, anti-social personality, with its most intense manifestation, psychopathy **(Chapters 35 & 36)**, and a third type called borderline personality disorder. An inmate with borderline traits believes that whatever feeling they are having right now is their only possible reality. For example, an inmate is accidentally bumped in the lunch line. Instead of brushing it off, he explodes. This is a borderline reaction. On the flip side, he meets his new attorney's assistant, and within five seconds, he knows that she is the love of his life.

Any of us can be overcome by feelings that seem beyond our control and make emotional decisions that are not in our own best interest, such as falling in love with the "wrong" person. We are sometimes impulsive, and sometimes we get angry, even enraged. For us, however, such experiences are an aberration, while for the inmate with borderline personality disorder, they are an everyday occurrence.

Those on the mild end of the spectrum will be quite emotional, over-reacting to things that others could take in stride. With those whose disorder is more severe, it is as if their nervous system, at least that part which regulates emotion, lacks any protective sheathing. Imagine trying to live your daily life with two layers of skin peeled off. That is borderline existence on an emotional level. Whatever one feels is inescapable. The borderline person lives with the intensity and the lack of emotional resilience of a toddler. They experience the world and the people in it as good and bad, perfect and foul. They are frequently arrested for domestic violence, road rage, and impulsive fights ("What are you looking at!").

Figure 34.2 Examples of People With Borderline Personality Traits

The two main characters in the movie, *Monster,* starring Charlize Theron and Christina Ricci, are portrayals of women with two types of extreme borderline personality disorders. Theron plays Alicia Wournos, a woman who came from a horrendously abusive background, drifted into prostitution, and then murdered six "johns." She had the emotional stability of a toddler, shifting from sweetness and trust to hair-trigger rage. Whatever she felt at that moment was her only reality. Some of her murders, at least, were based on the threat and abuse she *felt* she was experiencing from the johns.

The Ricci character was a woman of almost no character at all. She templated to whomever she was with at the time. Rather than an "active" borderline like Wournos, she was passive. Like Wournos, however, all her actions, too, are based on feelings alone, not on any rational evaluation on what was good for her, in this case—bonding with a dominant, violent individual, and then, later, betraying her to her law enforcement interrogators.

Because of this combination of character traits, inmates with borderline personality disorder frequently find themselves in various crises. Among them are genuine suicide attempts as well as para-suicidal acts—self-mutilating behaviors or repeat suicide "gestures" staged for discovery and attention **(Section VIII),** *impulsive* acts of assault, and brief psychotic episodes **(Chapters 41/42).**

Typically, other correctional officers, case managers, lawyers, psychologists, and nurses disagree how to respond to a borderline inmate, even to the point of arguing about whom is at fault for their current crisis. In particular, those involved in a therapeutic relationship with the inmate, often lean to "contextualizing"—explaining away or excusing their behavior, especially when the inmate has a previous history of trauma or abuse. When the team associated with a borderline inmate get tangled up in intense disputes about what is best for them, this type of conflict is called *splitting*.

Splitting doesn't happen in a vacuum. The inmate, although not really conscious of what they are doing, presents different facets of their personality to each person with whom they interact. Whether the inmate is aware of it or not, this is strategic, a "divide and confuse" tactic. If people are arguing about you, they can't gang up on you.

It is not surprising, really, that an inmate will appear quite different to a counselor trying to build a supportive relationship, as opposed to a case manager trying to help them negotiate their way through the jail system with a minimum of conflict, and to the correctional officer, who is responsible for the establishment of order and safety within the jail.

The correctional officer can, of course, unilaterally make a decision based on concerns of correctional safety and place the inmate into a higher custody setting. However, if all members of the team responsible for the inmate remain at odds, the "victory" by the officer will be short-lived. You will be working with the same people on other cases, and you will most likely continue to work "at odds together" regarding this inmate. Thus, whenever a team gets intensely at odds regarding a single inmate, suggest the possibility of splitting, and see if you can, by comparing observations, see if the inmate's interactions with various people have created the adversarial situation in which you find yourselves.

Borderline inmates are, not surprisingly, quite reactive to other people's emotional reactions. If you elicit a feeling, you "made" them feel it. If they are happy, they are sure you love them. If you anger them, then you are scum, trash or evil. Like a toddler, whatever they feel, they become. Therefore, the attitude of the correctional officer should be someone who wishes the inmate well, yet undeviatingly enforces the rules. By maintaining a type of "warm emotional distance," you won't get emotionally worked up over things, and the inmate will find less to react to as well.

CHAPTER 35

Bad Intentions: Recognizing the Strategies
of Opportunistic and Manipulative Inmates

In order to satisfy their need for instant gratification, many inmates attempt to manipulate nearly everyone with whom they come into contact. Some use manipulation as a means of furthering criminal actions. A few live for hate and destruction, and delight most in duping people so that they don't even know how "dirty they were done." Some manipulative inmates lie so that no one can pin them down, using a "divide and disappear" strategy so that the more powerful beings in their life argue about them, instead of focusing directly on what they are really doing.

Manipulative Strategies

Manipulative strategies can result from a variety of emotions and intentions, such as those born of revenge, malice, desperation, laziness, guilt, or as the result of drug and alcohol use.[31]

Correctional officers should be wary of inmates who appear to be overly compliant, especially those inmates who have committed serious offenses, such as sex crimes or offenses involving the use of weapons or violence. Quite often, some of the most dangerous inmates will be the ones who are, apparently, agreeable, low-risk inmates, complying with any requirements in their custodial setting. Their motives are hardly altruistic. This seemingly compliant behavior may in fact be nothing more than an attempt to manipulate and control *your* behavior. <u>Require proper verification of any information given by the inmate.</u> Remember, inmates realize how busy and overworked you are. What the compliant inmate is likely trying to accomplish is to manipulate you so that you do not see what they are up to. After all, why would an already harried correctional officer bother to focus much attention on a truly compliant inmate!

Inmates sometimes use stories to overload you with information to keep your attention away from what they are doing, either in your presence, or generally speaking, out in the community. They try to charm you so that you actually look forward to contact with them, yet remain unaware of what is really going on.

Manipulative inmates ask correctional officers for personal information, such as marital status, children, in which part of town the correctional officer resides, and so forth. These questions appear innocent enough. What the manipulative inmate is doing, however, is gathering information, something that they can use either for themselves or as a medium of exchange with other inmates. Redirect any questions that touch on personal matters back toward your professional duties.

Inmates are also masters at quietly hanging around officers' conversations, harvesting revealing personal information. This is the easiest way to find out who could be vulnerable to manipulation whether it is through love ("my husband and I are having troubles"), money ("I had to take out a loan to make my house payment") or any other information that could be used for leverage in the future. How many officers talk about their kids at work? Are there any inmates hanging around while you talk?

- "I took my boy hunting last week."
- "She scored three goals."
- "Yeah, he's doing better now. The doc says he'll be off chemo in three months.")

Manipulative inmates are also quite adept at reading body language. They are particularly interested in potential victims, those who are easily intimidated or frightened, including other inmates. They are also intrigued in those who put up any kind of a front, including an attempt to appear tough. All the manipulative inmate has to do is challenge them, and the "fronting" correctional officer begins reacting like a yo-yo on a string, trying to keep up appearances, to an inmate who has already read them inside and out.

Manipulative inmates are also likely to blame others for both their failures and their behaviors. Nothing is ever their fault: they were simply in the wrong place at the wrong time; they didn't know their "cellie" had a shank under the mattress; it is the correctional officer's fault for them losing their "good time."

Another means of manipulation is that of flirtation and sexuality, which can manifest in any gender configuration, including same sex. All correctional officers must address flirtatious behaviors or sexual innuendo immediately and the officer must follow through with appropriate written documentation on the inmate's behavior. While this may be embarrassing, it is the only way an officer can let their administration know, formally, that the inmate's behavior was addressed and boundaries were enforced. Firm limits must be set as to the professional nature of the relationship, and what constitutes acceptable conversation. If this issue is not addressed instantly, the inmate will view it as implied acceptance, which may lead to further advances or even attempted blackmail. It may also lead others, both inmates and co-workers, to assume that something is actually going on. By following through with written documentation, this allows the officer's supervisor to take further action if the inmate's behavior continues. Some inmate's security classification should be enhanced, if they show a pattern of trying to flirt or "hit on" staff. This is yet another of the many reasons that correctional officers should not be isolated while interviewing inmates, regardless of gender.

Manipulative inmates view relationships as transactions, with an eye toward gaining an advantage or placing the other individual in their debt. The manipulative inmate will sometimes deliberately make things difficult, only to then suddenly "give in," or become compliant. The likely purpose for their new-found compliance is to engender a sense of gratitude within the unwary correctional officer, or at least a lessening of frustration, toward the inmate. Along with a sense of gratitude however, can come a lessening of supervision or investigation. Officers should always be wary and always be thinking about what an inmate has to gain from any interaction with staff.

Figure 35.1 Examples: Strategies Used to Keep Officers Away

Inmates sometimes find a "theme" that either gets them out of trouble or is threatening enough that officers either chose not to deal with them or excuse their behavior. Female inmates that continually accuse officers of raping them or touching them inappropriately generally cause male officers to shy away from them, refuse to deal with them, or pass the inmate's bad behavior off to another officer. This creates dissention among the officers and reduces those dealing with them to only women officers. Think of the sense of power this engenders in the inmate—"All male officers are afraid of me!"

Other inmates tell officers that they are HIV positive when they are not. This is especially effective for the inmate in use-of-force situations as officers do not want to be exposed to bodily fluids. Inmates using this theme will often attempt to spit on officers. Because inmate's medical records are not available to officers, no one wants to deal with this inmate's bad behavior as their HIV status cannot be verified. Inmates cannot be compelled to take an HIV test without a court order. Officers will often let these inmates get away with much more than they would tolerate from any other inmate.

CHAPTER 36

Tactical and Safety Considerations Related to the Supervision of the Psychopathic Inmate

---

Figure 36.1 Authors' Note: Psychopaths Stand Alone

There is considerable overlap in this chapter with the safety recommendations made throughout this book, particularly in the last chapter on manipulative behavior. In **Section XII**, we will discuss what to do when facing someone presenting with Hot, Predatory, or Aggressive-Manipulative Rage—all modes that the psychopath can manifest when they become dangerously aggressive. Here, the authors are highlighting the most salient point's specific to psychopathic individuals. We believe that this information is so important to officer safety that it must be presented as a stand-alone chapter for easy reference.

The terms psychopath and sociopath are interchangeable. They evoke very strong reactions. Estimates are that 1-3 percent of any population, and perhaps 40 percent of the jail population is psychopathic. A small percentage of inmates commit most of the crimes in any society, and although there is a sociological component to crime, the psychopath, to a remarkable degree, seems independent of such factors.

The entertainment media as well as sensationalized news accounts of horrendously violent killers and rapists have introduced an image of the malevolent criminal mastermind and the sadistic predator into the public's consciousness. Without a doubt, violent psychopaths do exist, but they are often rather mundane in appearance, blending in with their surroundings without attracting any undue attention.

Figure 36.2 Examples of Psychopaths in the Movies

Instead of thinking of some movie monster such as Hannibal Lector, a much more useful image would be Johnny Depp's character in *Pirates of the Caribbean*. In his role as Captain Jack Sparrow, Depp plays an aggressive narcissist; he is attractive and likeable, but also utterly selfish and quite willing to violate social norms. A second image would be the Matt Damon character in *The Talented Mr. Ripley*, an inoffensive chameleon-like con-man, who has no particular desire to kill anyone, but when circumstances "require" it, he does so without hesitation.

Although psychopathic inmates can be charming and ingratiating, they can also be violent, provocative, dishonest, arrogant, and quite willing to break any rule. Although some are remarkably talented, even brilliantly creative, the only thing they truly care about is themselves. The psychopath presents problems far beyond what you will experience with the "ordinary" criminal inmate, however manipulative **(Chapter 35)** the latter may be.

Just as a leopard or a cougar is known to attack whenever a vulnerable animal exposes its neck, psychopathic inmates feed off vulnerability. Because of their manipulative charm, they can easily get under the defenses of others. They will gravitate to the most vulnerable people on your team. They study everyone with whom they come into contact, making note of any apparent weaknesses and developing new strategies of manipulation and control, either as a direct point of attack ("When I raise my voice, Officer Grohl flinches."), or as a new weapon to use against others ("When Officer Gibbs tilts her head and smiles while I'm talking, I find myself relaxing a little. I can use this the next time I'm trying to get close to that kid in D Block.") Not only do they lack a sense of remorse at the harm inflicted upon their victims, they often take delight in it.

They view themselves as utterly unique and special (grandiose narcissism), and therefore, do not view themselves as being incarcerated for the purpose of rehabilitation. They view the entire criminal justice system—from correctional officers to treatment programs—with contempt.

Because such inmates are easily bored, they deliberately flame up other inmates so that they come into conflict either amongst themselves or with correctional officers. Many, parasitic rather than violent, revel in the instigation of emotional drama or conflict, through the use of lies, rumors, and/or intimidation. Another purpose of these "set ups," is to create a unit chaotic enough that they are able to accomplish their own deeds unseen, with officers preoccupied with other inmates.

Without a doubt, the most dangerous are the sexually violent psychopaths, who use their guile to groom others for exploitation, prior to enacting sexual assaults. Although common sense would dictate against a correctional officer ever fostering a personal relationship with an inmate, it happens all too often. A psychopathic inmate may attempt to groom and seduce a correctional officer, just for the thrill of destroying their career, or for the purposes of blackmail or privilege.

Such inmates owe their allegiance to no one, although they may form quasi-sentimental attachments that last until a stronger interest or desire pushes them onwards to something else. This loyalty is on the level of, "Who do you think you are, patting my dog without my permission!"

As with many criminal inmates, psychopaths are often impulsive, and their sense of invincibility often leads them to ignore consequences. Their impulsivity and sense of entitlement can also result in explosive violence if they don't get what they want. Other psychopaths are "instrumentally violent," using it as a tool: "just business," so to speak. For others, the violent act itself is gratifying; they are sadistically violent. In sum, psychopathic inmates' propensity for physical and emotional violence, coupled with their charming manipulativeness and the fact that there are **NO** therapeutic interventions that can "cure" them, means that correctional officers must remain observant and wary at all times when dealing with them.

When supervising and interacting with the psychopathic inmate, correctional officers need to remain conscious of the fact that these individuals are quite skilled in reading other people, in light of how strong they are, their susceptibility to manipulation, and most significantly, what danger they represent to the inmate. Quite simply, they are out to destroy you by one means or another. The authors recommend Robert Hare's illuminating work, *Without Conscience: The disturbing world of the psychopath* for a detailed discussion of this subgroup of inmates.[32]

Figure 36.3 Substance Abusers May Present as Psychopaths

Substance abusers often act like psychopaths while using. Addicts in remission who *truly* are engaged in treatment usually begin to abandon manipulative and strategic behaviors. Psychopaths, on the other hand, don't fundamentally change. They may use different strategies when they are sober, but they will never abandon a tactical, manipulative approach.

Tactical and Safety Considerations

1. **You will be attacked through your "best" and your "worst" points.** Of course, the psychopathic inmate will attack your weak points. If you are insecure about your personal appearance; for example, the psychopath will either make you feel more insecure, or in a more sophisticated tactic, reassure you that he or she, at least, finds you very attractive. What is harder to notice is when you are attacked through your best points. For example, if you appear to be physically fit, they will try to consult with you about your exercise regimen, or ask where and when you work out. If you love children, they will find a way to ask your advice on an alleged phone call from their ex-wife about putting their child on medications. They might really have a child who needs medication. But they are asking you in order to gain some traction, not to get your help. For such an individual, anything can be leverage. Remember, they don't even have to lie. The truth is an even better tool!

2. **Notice when others start making excuses for the inmate.** When manipulated, people often find a way to rationalize what the psychopath is doing. For example, after a near assault during his substance abuse treatment group, a counselor says, "You have to understand. He was brought up that way. When you threatened him with a violation, it was like a flashback to the way his father treated him." Don't allow others to sway your opinion or prevent you from attending to your professional duties.

3. **Track any manipulative strategies, document them well, and alert all other members of your team to the tactics an inmate is using.** Consult and consult again. Don't discount the observations of other officers. They are often very important, especially those of correctional officers, who interact most directly with the inmate in question. Consult yet again.

4. **You may be intimidated.** The most obvious manifestation of intimidation is fear. <u>There is always a reason for fear.</u> If you are frightened of an inmate, consult with your fellow officers or supervi-

sors immediately. What is more difficult to recognize is an unconscious attempt to avoid being frightened by giving in to the demands of the psychopath! Ironically, the intimidated officer may sometimes claim that they have a working relationship or special rapport with the inmate, when, in fact, all they are doing is giving the predator exactly what he wants.

5. **Be aware of grooming behaviors.** The "grooming cycle" is a pattern of behavior designed to alleviate the intended victim's fears and apprehensions, all the while targeting them for attack. The inmate will make their target feel a little off-balance, making them anxious, scared, or flattered. Then they lessen the pressure while making a request that the correctional officer would have granted anyway. The inmate begins to "train" the correctional officer to experience a sense of relief when granting a request.

Figure 36.4 An Example of Grooming

The inmate stands too close to you (slightly, not enough to require you to issue a command that they back up). Then, simultaneous to moving back to a more comfortable distance, he asks permission to get a drink of water. His goal is to cause you to associate granting a request with a release of tension. Hard eye-contact, shifting to friendliness, is another common grooming tactic.

If successful, the inmate will make requests that get closer and closer to a moral or ethical line. Once he can get you to do something *over* the line, however, slightly, you are now compromised: an object of blackmail or worse. An example of this would be, once groomed, you let the inmate have "just one minute" on the phone, past curfew, to say goodnight to his kid. Once you start bending the rules, breaking them isn't so far off.

6. **Guard all personal information.** As discussed previously, personal information can be used in a variety of ways. The psychopath can use such information to determine points of leverage against you. They can talk publicly about you, apparently displaying intimate knowledge of your affairs. In the worst case, such information can be used to track you down outside of your professional life, or make you fear for the safety of your friends and family.

7. **Don't get beyond the horizon line.** <u>Don't meet psychopaths alone!</u> Don't close your office door when interviewing them, and either have back-up present or in immediate contact. You are vulnerable to false accusations. You are vulnerable to manipulation when no one is present to witness and monitor the interaction with the inmate. You may not even perceive manipulation is happening. You are also vulnerable to physical attack at any time the psychopathic inmate believes that it is to their advantage, if their rage is triggered, or simply because it would be enjoyable.

8. **Detecting calculated splitting.** The psychopathic inmate uses gossip, rumors, misdirection, and blatant lying to set all the stakeholders involved in their supervision and treatment against each other. Regular communication and consultation with the various members of the treatment team is the best way to detect and confront splitting.

SECTION VII

Communication With Inmates
That Have Severe Mental Illness
or Other Conditions That Cause
Severe Disability

CHAPTER 37

Overview of Section VII

This section offers detailed descriptions of the most significant *behaviors* that severely mentally ill inmates may display, regardless of diagnosis. Along with each description will be suggestions on optimal communication strategies. Some are generally applicable, therefore overlapping among various sections, while others are specific to only one type of behavior/symptom. Just because you might be reading about paranoia for example, doesn't mean that paranoid inmate is not also disorganized, delusional, or manic. What you are trying to develop is a range of communication tactics that cover as many situations as possible.

It is a common misunderstanding that all mentally ill individuals are severely impaired individuals, who manifest severely disordered or unusual behaviors. That is not necessarily so. Even the severely mentally ill can have many periods throughout the day where their illness is not predominant. Furthermore, most contacts with mentally ill inmates are not emergencies. Nonetheless, the basic principles of communication presented here will serve you just as well with those who are manifesting a mild level of disorder, as well as those who are on the extreme end of the spectrum.

As the establishment of safety and the de-escalation of aggression are the primary purposes of this book, we focus on general patterns of inmate behavior, **regardless of the cause**. Mental illness, in this vein, does not refer only to such disorders as schizophrenia, bipolar disorder or depression. For example, intoxication can be considered a time limited, substance induced mental disorder. Beyond any medical condition, people, otherwise normal, can display acute, "out of character" behaviors, due to problems or stressors in their lives, and jail itself is certainly stressful. Thus, for the sake of this discussion, substance abuse, distinct neurological disorders, so-called character or mood disorders, as well as atypical episodes brought on by stress or other factors, all function as mental illness, sometimes of "time-limited" duration. The cause may be relevant if making appropriate referrals for treatment; the correctional officer, however, should most emphatically focus on the behaviors, whatever the cause.

Speak to the Person, Not the Illness

You are walking outside on an icy winter day. You slip suddenly and spin toward the pavement. You thrust out an arm that breaks your fall. It also breaks your right wrist. Your life, for a few weeks or months, is different. Even the simplest tasks are difficult and may require assistance. Still, even though you are inconvenienced, and the injury probably changes your mood quite a bit, you are still "you," the same person as before your injury. Your injuries will eventually heal, the accident forgotten, as you continue through life. Such is not the case with mental illness.

Severe mental illness can cause mental and emotional disturbances far more profound than the temporary inconveniences brought on by physical injury. One's ability to think is distorted, and with delusions, reality is skewed. Perceptions may be bizarre, even hallucinatory. Emotions swing from high to low, or shift into realms at odds with one's immediate circumstances. Even so, as bad as such an illness may be, **there is a still a person behind the symptoms.** The inmates under your supervision aren't simply bundles of raw emotions or distorted cognitions. There exists an essential part of each of them untouched by their mental illness. **We can choose to speak to the illness, or speak to the *person* who is ill. For both humane and tactical reasons, it is that core part of his or her psyche that we are trying to reach.**

CHAPTER 38

Struggling in a Fog:
Dealing With Symptoms
of Disorganization

Figure 38.1 Author's Note

See **Chapter 67** for a detailed discussion of de-escalation of disorganized inmates in a state of chaotic rage. See **Chapter 71** for information dealing with agitated developmentally disabled inmates.

Understanding Disorganization

Disorganization is a general term used to describe what it is like when inmates can't adequately organize their thinking, perceptions, behaviors and/or emotions so that they can function well in the real world. This can include those who are developmentally delayed, profoundly psychotic, head injured, those suffering from any kind of dementia or delirium, as well as those who are severely intoxicated (chemically induced disorganization).

Due to their cognitive limitations, developmentally disabled inmates are not skilled at problem-solving situations. Furthermore, they often lack the maturity to manage complex or frustrating situations, and jail is nothing if not frustrating, confusing, intimidating, frightening, etc.

Psychotic inmates also become disorganized when they deteriorate. Oddly enough, their delusions may have served them as an organizing principle. For example, if you believe yourself to be surrounded by enemies, or are on a mission to save the world, you have to concentrate, because of your mission, as delusional as it may be. When one becomes disorganized, even delusions break down into chaotic thoughts, which are often manifested in incoherent speech and disorderly behavior.

Figure 38.2 The Near Impossibility of Communication

You will know you are dealing with a disorganized inmate because they are incoherent, or it is otherwise nearly impossible to communicate with them. They may seem to shift from one emotion to another, for no logical reason, and it is very hard, if not impossible, to hold their attention. Disorganization is an "over-arching" category, including aspects of almost syndrome described in other chapters. A disorganized person can be latent and/or concrete, have mood swings, paranoia, anxiety, extreme agitation, confusion, delusions, hallucinations, and information processing problems, to name only a few traits that are discussed elsewhere in the book. This chapter is concerned with the overall phenomenon of disorganization.

Small Bits at a Time

To better communicate with disorganized inmates, officers should divide tasks and instructions into small bits. Make sure that you are very specific concerning what you expect them to do. There is no point in being irritable with them. That just makes things more difficult and confusing because they usually don't know why you are upset.

Be realistic about what they can do. Correctional officers should not expect severely disorganized inmates to do something that is beyond their individual skill level, or their current mental status. Of course, the inmate should still be held to a high standard; just don't make it an impossible one.

Creating Room for Success

Although supervising disorganized inmates can be frustrating, inmates should be rewarded for positive behaviors, not just punished for negative ones. Indeed, your positive feedback may be the first they have ever received, and it will often help them adjust to incarceration in a positive manner.

Over Stimulation

Loud noises, the presence of many people (particularly if more than one is talking), too much background noise or even bright fluorescent lights, will both distract and further agitate the disorganized person. Given the conditions in most jails, it is hard, if not impossible to address this problem, but whenever possible, move the individual to a less stimulating environment. **It is particularly important with disorganized inmates that, when you are trying to elicit compliance, only one person speaks to them at a time.**

Keep It Simple

The disorganized inmate pays far more attention to non-verbal communication. Self-control is particularly important when de-escalating disorganized inmates. Your sentences should be short and each should only have one "packet" of information. Keep the emotion out of your voice, and limit your physical gestures.

Let Me Repeat Myself

When we are not understood, our usual impulse is to elaborate. We use different words, expressive hand and facial gestures, and the emotional tone of our communication intensifies. This makes things worse with disorganized inmates. **Rather, simply repeat the same statement or question word-for-word, with the same gesture and facial expression**. When their disorganization is profound, you may need to repeat information and statements several times. The aim is not to browbeat them. You should not shout at them to "get through." Repetition can be a touchstone of stability. However, if you change your vocal tone or get irritated, you will defeat the purpose of the repetition. Rolling your eyes, making side-long glances of amusement at your back-up, sighing, raising your voice, pointing, standing close to them to get their attention, snapping your fingers, or suddenly clapping in front of their face, to name only a few, undermine safety, whether you are repeating the same words or not.

By repeating yourself several times, with a clear measured tone of voice, telling the inmate exactly what you want them to do, you provide a verbal lifeline that they can focus on rather than the chaos that is otherwise overwhelming them.

Magical Thinking

"Magical thinking" (mentioned in **Chapter 2** as "speaking into being") is telling stories which you then believe. It is most common among small children, senile and demented adults, and developmentally delayed individuals. Inmates displaying magical thinking don't show the same fixed quality of delusional inmates **(Chapters 41/42)**, where a fundamental truth is suddenly revealed and then locked into place in their mind. Rather, the disorganized inmate verbalizes his fantasies, repeats them, and then believes them to be reality.

You will usually observe magical thinking in a developmentally disabled inmate, often as a kind of fable making, the kinds of stories told by very young people, either young in age or young in mind. Once you have established that a claim or statement is not true, there is little to be gained by arguing with the inmate about it. Sometimes just let it go. Other times, you can say, even with a little tiredness in your voice, "I've heard that story before. You don't have to tell me again." Then, simply move on to the next topic at hand and shift the inmate's focus toward the actual issues of concern regarding their supervision plan.

Figure 38.3 A Note on False Confessions by Developmentally Disabled Individuals

Important: Research on false admissions to crimes reveals that a large number of such confessions are made by developmentally disabled individuals. The developmentally disabled inmate may do something similar, when feeling emotionally pressured or if they are trying to impress or please you. During investigations with developmentally disabled inmates, you will get the most accurate information when they are calm and feel safe.

Figure 38.4 Dealing With a Disorganized Inmate

You will know you are dealing with a disorganized inmate when he or she is:

- Nearly incoherent, or otherwise impossible to communicate with.
- Shifting from one emotion to another with no logical reason.
- Distracted and you cannot hold their attention.
- Acting in a bizarre or chaotic manner.

When dealing with a disorganized inmate you should:

- Divide tasks into small bits.
- Give simple, specific instructions.
- Be realistic about what the person can and can't do.
- Repeat your instructions rather than elaborate on them and don't change your vocal tone.
- Don't argue with magical thinking—redirect them to discussing what, if anything is emergent.
- Allow only one person to speak to the disorganized inmate.
- Particularly in crisis situations, minimize environmental distractions when possible, such as the TV in the background, other people talking, and bright lights, etc.

CHAPTER 39

Latency: Dropping Stones
Down a Well

Latency is a behavior in which inmates respond in a much-delayed manner. It is often a manifestation of disorganization, but because of its confusing nature, we have chosen to discuss it as an entity of its own. With latent inmates:

- You ask a question, and they talk to themselves quietly as they puzzle out what you might be saying.
- They may not even make eye-contact, or engage in odd movements in the air.
- Some latent inmates may simply stare away, a vacuous look on their faces.

Figure 39.1 How to Recognize Latency

You will recognize latency when the inmate to whom you are speaking not only delays his or her answers for a long time, but also when they do reply, their communication is somewhat odd and disjointed. You will notice that they do not really respond to the questions asked. This is different from being silent or defying you. You get the sense that they are not "there," that it is about something going on inside of them, not about you at all.

Figure 39.2 Example of Latency

The correctional officer comes upon an inmate, tying himself to the bars of his cell with his shirt:

- **CORRECTIONAL OFFICER.** "Why are you tying yourself to the bars?" (*30 seconds pass with the latent man standing and staring at the ground, frozen.*)
- **CORRECTIONAL OFFICER.** "Why are you tying yourself to the bars?"
- **Inmate.** (*The mentally ill man slowly raises his head, and his eyes vacant, slowly speaks.*) "Uh, bar fly." (*He then resumes tying himself to the railing with thin string.*)
- **CORRECTIONAL OFFICER.** "I can call for help so you can go to the clinic. I know there is someone there that is able to help you."
- **Inmate.** (*The mentally ill inmate stops tying himself, his hands still holding the string in mid-knot. His lips move as if he is talking to himself. He raises his eyes, lowers them, and raises them again. He speaks.*) "Don't take me steal me." (*He then resumes his activity without eye contact.*)

Note the CORRECTIONAL Officer's exemplary patience. This contact is not a failure. The officer has ascertained that the individual is so profoundly ill that he is unable to communicate. That the officer is calm probably keeps the inmate from becoming fearful or combative in response.

Note also that the officer did not try to analyze this, for example, asking the inmate if he is afraid he will fly away, and that's why he's tying himself to the bars. Given how impaired the inmate is, figuring things out is unnecessary.

Coping with Latency: Keep Things Simple

Although communicating with a latent inmate can be frustrating, as well as time consuming, the correctional officer should remain calm. Indeed, any frustration or anger you display will only further confuse them. Keep your sentences and instructions short and direct. Minimize the use of qualifiers, such as "you might" "maybe" "kind of," etc., that you ordinarily put in your sentences. Officers should also minimize the use of hand gestures or changing facial expressions. Don't speak robotically; simplicity is best.

It is useless to try to "get through to them" by yelling. All this does is drive them further into the latent state, as they get more frightened, overwhelmed, or confused by the irate officer yelling incomprehensible things at them.

Latent inmates usually don't need things explained in further detail; they just don't "get it" the first time. Say the same thing again and again, with a slow measured pace.

Figure 39.3 How to Speak and Respond to a Latent Inmate
- Keep your sentences short.
- Don't change your vocal tone.
- Repeat the instructions using the same words and the same tone of voice.
- Pause between sentences, giving the inmate time to process what you have said.
- Try to get the inmate to repeat back your instructions (No guarantees on this item!)
- Contact medical. Changes in mental states may indicate the recurrence or onset of serious mental illness.

CHAPTER 40

Withdrawal from Intoxicating Substances

Figure 40.1 IMPORTANT NOTE: The Question of Co-occurring Diagnosis

Given all the attention usually paid to this subject, the reader may question why we have not devoted a large section specifically to the behaviors of inmates with both substance abuse and mental health issues as a separate concern. There is no doubt whatsoever, that co-occurring diagnosis can profoundly affect every aspect of an inmate's life, including their success or failure in a corrections setting. Substance abuse makes it much harder to heal from or even manage mental illness, and mental illness makes it much harder to recover from substance abuse. And both affect their ability to maintain themselves in general population.

This book, however, is concerned with the issues of safety and de-escalation from extreme states. Imagine all the pages that would be necessary to distinguish between, for example, a solvent-inhaling inmate with bipolar disorder, a marijuana-smoking inmate with social phobia, and a schizophrenic who shoots up a mixture of cocaine and heroin. To be sure, each and all of these concerns are relevant when it comes to treatment, but whatever substances they may have ingested, whatever illness or syndrome they may be suffering from, we are concerned with the behaviors that they are displaying. **Deal with the behavior, not the cause**.

Many mentally ill inmates actively use or are addicted to drugs and/or alcohol. These inmates are "dually diagnosed;" that is, they have been diagnosed as having a mental health disorder as well as substance abuse issues. The abuse of drugs and/or alcohol not only complicates their recovery, but also can be life threatening if the mentally ill inmate experiences a severe reaction brought on by mixing drugs and/or alcohol with their prescribed medications. Others develop conditions (amphetamine psychosis, for one example) that function exactly like mental illness, although the primary cause of their illness is different. Many of these substance-induced disorders continue long after they have discontinued use of the drug, due to damage to their neurological system.

Many mentally ill inmates have been abusing drugs and/or alcohol for years before they were even diagnosed with a mental health disorder. Breaking the cycle of addiction for long-term drug users, while attempting to get them to address their underlying mental health issues, can be a Sisyphean task,[33] where you work like that mythic figure, pushing the inmate up the slope of addiction treatment only to have him or her fall down the slope of decompensation into mental illness, and then when you push them back up *that* slope so that their mental illness is under some control, they relapse again on drugs.

Unfortunately, certain inmates enjoy the effects of combining illicit substances with their prescribed medications, such as opiate abusers enhancing their "high" by taking the prescription medication Klonopin. Other inmates may be too addled by drug and alcohol use to remember to take prescribed medications, while others simply prefer the drug-induced state of consciousness to that of being properly medicated. In any event, correctional officers are encouraged to not only obtain a working knowledge of the various psychotropic medications that their inmate's may be prescribed, but also to familiarize themselves with the wide array of illicit substances and prescription medications used (and abused) by many inmates. Being familiar with the symptoms of drug use, either independently or in conjunction with prescription medications, will better prepare the officer to de-escalate an inmate who is going through withdrawal.

Withdrawal Is a Medical Emergency

First and foremost, alcohol and drug withdrawal is a medical emergency. There is no specific "withdrawal rage." Use whatever tactics necessary to de-escalate and control them, <u>based on their behavior</u>, as described in the latter sections of this book. The correctional officer should summon medical attention immediately, and then focus on keeping the inmate calm while waiting for medical assistance.

Inmates in withdrawal are often in pain or feeling quite ill. They are also frightened or irritable, and very much focused, in a completely entitled way, on getting their needs met. This may include a high level of resistance to seeking medical attention, or assurances by the inmate that they are well enough to be left alone. The signs of withdrawal can include:

- **Unstable Coordination.** Try to get inmate to sit or lie down for their safety.
- **Restlessness and Agitation.** Try to reduce any stimulating input.
- **Unpredictable and Sudden Actions.** Keep your movements calm and slow so that you don't elicit a startle reflex on their part, which can easily turn into an attack.
- **Slurred or Incoherent Speech.** Speak to them in a calm, quiet voice and make an extra effort to understand what they are saying. Provide short explanations.
- **Abnormally Rigid Muscles.** It is hard to sort this out from a pre-assault indicator. Be on guard for an attack.
- **Being Argumentative and Demanding.** Try to redirect them or de-escalate depending on the mode of anger or rage they exhibit.

Figure 40.2 Calming Inmates in Withdrawal

Be calm and firm. Redirect them when they get very demanding. Reassure them that help is on the way. You are simply trying to delay things until the ambulance and/or back-up arrives. To reiterate, this is a medical emergency. A person in withdrawal—at least from some drugs—may die without help.

There is no specific withdrawal rage. They will display terrified, chaotic, hot, cold, or predatory rage (**Section XII**). Use the tactics that best fit the mode of rage they are experiencing.

CHAPTER 41

Psychosis: Delusions and Hallucinations

Whatever the diagnosis (i.e., schizophrenia, bipolar disorder, trauma-induced, depression, drug induced), the syndrome of psychosis is typified by delusions and/or hallucinations. A **delusion** is first and foremost a belief that does not fit reality. A **hallucination** is an unreal perception through any of the senses.

What Is a Delusion?

A delusion is actually a lot more than a belief that does not conform to reality. People from different cultures have different beliefs. Shared cultural beliefs, however, are not delusional, even if you can't conceive how others could see the world as they do. There is sometimes nothing weird about the delusional belief either, except that it is not true. For example, everyone knows the FBI follows people, but "Is the FBI following this particular person?" Lots of people have eccentric beliefs: unconventional religious rites, non-traditional dietary and health habits, a belief in aliens, crop circles, or telepathy, etc. Some are possibly *your* beliefs: they are eccentric to others, but not to you. Unusual ideas and beliefs are not necessarily delusional.

A delusion is a <u>fixed</u> belief that is not reality based. Having a delusion is like being a member of a one-person cult. All the confusing thoughts the inmate may have had, all their worries, prayers, fantasies, or ideas suddenly coalesce into **BELIEF**. Such beliefs are unshakable, inarguable, and unaltered by conflicting evidence. The difference between a cult and a delusion is that cult beliefs are externally imposed: even confirmed cult members can, in a single moment, realize the beliefs are false and abandon the cult. Delusions, however, are internally generated. One cannot simply stop being delusion when presented with an alternative belief system.

Types of Delusions

The following is a list of the different types of delusions:
- **Grandiose.** A belief that they have been appointed to a special mission, that they have extraordinary or unusual powers, or are special, remarkable beings.
- **Religious.** Often linked with grandiose delusions, an inordinate preoccupation with religion, focusing all their attention on their beliefs, which may be self-made or associated with mainstream doctrines. To reiterate a previous point, it is not the religious belief itself that makes it delusional, because religion is based on faith, not knowledge. It is the locked-in quality of the belief. In a

religious delusion, one is locked into the belief by one's own mind, just as, in a cult, one is locked into an unshakeable, group belief.

- **Jealous.** A belief, against all evidence, that their partner is unfaithful to them. Jealous delusions surpass the almost always irrational nature of ordinary jealousy. The jealous delusional inmate concocts infidelity out of the slightest glance, a change in clothing, or a five-minute delay in meeting when promised, etc. Perpetrators of domestic violence, particularly those with a paranoid **(Chapter 33)** or borderline character structure **(Chapter 34)**, often manifest this type of delusional psychosis in periods of stress. Some of your inmates will display such delusions focusing on someone on the outside; others will display it towards another inmate.

- **Delusional Stalking (Erotomania).** A belief that another person is in love with them, is married to them, or has been somehow designated as theirs, whether they know it or not. Special requirements for communicating with those who display erotomaniac stalking behaviors will be discussed below.

- **Persecutory (Paranoia).** A fixed belief that people, institutions, or other powers have hostile intentions toward them or have committed evil actions against them, that others are sending energy toward them, thinking about them, talking about them, or looking at them with malevolent intent. In addition to general strategies for managing any psychotic inmate, there are specific strategies for communicating with a paranoid inmate **(Chapter 33)**. The paranoid delusional individual is a "special victim," singled out for persecution by powers beyond them.

What Are Hallucinations?

Hallucinations are false perceptions through any of the senses. Hallucinations are often, but not always, accompanied by delusions. It is possible to perceive a hallucination, but be neither delusional nor psychotic. For example, people suffering from several days of jet-lag may complain of hearing voices. However, they are quite aware that the voices are caused by sleep-deprivation, and pay them no more heed than people do when they have a song "stuck" in their head. However, most of your inmates who experience hallucinations will be psychotic.

Types of Hallucinations

The following is a list of the different types of hallucinations:

1. **Auditory.** There are two levels of hallucinations perceived through hearing. The first level is *auditory distortion*. One mishears what is said, something that is frequently part of persecutory delusions. For example, a paranoid inmate is sitting near someone who says, "I like chicken and ribs." They hear, "I'd like to get this chicken in the ribs." The second level is true *auditory hallucinations*. In this case, the voices are as real to them as the voice of your coworker or spouse is to you. Brain scans reveal that the neurons of a person experiencing auditory hallucinations are "firing" just as those of a healthy person do when they actually hear something. The psychotic in-

<u>mate actually *hears* the voices.</u> That is why you can't simply say, "The voice isn't real:" that makes as much sense to them as someone saying to you that your foot isn't real. <u>Paranoid inmates, in particular, often display a "listening attitude.</u> They enter a situation that evokes their paranoia, and expect to be victimized, accused, talked about, and/or assaulted. They then either mishear people, based on what they expect to hear, or in more severe cases, actually hear hallucinatory voices uttering just what they expected or feared.[34]

2. **Visual.** Psychotic individuals may experience ***visual distortions***. The distorted visual image appears to move, melt, emerge toward them, or even speak. Think of a Salvador Dali painting in which the objects melt and flow. The second level is true ***visual hallucinations,*** in which objects or beings appear that no one else can see.

3. **Olfactory.** This is sometimes a result or symptom of brain injury, as the part of the brain that detects odor(s) is at the front of the head, a frequent target of injury. <u>If a previously non-psychotic inmate complains of hallucinatory smells, get them immediately checked medically.</u> This is often an emergent situation that, if not addressed, can result in permanent brain damage, something particularly important with incarcerated active military and veterans. Other inmates, without head injuries and purely psychotic, can get focused on their own body smells, and believe, for example, that they are rotting away. Others believe they can smell poison gas seeping through the walls.

4. **Tactile.** These are sensations felt within the body. Formication, the sensation of bugs crawling under the skin, is a frequent side effect of such drugs as methamphetamine or cocaine. Tactile hallucinations can also be a side effect of the inmate's psychiatric medication. A medical doctor should always check this symptom, because individuals with tactile hallucinations are frequently very irritable or aggressive. Be especially on your guard when dealing with them.

The Torment of Hallucinations

Hallucinations torment their victims in a variety of ways:

1. For unknown reasons, hallucinated voices are almost always cruel. Inmates can be ordered to do degrading things, or they may simply hear awful sounds and demeaning words. Visual hallucinations can be as haunting as ghosts. Olfactory hallucinations are often foul, and tactile hallucinations are almost always very unpleasant sensations.

2. Inmates try to tell others what they perceive, but their experience is denied over and over again. They can be teased or laughed at. Ironically, the people they tell often torment them in ways similar to the torment of the hallucinations.

3. Psychotic inmates find that their worldview is called into question every day. They don't know what is real and what is not. Imagine reaching to pick up your coffee, and not knowing if the liquid will disappear from the cup, or if the handle will suddenly twine around your finger like a little snake. Imagine this is true of every object in your life. In such circumstances, the inmate finds it difficult to trust anything at all.

CHAPTER 42

Communication With Inmates Experiencing Delusions/Hallucinations

Disengage

It can be very draining to talk with a delusional inmate. Like a cultist trying to convert you to their group, the inmate may try to convince you that what they believe is real. They may insist that you accept their beliefs, or even more problematic, insist that you *do* believe, but simply won't admit it. They become focused on debating your resistance, or furious that you deny what is, to them, absolutely true. There is often no good reason to continue such a discussion. Delusions are not like some sort of backed-up fluid that you vent and drain away. The more the delusional inmate talks about it, the more preoccupied he or she becomes, and more agitated as well. While delusional inmates may feel locked in their inner world and desperate to communicate what they are experiencing, discussion and argument seem to cement the delusions even further.

Figure 42.1 Rule 1: Disengage

There are many occasions when nothing at all can be accomplished by talking about delusions or hallucinations. There is no emergency, and no need for investigation or information gathering. In such cases, disengage.

Islands of Sanity

Imagine being dropped overboard into the ocean. It is cold and rough among the waves, and there are all sorts of sea-life that demand your attention, everything from sharks to jellyfish. There seems to be no way to escape, and it is so overwhelming that you can't take your mind off of it.

Even in the ocean, however, there are islands. If you can only get to them, you can put your feet on solid ground. For psychotic inmates, too, there are "islands of sanity," areas of their lives where they are not delusional. They may be convinced, for example, that someone is poisoning their food, or that someone is beaming messages directly into their brain. But when you bring up the subject of football, and the two of you begin talking about how the Steelers' destroyed yet another opponent, the inmate takes his mind off his delusions, and for a brief moment, has a moment of peace. If you steer conversations toward these islands of sanity, they may begin to see the correctional officer as the most stable person in their life, someone with whom they can have moments of clarity.

Figure 42.2 Rule 2: Move Toward an Island of Sanity

Pay attention to subjects where the inmate is not delusional, so-called "islands of sanity," and whenever possible, direct your conversation there, rather than allowing them to focus on delusional subjects. Make links, when you can, with other subjects that are also not tainted by delusions. Think of yourself as expanding the size of the "land-mass"—making an area where it's predictable and safe. If the inmate gets stuck within his or her delusions, you may find that changing the subject requires real finesse. Nonetheless, do so whenever you can, because talking about delusions makes it worse.

NOTE: These "islands of sanity" are not necessarily "nice" subjects. One of the authors worked with a very dangerous man for nine months and the only subjects we could talk about where he was not floridly psychotic were bar fights and motorcycles. It was safer talking about the sound of a cue ball impacting on someone's skull than what he had for dinner or what his childhood was like.

Threat Assessment: When *Should* You Talk About Delusions Or Hallucinations?

With some of the more dangerous mentally ill inmates, it is necessary to do a brief threat assessment every time you see them. Imagine a delusional inmate who is sure that he is the Archangel Michael. If you recall this biblical story, Michael, the righteous sword of the Lord, casts Satan out of Heaven. Further imagine that this man believes he perceives Satan's work in the behavior of other inmates. Based on his past history, you must intervene when he gets preoccupied with his delusions, because some time ago, seeing evidence of Satan's corruption within his cellmate, he tried to cut out his heart with a shank. The cellmate managed to fight him off, long enough for correctional officers to arrive and stop the assault.

Therefore, whenever this inmate begins to talk about God, angels, Satan, or anything similar, it is a good idea to ask questions about that which he is preoccupied. Some questions you could ask him follow:

1. Inmate. "Hampton, are you telling me that you think you have seen Satan?" "Where?"
2. "Why do you think that this is Satan's work?"
3. "Do you think you should do anything about this?"
4. "What do you think you should do?"

If the inmate's answers are bland and not aggressive, change the subject to an "island of sanity." If, however, he were to say, "Don't call me Demon-spawn Hampton! I'm Michael, the Lord's most beloved angel. Satan will have no place on this earth when I take my righteous blade in my strong right arm!" You need to take action immediately.

Dangerous answers require the correctional officer to alert other officers, and conduct a search of his cell/dorm area for weapons, or perhaps ensure he gets a psychiatric evaluation. He may have to have his medications adjusted, or need to stay in a crisis care unit or treatment facility for an extended period of time. Whatever the appropriate response, you must intervene when such an inmate is acting or thinking dangerously. And consider this, the mightiest angel in Heaven is likely to object when you try to take him into secure custody. Be very alert to danger! (And once you have him under control and are waiting for medical to arrive, shift and talk about an island of sanity if you can).

Figure 42.3 Rule 3: Talk About the Delusions to Assess Risk

Talk about the delusions as a means of threat assessment. Ask direct questions, particularly in regard to the person's intention to hurt him/ herself or others. When contacting such an individual bring up the issue of concern yourself, if they don't do so on their own, just to see if they have become seriously delusional again. For example, "The last time we talked, you told me about the Angel Michael and Satan. Are you worried about the Devil today?" Remember, the distinction between this rule and the previous two is that in this case, you are assessing risk, not just indulging in a conversation about inmate's preoccupations.

Don't Agree: At Least Most of the Time

It might seem to be easiest to take the line of least resistance: simply agree with the delusions, or pretend that you, too, perceive the hallucinations rather than get caught in arguments with a mentally ill inmate about reality. However, there are a number of problems in doing so. Some of these problems are listed below:

- Agreement with delusions and/or hallucinations will entrench them even more deeply into the inmate's belief system.
- Agreement can also lead to the correctional officer being *incorporated* into the delusions and hallucinations. Sometimes this can be merely wearying, as the inmate wants to talk incessantly about their delusions with the only person who seems to share their point of view.
- This can also become dangerous if the inmate decides that you are in collusion with their perceived enemies, or they may perceive you as either scamming them or making fun of them. In almost all circumstances, don't agree with the delusions.

Figure 42.4 Example: An Exception to the Rule

Sometimes the mentally ill inmate will incorporate their correctional officer into their delusions in a positive way. For example, an inmate believes he has a secret team of advisors who tell him what to do. Recently, he announced that one correctional officer was on the team, and he had therefore decided to listen to what she said and follow her advice. Don't try to "prime the pump" by claiming a positive role in their delusions, or simply accept it if the inmate so "appoints" you. Rather, consider this development from all sides. It may be worth consulting with the treatment team or a mental health professional. You have to assess if there is any risk that the delusion might "mutate" in a dangerous way. If, in your considered judgment it does make tactical sense, at *most* that you tacitly accept this information. In the example above, you might reply, "Well, all I know is that if the doctors think you should take your medications, then I think that's a very good idea."

In another example, let's say an inmate is convinced that demons will try to enter his cell to harm him. If you find out that he is, in his own way, a Christian, there is nothing wrong with suggesting, "If you are concerned about that, it's okay to put a crucifix on your wall."

However, don't assume that a delusional person is suggestible, and anything you tell them will work. One of the authors recently spoke to some police officers who had detained a psychotic naked woman who was convinced that bugs were crawling in her clothes. After some struggle, they got her under control and then with the help of EMS, strapped onto a gurney. She was still naked, however, and began screaming and fighting when an EMT tried to put a blanket over her. Trying to be slick, he said, "Don't worry, it's a Jesus blanket." The woman stopped screaming, looked him dead in the eye and said, "What the fuck are you talking about, that's the stupidest thing I ever heard," and then began screaming again to get the blanket off her.

Figure 42.5 Rule 4: Don't Agree With the Delusions

In almost all circumstances, don't agree with the delusions. At most, if you have a consensus that it is worth the risk, passively accept their perception in the interest of their complying with something that will keep everyone safer.

Don't Disagree: At Least Most of the Time

The problem with arguing with delusional or hallucinating people is that you are telling them that their perceptions are lying to them. If they had any trust in you before, it is unlikely that telling them that the world as they see it is not real will improve that rapport.

Sometimes, however, a delusional inmate may ask, or even plead with you for disagreement because they don't want to believe what their delusions seem to tell them. At other times, a hallucinating inmate can make a tenuous distinction between real perceptions and hallucinations and will ask if you think something hallucinated is real. In these cases, *when you have been invited*, you may state that not only do you not perceive or believe the hallucination or delusion, but you also don't think it is real.

Figure 42.6 Rule 5: Don't Disagree—At Least Most of the Time

Don't engage in arguments about whether the psychotic inmate's perceptions are real. However, if they <u>ask</u> you for a "reality check," then you can state that you don't believe that the delusional belief is correct or the hallucination is real. In this case, you are helping the inmate understand that what he or she perceives is not the "rule" of the world.

Important Exceptions to the "Do not Disagree" Rule: Delusional Stalking

Stalking delusions are dangerous because they involve another person as the victim.[35] The inmate is often possessed of an absolutely entitled sense of their right to approach or harass the victim. Such advances may be criminal in nature, and the inmate must be confronted about their behavior immediately. It is very likely that the psychotic stalker in a jail is incarcerated *for* stalking or felony harassment. Correctional officers have an important responsibility to make sure that nothing they say could possibly be construed as support for the inmate's delusions. This would put the victim at greater risk.

If the inmate has succeeded in contacting a celebrity or other public figure, or verbally fantasizes about this, correctional officers must flatly, but directly, inform the inmate that the subject of their delusions is not destined for, in love with, or otherwise involved with them. Calmly and directly tell the inmate they have no right to the victim they stalk.

For inmates convicted of stalking, harassment, domestic violence, sexual assault, or similar offenses, their supervision plan will likely include a "no victim contact" stipulation, giving the correctional officer a solid legal basis for any necessary violation proceedings, including temporary segregation and/or crisis care placement of the inmate. Other times, criminal charges can be filed. Public, institutional, staff and inmate safety, including that of the victim, is the correctional officer's paramount concern.

Particularly if the object of the inmate's delusion or obsession is another inmate or jail staff, and if the inmate threatens or hints at committing an act of violence against the subject of their delusions, correctional officers should conduct a search of their cell or dorm to locate weapons or other contraband. In addition, the correctional officer should contact the other members of the treatment team to alert them of the inmate's delusional thoughts and behaviors. In the event that the correctional officer becomes the subject of an inmate's delusions, suitable safety precautions must be taken, including, in many cases, moving the inmate to another unit: such delusional ideation or other types of stalking must be regarded as a high risk factor in assault on correctional officers.

Figure 42.7 Rule 6: Exception—Disagree with the Delusion of Erotomania

Calmly and directly tell the delusional inmate they have no right to the victim they stalk. Define to them that what they are doing is stalking. Do whatever you can to ensure the safety of the victim, whether they are a correctional officer, another staff person, an inmate, or someone outside the jail.

Differentiation: Distinguish Between Your World and Theirs

Delusional beliefs are nearly inescapable. When an inmate experiencing psychotic symptoms attempts to talk about their delusions, they are often brushed off, minimized, or even ridiculed. If you should neither agree nor disagree with their delusions, how can you respond in an effective way to the inmate's delusional thinking, while also trying to get them to recognize the distinction between your world and theirs?

Differentiate yourself from them. To differentiate is to perceive or express a difference. While also informing them that you don't share their perceptions or beliefs, you are not arguing about them. You are, however, attempting to help the inmate grasp that other viewpoints do exist. Here are some examples:

1. Alice, I see the bunk and the bars, the picture on the wall, and the books on the floor, just like you do. But I don't see a vat of boiling oil in the corner of the room. No, I'm not saying you don't see it. I believe you do. I'm just saying that it is something you see that I don't. I don't know why, but that's the way it is.

2. Sal, I only hear two voices in this room, yours and mine. I don't hear a woman's voice at all. What do you hear her say?

3. Jamey, I know about the Democrats and the Republicans. I've never heard of the Illuminated Ones. I'm not arguing with you. I'm just saying that I've never heard of them, so I'm not the person to talk about them.

Remember, the point here is not to convince the inmate that their delusions are not real, or even that they are wrong. Differentiation simply helps you keep the lines of communication open. Think of two people from different cultures, trying to explain what it is like to live in their respective worlds, or even two beings from different planets. If the mentally ill inmate finds himself or herself shut-down or discounted when he tries to talk about perceptions or beliefs, it is very unlikely that he or she will be open about any other area of concern to the correctional officer, like if he is planning an assault because of what the voices are telling him. In some circumstances, you can act in concert with their belief without endorsing it. For example, "I can't see the laser beams, but I know lasers don't pass through solid objects. Maybe you will feel safer in that room (crisis unit, for example) instead of sitting out here in the yard."[36]

Figure 42.8 Rule 7: Differentiate

Give the inmate the "right" to their own perceptions and beliefs. Inform them that while you don't perceive what they do, you are not arguing with them about what *they* see or believe. In some cases, take their delusions into account without agreeing with them. Example: "I don't see any razor blades on the bars in inmate Jackson's cell, but if I did, I wouldn't walk over there. I'd stay in my own cell area, over here." Please note that, in this case, and others like it, this may be a psychotic, symbolic attempt to inform you of some real danger (for example, Jackson is so scary, it is as if he has razor blades all around him), so view such communications from several perspectives. He may have been trying to warn you of danger and you didn't get the message.

Steam Valve: Take the Time to Save Some Time

Some inmates, either psychotic or manic (**Chapter 43**) are so full of things to say, think, or feel that they seem like they are going to explode from the pressure. Their speech can become pressured as well. Words burst out of them like a waterfall. Sometimes they make sense, but they totally dominate the "air time" in the room, talking over other people. Even if there is a task to be done, they can't focus and they make it nearly impossible for you to focus as well. Other times, they make no sense whatsoever. Their words may sound like poetry as they link words by sound, not by meaning. They may jump from idea to idea, in what are called "loose associations," or "tangential thinking."

You can't allow the inmate to dominate the air, even if they are ill. The correctional officer must regain control of the interview. Sometimes the officer simply has to say, "You have talked enough for a while. We need to move on to ____." For some inmates this works quite well; it is honest, it is direct, and it sets a limit.

At other times, particularly when the inmate is more pressured or intense, one needs to let out a little pressure like opening a valve in a steam pipe. Then you take over saying one portion of what you have to say:

- Let them speak for a little while about their preoccupations. In the process, they let out a little pressure, like a steam valve.
- Put out a hand, palm down, fingers curved at waist level to interrupt them. If they do not perceive it, put up both hands, using a little drama in your facial expression, to get their attention and interrupt.
- Sum up what they said in a sentence or two. Put a little energy in your voice to prove that you are really "with" them. Then, ask or say something, getting either some compliance or a bit of information. "That is serious. Politics right now are terrible! You HAVE to tell me more about the left-wing conspiracy, but before you do, did you take your pill last night?
- In return, let them return to their cascade of ideas, allowing a little more pressure to be released.
- Once again, firmly interrupt, sum up in a phase what they are saying now, and ask the next question or get agreement on the next item on your list.

In essence, you sum up what they said to prove you were listening, and *then* ask your question or make your statement. "Steam-valving" is for the purpose of letting the inmate say enough of what is pressuring him or her internally so that he or she does not fight you for the conversational floor.

Figure 42.9 Example of the Steam-valve Technique

Inmate. "I was looking outside my window at the thistles, and they were covered with gold finches. The lemony yellow just burned my eyes so badly I closed my eyes. My eyes were burned by the fiery birds."

CORRECTIONAL OFFICER. *(Interrupting firmly)* "Charley, I want to hear more about those birds. I haven't seen any goldfinches this year. But first, have you been taking your meds."

Inmate. "Yes, I did, behind my closed eyes, where the birds couldn't burn my eyes out. I talked to a very nice nurse about my meds last week. They have a sound that is piercing to the brain, and a single glance can burn your eyes to a crisp—the birds, not the nurses."

CORRECTIONAL OFFICER. "I can see you are worried about your eyes. That's why you have your hands on your face, huh? I want you to tell me how your eyes feel, but first, when do you see the nurse again?"

Inmate. "It's on a Thursday, but I don't know when, or what time. I'm burning among the birds, you see, with their lemony scalding flame."

As you can see, the correctional officer was able to get the information that the inmate actually did talk to the nurse, but it's obvious he's getting worse, and his next appointment is not until Thursday, three days away. At this point the officer would contact medical staff so that the inmate can be assessed more immediately

---

Figure 42.10 Rule 8: Steam-valve

This is useful with inmates whose speech is a cascade of words and ideas that are either all over the place (zigzag) or delusional. Listen and then interrupt. Sum up what they said, and tell them you want to hear more, but before they do, you have a question (or instruction) for them. Then let them return to their cascade of words. Listen a bit more, and then interrupt again. Sum up what they just said. Continue with multiple sequences of release of pressure, interruptions, and questions until you get the information you need.

Physical Space, Physical Contact, and the Use of the Eyes With Psychotic Inmates

Concerns about eye contact and physical contact are incredibly important in regard to inmates with psychosis. Even more than in ordinary circumstances, be aware when you are inadvertently "pressuring" the psychotic inmate by standing or sitting too close to them, looming over them. Consider this *your* responsibility. Don't expect them to necessarily tell you. The first sign that you are too close, **if you are not paying attention**, may be an attack because the psychotic inmate believes they must protect themselves from your "invasion."

Other psychotic inmates are not aware of personal space and stand or sit too close to you. Firmly, without aggression or heat, tell them to move back. "Inmate McDougal, I really want to hear what you are saying. But you are standing too close to me. Take four big steps back and tell me more." After all, officer safety is the primary goal here whether the interview is conducted in the office, inmate jail mainline, or housing area. In the office setting, correctional officers can control spacing issues more easily with proper furniture placement and other physical site safety procedures. While conducting interviews in the jail mainline or housing area, correctional officers have to remain alert to their surroundings in this regard. Do not allow yourself to be maneuvered into an enclosed area or otherwise cut off from an escape route.

For many psychotic inmates, direct, sustained eye contact seems to pierce them to the brain. It's as if you can read their thoughts. Other mentally ill inmates can misinterpret direct eye contact as aggressive, threatening, or seductive. Therefore, if they are uncomfortable with being looked at directly (you will know it), occasionally "touch base" by making brief eye contact, and then shift off to the side of their face, where you can still see their hands, feet, and facial expression. Ease your eyes away and back again, smoothly. Of course, never take your eyes off of the inmate so that you are unaware of any precursors to assault. Furthermore, in the event of aggressive behavior, you **MUST make direct eye contact, whether they are psychotic or not.**

Figure 42.11 Rule 9: Body Spacing, Body Contact, and Eye Contact

Be aware of physical spacing—don't stand too close, and don't accept the inmate standing too close to you. Most psychotic inmates are made anxious by direct eye contact, experiencing it as either a threat or a challenge. Limit direct eye contact unless the situation is emergent. If it is, then you will hold direct eye contact, no matter what their diagnosis, because you must establish control through command presence.

CHAPTER 43

Welcome to the Rollercoaster: Tactics for Dealing With Symptoms of Mania

Mania is a state of high energy. Manic inmates need little sleep, and can be excited, grandiose, agitated, or irritable. They often have flights of ideas, which can be either creative or completely irrational. Their speech is often pressured. Not only is it rapid, but there is a sense that there is more to say than they can get out.

They are usually extremely confident, even to the degree of believing themselves to be invulnerable. Manic inmates feel wonderful, and their own needs and desires are the only things that matter. Their judgment can be extremely poor and impulsive, and they engage in behaviors that can put them or others at risk.

The manic state is associated most commonly with bipolar disorder (manic-depression), in which periods of mania are one-half of a cycle in which the other is periods of depression. **Some drugs can also cause manic episodes (particularly stimulant drugs such as amphetamine, cocaine or "bath salts"), and not infrequently, mania can also be a side effect of psychiatric medications.**

Figure 43.1 Extreme Manic State Becomes Delirium

Inmates with different brain malfunctions can have periods of agitation that may look very much like mania, but this kind of delirium is usually more extreme than the classic manic state. Such inmates are usually quite confused and disorganized. On the other hand, manic inmates can get so agitated, called "manic excitement," that they shift into a delirium state. All such individuals are de-escalated using the strategies for Chaotic Rage (**Chapter 67**).

Manic inmates are particularly vulnerable because they are most susceptible to making harmful decisions when they feel wonderful. Imagine the best spring day of your life. You wake up and literally jump out of bed, and you have so much energy that it feels like there is champagne in your veins. You know you will make some new friends today, so you are going to go to the park, the club, the bar, whatever, and just hook up! Imagine that feeling day-after-day, multiplied by ten or twentyfold. Can you see how easy it would be to make unwise choices, how your confidence could lead you, for example, to hijack that freight train because you always wanted to be an engineer?[37]

When you feel this good, it seems like a good idea to feel *even better*. Thus, manic inmates very often want to party. Drugs and alcohol are always there, and, in a corrections setting, they can easily get into debt and then into terrible trouble. Their energy can turn sexual, and the manic person gets involved with people who may be inappropriate for them or even dangerous, or if they are also aggressive, turn to sexual assault. On the flip side, manic inmates—stimulant drug users or not, sometimes try to calm themselves with other drugs: barbiturates, heroin, and alcohol. Alcohol can have a "paradoxical effect" on some manic inmates, further exciting rather than sedating them.[38]

Manic inmates often talk in rapid cascades of words, a waterfall of ideas leaping from one area to another. Sometimes you can follow their thoughts, although they are speaking very rapidly, but at other times, they leap and zigzag, making connections that have little or no meaning to you. In extreme manic states, inmates can become psychotic, displaying, in addition to their mania, some or all of the symptoms of grandiose, persecutory, paranoid, and religious delusions that any other psychotic inmate might.

Some manic inmates become very irritable. They can have hair-trigger tempers, and may also be provocative. Rather than merely being reactive, some will aggressively tease and taunt other people. It may seem to be in good fun, at first, but it goes too far—way too far. Others may simply try to pick a fight, or explode into rage and violence.

Brittle Grandiosity

Manic inmates can act as if they don't have a care in the world. They spin ideas, one after another, and expect both agreement and admiration. They seem utterly self-confident. However, truly self-confident individuals are resilient; unfair criticisms seem to bounce off them. Think of manic grandiosity, however, as a fragile structure, like a tower made of spun sugar. It glitters, it glows, and it is huge! But tap the wrong strut or beam and the entire tower falls down in shards. It is **brittle**!

- If you bluntly criticize inmates who are manic, they can experience your criticism as a personal attack, and from giddy happiness, they suddenly turn on you in rage.
- If you tease them about their somewhat irrational ideas, try to joke around with them, or laugh at something funny that they said, they easily misinterpret these, too, as an attack, thinking you are making fun of them

WARNING! Boisterousness Is Not Happy

One of the warning signs of impending assault, particularly with manic individuals, is a loud happiness—boisterousness, where the manic inmate is the only one who thinks things are funny. They make their own fun, and violence can easily be part of it, because in the boisterous manic state, you are just something to mess with. Such people make life like an "itchy and Scratchy" cartoon (see the <u>Simpsons</u> TV show). No one gets "really" hurt in a cartoon—or at least, that's the way they see it at the time.

Watch Out! Mania Can Be Infectious

Although manic inmates can present themselves as brilliant conversationalists, witty, sexy, provocative, entertaining, correctional officers must be wary of being seduced by the their overt friendliness or entertaining demeanor. Don't allow an inmate's apparent personality (He's such a nice guy, a lot of fun!) to cloud your professional judgment and responsibilities.

Figure 43.2 Author's Experience: Be Careful—All is Not What It Seems!

WARNING: They may be acting like comedians, but they are not trying to be funny!

One of the writers recalls a little guy who had lined up over five thousand "matchbox" cars on every projecting surface of the inside of his house. None were glued, but they were perfectly balanced, even on the molding on the walls! Because he had overdosed, we took him to the hospital. He was given charcoal, and as he sat on a gurney, belching black fluid down his chin into a pan, he was talking non-stop, chirping like a little bird, asking why, if this medicine was so bad, they had given it to a man like him? Why not skittles instead? It was both a reasonable question and under the particular circumstances, funny. One of the nurses began to laugh, and he frisbeed the metal basin he was holding right at her head, arches of black vomit spraying all of us, and while we were all ducking, he grabbed her by the throat, screaming, "This isn't funny. Nothing's funny!"

If you accept, or laugh along with the manic inmate's actions without contradiction and appropriate limit setting, they will assume that their actions and behaviors, no matter how non-compliant, are acceptable. However, when you subsequently violate them for those behaviors, they will turn on you suddenly in betrayed anger.

Manic inmates can be very manipulative, while appearing to be friendly and engaging; they are only doing so in an effort to control the relationship. Remember, the manic inmate may be very provocative trying to set you up for an over-reaction or making you look like a fool. Think of Bugs Bunny and Elmer Fudd, or the Road Runner and the Coyote. You know which role the inmate puts you in.

As stated earlier, they often sexualize interactions; therefore, you must be very cautious that they don't perceive sexual interest on your part based on you letting pass some innuendo or mild flirtatious comment. This applies to same-sex interactions as well as cross-sex.

There is an old expression: "He's a drag," referring to someone who slows the party down. That is not a bad idea with the manic person. Remember, as a correctional officer it is not part of your job description to be liked by those inmates you supervise. Therefore:
- Stay centered.
- Don't get swept away or swept up in their energy.
- Focus on slowing things down. Speak slowly, and take things step-by-step.

The Medication Struggle: It Is NOT Like Diabetes

As stated earlier, mania is a unique state in which one feels wonderful, healthy, confident, and effective, when one is actually not doing well at all. If the mania is due to abuse of drugs, inmates must stop using if they are to heal. If their mania is a side effect of their medication, then they must see a doctor.

When the problem is a symptom of the inmate's bipolar disorder, medication can usually control the symptoms. However, some bipolar inmates believe, in some ways correctly, that they will feel worse when they take the medications. Yes, perhaps they will be calm, more organized, sleep better, and not get into trouble. They may avoid crushing periods of depression as well. But life will lose a wonderful glow, and the hours of each day will be more like lead than gold. Unlike almost any other condition, manic inmates feel best when they are most ill.

When encouraging a bipolar inmate to take medications, many people say, "It's a condition like diabetes. You need to take it every day. It's not like medicine for a sore throat that you take until you are cured, and then never have to take again." This is true, but there is a vast difference between diabetes and bipolar disorder. If a diabetic does not take their insulin, they quickly become seriously ill and they feel awful too. On the other hand, the manic person feels far better when they don't take their medications. The only way they will accept medication is if their medicated life is tangibly better to them than the un-medicated carnival of the manic state. Otherwise, it is highly unlikely that the inmate will be compliant with their medication.

Figure 43.3 Review: Dealing With an Inmate in a Manic State

You will recognize the manic inmate because they will display super high energy. They will often be talking very fast and their ideas will "zigzag" from one to another. They often act like comedians, with a rapid-fire delivery. Their behavior may also be either sexualized or hair-trigger aggressive. In either case, they will very likely be provocative.

- Remain calm and centered.
- Be conscious of their "brittle" state of mind, in spite of how confidently they behave. Grandiose does not mean healthy or psychologically stable!
- Don't bluntly criticize their actions.
- Don't tease or joke around. If you use any humor, it is for the purpose of slowing them down, not having fun.
- Don't join in what sounds like fun. It is not.
- Over boisterous happiness is actually a precursor to assault or loss of control.
- They may try to provoke you (think of the Road Runner and Coyote, or Bugs Bunny and Elmer Fudd).
- They can be very volatile, exploding into rage with the slightest provocation. Be relaxed but ready for the worst.
- If the manic inmate is also psychotic, that will probably take precedence. In these situations, you basically have a hallucinating or delusional person who also happens to be moving and talking very fast.
- Try to enforce compliance with their doctor's orders, particularly concerning medication.

CHAPTER 44

Communication With Inmates With Dementia (The Elderly)

The fastest growing population of incarcerated felons is that of the aged.

State jail inmates 55 years of age and older grew from approximately 2.9% of the state jail population in 1979 to near 5% in 2007. In federal jails, the inmate population 56 years and older grew from 5.1% in 1990 to more than 7% in 2009.[39]

With maximum sentencing guidelines, we are seeing more and more aging inmates, some lapsing into ill health and dementia. They are victimized by younger inmates, require special care, and are a tremendous drain on public resources. One can question if any purpose (rehabilitation, punishment, or public safety) is served by maintaining them in jail, but such questions do not help the situation. They are there and must be managed along with any other inmate.

Effectively dealing with elderly inmates, particularly if they are also mentally disabled is one of the most challenging situations an officer might face. Officers will almost always outweigh and outmuscle them, but even if the elderly inmate has retained substantial strength (tendon strength, hence grip, is the last to go), they may be physically fragile.

So what do you do with an elderly aggressive inmate? If you apply a come-along hold, for example, they easily can get a broken wrist or arm (one of the authors, and not the correctional officer, accidentally did this to a slender wristed woman while applying a level of force barely enough, he thought, to get her attention! The result was a broken bone!). If you find it necessary to tackle the elderly inmate or man-handle him or her to the ground, they may end up with a broken pelvis or thigh—injuries like this have killed elderly individuals!

Are there any verbal interventions that might possibly keep the situation under control at a lower level of force with an elderly, demented inmate? Remember, older adults are not a monolithic category. They are people—just like us—simply older. Every character type, every mode of aggression, every mental syndrome, and every de-escalation strategy applies to the elderly as well as those of other age groups. Despite their age, elderly people do assault others. Their rage can emerge from dementia, medical conditions, pain, adverse drug reactions, mental illness, pure meanness or hate, or any number of stressors.

Figure 44.1 Concerning Physical Force and the Elderly Inmate

If physical force is required to safely bring an elderly inmate under control, then it is required. However, because of the particular vulnerabilities of elderly people, your defensive tactics instructors should consult with medical specialists, particularly paramedics and emergency medical technicians, regarding the type of physical guidance and restraint that offers the least risk of injury. This should be integrated into your training scenarios.

The elderly inmate, rather than being demented or mentally ill, may be suffering from a complication from drug interactions, or, due to age and confusion, taking the prescribed medications improperly. Medical emergencies due to such medication problems are quite common.

Figure 44.2 Human and Tactical Concerns With Elderly, Aggressive Inmates

- Be aware that elderly inmates may be resistant to help or non-compliant with directives:
- When it is not an immediately emergent situation, take a little bit more time. Attempt to "nibble around the edges," talking about life, about family. Sometimes the volatile rage that elderly people display comes from a deep depression; they are isolated, confused, and no one seems to care if they live or die. This may be true. Many elderly inmates have lost everyone in their lives, due to a lifelong history of criminality.
- Be prepared to get enormously frustrated at their leaden stubbornness, that "they simply won't do what is good for them." This stubbornness may be fear. Remember that the biggest *change* in their immediate future is death. Any situation suggesting change evokes thoughts of the biggest change—death. **You may think they are defiant; they may simply be scared out of their wits.**
- Don't talk around or about the elderly inmate as if they are not present.
- Don't barrage them with choices, decisions, or too much information.
- Paranoia, **(Chapter 33)** whatever the cause, is one of the frequent triggers of rage in elderly people. As the person becomes suspicious, you can often change the subject, so that the object of their suspicion recedes from their awareness.
- The rage and violence that emerges with elderly people is frequently chaotic. Please refer to **Chapter 38** on details regarding communication with disorganized people and **Chapter 67** on de-escalation of people in chaotic states.
- Be aware that the inmate's behavior may very possibly be brought on by improper use of their prescribed medications.

SECTION VIII

Suicide

CHAPTER 45

Suicide in Jail

Few correctional officers are certified therapists. Nevertheless, correctional officers should be able to recognize the signs of distress and frustration that often lead to suicide attempts, and should also know what to say or do while trying to get them assistance. The truth is, the correctional officer is not only the "first responder" in cases of suicidal inmates—they are often the inmate's ongoing, day-to-day contact with the world of the living. Officers are also the "first noticers" of many suicidal inmates. Sometimes it is just a variation of the inmate's routine or a quiet withdrawal from activities. Only the officers who deal with inmates on a daily basis have the reference points necessary to detect when an inmate may be deteriorating.

The suicidal inmate is not the only individual for whom you should be concerned. Suicide is an act of aggression. The difference between suicide and homicide is often no more than what direction the weapon is pointing. The ability of the correctional officer to recognize and address signs of aggression and suicidal thoughts, which so often go together, is essential to your safety.

Why Would You Even Suspect That an Inmate Is Suicidal?

Suicide is a problem-solving answer to the seemingly unending pain, trauma, and frustrations of life. However, problem-solving activity that it may be, suicide is also an act of violence that, if successful, results in the death of a human being. Suicide is often expression of anger and always of desperation, and the suicidal inmate often uses a weapon to kill himself/herself. Given these facts, officers should use extreme caution when interacting with a suicidal inmate. Following any verbalizations of suicidal thoughts, especially if the inmate specifically states that they would use a weapon to commit the act, correctional officers should immediately conduct a search of the inmate's cell or living area, once they are safe and secure. You search just as diligently as you would in any case, but with the specific intent of finding a weapon, drugs, poisons, other means of suicide or a letter stating the inmate's intent. Of course, before that search, the inmate must be taken to a safe cell, searched for weapons or pills and given tear resistant clothing. The inmate should then be immediately placed in a higher custody crisis care unit for direct observation by staff pending a threat assessment and mental health evaluation.

Tell the inmate that you are searching them and moving them to a secure cell in order to help them.

Figure 45.1 Search the Cell With the Intent of Helping the Inmate

Rather than "tossing" the cell, keep things ordered. If you trash an inmate's possessions, he or she will not reveal their intentions to staff the next time they are suicidal—and by the way, if they are suicidal, will they be less so if their possessions are messed up, stepped on, or even damaged?

Warning Signs

Many books and training manuals on suicide present lists enumerating the suicide rates among various ethnic groups, age, educational and economic status, traumatic life events, and so forth. Although such general information can suggest some viable warning signs, you need to notice what is significant about the individual inmate at hand, not merely to which category he or she conforms. Examples include:

1. Inmates brought into booking under the influence of alcohol or drugs are at a higher risk for attempting suicide, as they don't have the clarity of thought needed to reason themselves out of it. This situation is compounded if the person has some standing in the community and/or the crime is one that would bring more than the normal amount of shame on the person, such as rape of a child.

2. Significant negative changes in the inmate's life, such as divorce, break up of a relationship outside or *within* the jail, the death of a loved one or significant other, problems in the jail which can include difficulty due to a debt owed, pressure from a gang, sexual assault, or other threats to life, limb or integrity, and disappointments such as losing visiting privileges, or placement in segregation. Of course, another major stressor is the possibility of a longer term, especially after a recent sentencing.

3. Other warning signs may include a radical change in appearance, weight loss, loss of appetite, removing themselves from a work detail, hostility towards peers, workmates, or services staff, alienation from family, social isolation, the giving away of prized possessions, writings or drawings with morbid or despairing themes, a depressed demeanor, and allusions to a lack of a future or to the "pointlessness of it all," or paradoxically, reassuring statements when you know nothing has changed for the better, such as: "You don't have to worry about me anymore. I'll be taking care of things. It's not an issue, anymore," etc.

4. Sometimes, without knowing why, an officer has a sense of foreboding, or at other times, they think something "ridiculous," like, "I don't think that guy will live out his sentence," or "I wonder if this is the last time I will see this inmate." Such thoughts are often an intuitive sense that something is very wrong.

Figure 45.2 It's not Just About Inmates

Nearly every warning sign regarding suicide with inmates is directly applicable to the officers with whom we work. Correctional Officers are twice as likely to kill themselves as they are to be killed in the line of duty. The main rule for corrections officers is that everyone goes home at night, and this should include the caveat that our fellow officers are safe after they've left work as well. Keep your eyes and ears open for warning signs in your fellow officers, and be ready to offer a hand. This requires a particular kind of courage—to step up and ask the hard questions to someone, perhaps a friend, who may act as if they do not appreciate your concern. They may resent it intensely, but if they are genuinely suicidal, they are no longer the best judge of what is in their own interests, much less that of their loved ones, who would have to suffer the terrible consequences after they killed themselves. Therefore, pay close attention to the subsequent chapters in this section. Given the terrible stresses that this job can impose, officer safety *must* include the willingness to help protect brother and sister officers from violence to themselves.

CHAPTER 46

The Basics of Intervention
With an Inmate
Who May Be Suicidal

As a correctional officer, you are not qualified nor expected to make a diagnosis of any inmate who has indicated or appears to indicate suicidal ideation. You are expected, however, to immediately seek the intervention of a qualified clinician. In the meantime, the correctional officer should, after notifying staff and supervisor, either place the inmate on a constant and direct observation suicide watch or maintain the inmate in the clinic or infirmary pending clinical evaluation. Do not leave the inmate alone! The correctional officer should also document the occurrence, providing as much detail of his or her observations, intervention efforts and referral to further clinical evaluation.

The officers' documentation will show a continuum of treatment and response to crisis of the particular inmate. It is also important for future case management and/or any agencies with oversight responsibilities such as a court appointed receiver, community corrections officer or case manager

When attempting to speak with an inmate whom you expect or know is suicidal, you must ask yourself if you are the proper person to ask this inmate any questions at all. Don't believe that because you are "good with the inmates," that this man or woman will open up to you. Does this particular inmate respect you? Have you acted in ways in the past that would lead them to feel otherwise? Perhaps another officer would do a better job speaking with this particular individual. We also recommend you document your concerns, complete with the reasons why you believe another officer should speak with the inmate. Don't get your feelings hurt, just get the inmate to the person they might talk with and do not leave them alone if you are convinced the inmate is suicidal.

If time and circumstance require that you are the person to speak with them, at least initially, see the list below for helpful information on what to do when speaking with a possibly suicidal inmate. Some of these strategies may seem contradictory, read one after the next. They are not a checklist—they are a list of possible strategies, one or another that may best suit communication with a specific individual. As you read them, you will probably be able to imagine or recall the type of person you should approach in that specific way).

- **Location.** You need to assure the inmate some privacy, but you don't want a place that is so private that you and the inmate are isolated.
- **Demeanor.** Too much direct eye-contact, or close physical proximity, may shut them down. Speak easily but not overly confidently. If you present yourself as too "together," they may expe-

rience this as an implicit judgment on them, their misery contrasting so dramatically with your confident demeanor. Sit or stand at an angle, with only occasional direct eye contact with the inmate. Your occasional eye contact will then have significance, rather than being experienced as a constant, intrusive examination. Don't forget your tactical training. Position yourself so that you have an exit strategy.

- **Meander.** With a wary inmate you may wish to "wander around," talking about this and that. As long as they are talking, they are not killing themselves. This gives you time and also helps to build trust.

- **Ask Direct Questions.** When you have a real concern that an inmate is considering or planning suicide, you must be more direct. Don't tiptoe around the subject. Instead of asking an inmate, "are you thinking of hurting yourself," ask, "are you thinking of killing yourself?" Such direct questions often come as a relief because it indicates that there is someone who is strong enough to listen to what is really going on inside them. If the inmate is not suicidal, they will let you know. If they are outraged by your questions, explain why you believe they might be suicidal. They should be able to give you a clear explanation why you don't need to be concerned. <u>One final point: asking them if they have thoughts of suicide won't put the idea in their head if it was not already there.</u>

- **Voice Tone.** Speak in a calm matter-of-fact tone of voice. If you sound nervous, you will appear unreliable. If you are joking or off-hand, the inmate will feel that you are not taking them seriously. If you are overly concerned, overly warm, or sensitive, you will sound like a hovering counselor, that soft-voiced, gentle soul who can't be trusted to stand up and fight, but seeks refuge only in being "nice." A calm, matter-of-fact tone shows that you are not panicked by their situation, and that you can handle anything they say.

- **Take Your Time.** Act as if you have all the time in the world. If you act like there is little time, the inmate will believe you, and they will rush to a decision or conclusion. *When you take time, you give time,* and the suicidal inmate begins to believe that there is <u>enough</u> time to figure out a better solution than suicide.

- **Don't Give Advice Too Soon.** Until you become more familiar with the situation, don't hand out advice. Even then, keep it to a minimum. For example, if you immediately say, "Think of your family," the individual might think, "Yeah, they'll be sorry. They haven't visited me in seven years. Their tears dropping on my grave are the best payback I can think of!" The assessment process is a means to get them to reveal themselves, so they feel less isolated, and furthermore, so you know the right thing to say.

- **Never Dare Them to Do It.** That kind of stupidity only works in the movies. The ultimate stupid sentence is, "Cutting? If you were serious, you would cut your wrists lengthwise, not crosswise." The idea here is to "scare the person straight." It is obvious the aggressive intervener thinks, that the suicidal person is attention seeking and not serious, and they try to shock them with the reality of what they are doing. In all cases we can recall, such "interventions" are born out of frustration, irritation, burn-out, or plain dislike of the often repeatedly suicidal person. It is a statement for us, not them. One of the authors met a man who took such advice. His crippled arm looks like corduroy, due to seven elbow-to-wrist razor slashes down to the bone.

- **Don't Debate.** Some inmates use suicidal behavior as a way of attaining some personal power in a world over which they have little control. Debates about the meaning of life, religion, or the immorality of suicide will *break* rapport, particularly if you are "winning."
- **Protect Yourself Emotionally.** Quite often the stories that suicidal inmates tell are very painful. However, this can also be a very sophisticated type of manipulation, and inmates who dramatize their problems, only to later minimize them or discount those who tried to help them, can enrage or frustrate us. The authors are not encouraging cynicism here, but as correctional officers, you can't allow yourselves to become so emotionally involved that you feel betrayed, or simply burned out, if the inmate rejects your efforts to help.
- **Identify Other Intended Victim(s).** Identify the intended victim(s), beyond themselves. Try to ascertain who the suicide is intended to hurt. You will get a better sense if they are also homicidal, intent on taking others along. You can tell if others are intended to suffer by asking "Who will be at your funeral?" Some people are shocked at the question, so preoccupied with their own pain that they didn't even think that a loved one would have to bury them. Others describe that same scene with happiness, imagining people weeping at the gravesite.

Figure 46.1 Dialogue Is the Lifeline.

The most powerful intervention with suicidal individuals is that you are talking. Suicidal inmates feel profoundly alone. They believe that nothing can end their pain, but death. They are often depressed or very bitter and angry. When one is isolated, one does not even feel half-alive, because to be human is to be in relationship with others. When you are able to begin a dialogue with the suicidal inmate, <u>the power, beyond anything you say, is that you are speaking</u>. A sustained, respectful conversation conveys on an almost primal level that they are still worth something—because you, who are worth something, find them worthwhile by speaking to them. By definition, the inmate is no longer alone. Someone is hearing them out. Someone grasps how terrible life is for them. As time passes, the very fact of talking with you can make them feel alive again, and this gives hope, even when their situation has otherwise not changed.

CHAPTER 47

Essential Questions

The Basic Questions

The following are the standard questions for assessing suicide risk.[40] There is a progression in which greater specificity indicates greater danger. You are not in the role of a therapist, but even if you were, the basic questions would be the same. You are assessing if the inmate is safe, and determining the need to contact a mental health professional. Don't use the following questions as a mere checklist. Instead, use them in the natural flow of the conversation while understanding that the inmate may wander off on all sorts of tangents before being ready to answer the next question.

The Four Questions

Question One. "Are you planning to kill yourself?" If they answer no, follow up with questions and statements why you believe they might (Perhaps you received a kite from another inmate who stated that the inmate was going to "end it all"). If they can't counter your suspicions satisfactorily, then you need to call emergency response to assure their safety despite their denials.

If the inmate replies something along the lines of, "I don't want to kill myself, but sometimes I pray that I won't get up in the morning," this could be termed passive or soft suicidal ideation. Don't minimize this, as the inmate's pain is very real, although their lack of an immediate plan usually allows you sufficient time to refer these inmates for a mental health evaluation. Should the inmate refuse to answer, but you have reason to believe they may be suicidal; a referral for a more detailed mental health assessment is necessary.

If the inmate answers "yes" that is a clear sign of their thought processes and intent. Follow up this answer with more detailed questioning, or take immediate action to ensure the inmate's safety, perhaps even taking them into higher custody or to a crisis care unit for further evaluation and stabilization. Do not leave the inmate alone.

Question Two. "How would you do it?" Obviously, this question is asked in response to the inmate answering "yes" to question one. If their response is "I don't know," then you should have time to address the issue by negotiating an agreement to accept treatment. If the inmate says that they "could do it all sorts of ways," and offers a long list of possibilities, or simply says, "I'm not telling you that,"—this is manipulation. This doesn't mean they won't make an attempt, but their response usually stems more from an "I'll show you I'm serious!" attitude. At this point, you must make it clear to them that such suicidal threats are taken seriously and have them evaluated by a mental health professional rather than dancing around, so to speak, trying to coerce from them how serious they really are. If the inmate specifies a particular method (poison, overdose, hanging) or weapon (an edged weapon), the level of risk has just increased exponentially.

Sometimes, the suicidal inmate will offer a plan and a back-up plan, for example, "I want to jump off the tier, but I think I don't have the guts. So, if I can't, I'll just get some drugs on the yard and overdose." This is usually not a manipulative strategy because it denotes careful planning. Among other responses, you will check his cell for stockpiled drugs. (Sometimes inmates "sort of" tell the truth; in this case, "I'll get some drugs" really meant, "I've got some drugs." Once again, you should immediately conduct a search of the inmate's person, cell, and living areas for possible weapons or other validations of the inmate suicidal intent).

Question Three. Often suicidal inmates may have decided on a method, but it is one that they have not yet acquired or have access to. Be sure to ask follow-up questions to ascertain if they have access to the method they have named. Examples of follow-up questions follow below:

1. "Do you have any pills?"
2. "What kind?"
3. "Where are they?"
4. "Do you know what would happen if you took them all?"

Question Four. "When will you do it?" This question helps you gauge immediacy, and to determine if the inmate has established the plan to make others suffer, and if there is anyone else who is "timed" to suffer, e.g., "on my mom's birthday." The more "positive" answers you get to these questions, the greater the risk of a lethal outcome.

Follow-up Questions

In most cases, particularly when interviewing an inmate regarding suicidal risk, you will have fully accomplished all that you need to do. You know that the inmate is or is not suicidal, and how close to the act they are. In many cases, however, you may have to keep talking for the following possible reasons:

- They trust you and want to talk more.
- It is a barricade situation, and the inmate is talking on the other side of a door.

As inmates continue to talk, they often pull back from the intent to kill themselves on his or her own, or they will be more amenable to de-escalation because they feel that, at last, someone is willing to listen. Simple communication brings people away from suicide, even without a solution to the problems that drives them toward it. Below are some follow-up questions that may prove helpful:

- "Have you tried to kill yourself before?"
- "Have you ever tried to kill yourself another way?" Desperate people become very concrete and literal, only thinking of their chosen method. They may have made several attempts before, by other means.

- "Have you ever *felt* like killing yourself before?"
- "What stopped you?" "Who stopped you?" Be sure not to make them feel like they "failed" when they were not successful in a previous attempt. When they recall someone or something that stopped them, this may help them regain a sense of responsibility for the people who care for them, or some other factor that kept them alive in the past.
- "Has anybody in your family or someone you cared about ever tried to kill themselves?" Such people have 'shown the way.'
- "Have you been drinking? Using any drugs?" *(Don't push this one if you have a sense that the person will be more worried about getting violated for use or possession than finding a solution to the situation.)*
- "What's happened that things are so bad that suicide makes sense?" OR "What happened TO-DAY that you decided to kill yourself?"
- "What else have you tried to do to get yourself out of this situation?" (Be careful—a defensive person could respond by thinking or saying, "Oh, so you think I'm stupid" or "Now I have to explain myself again—I don't **know** why having a girlfriend waiting for me and getting released in three months isn't enough!!!!!!!"
- Other areas to talk about include if the inmate has suffered any recent losses, is ill, or has little or no social/family support or has been recently diagnosed with severe health concerns

Despite whatever assurances these questions might engender regarding the inmate's real abilities to commit an act of suicide or not, the questions by the correctional officer should be immediately followed by a mental health evaluation by a trained and licensed clinician who will then make a decision as to whether or not the inmate requires further staff intervention strategies.

The Taxonomy of Suicide

This tool can be used to help gauge the seriousness of the inmate's suicidal intent, and what type of suicide it might be. Given that suicide is a form of murder, let us categorize the act in roughly the same manner as a homicide. See below:

- **Aggravated First Degree Suicide.** This would include killing oneself in a heinous or torturous way, because the person believes he deserves to suffer. Another example would be a suicide calculated so that a loved one will see a mutilated body. A third would be a murder-suicide. The latter is seldom encountered within a jail or jail because the individual seldom has sufficient time or privacy to follow through with the act.
- **Premeditated First Degree Suicide.** This would include any planned suicide. This is the typical pattern for a suicide while incarcerated.
- **Second Degree Suicide.** You usually see this type on a monitor as they are carrying out the act, or come upon their body later. When incarcerated, this form of suicide is usually precipitated by an extreme emotional occurrence, such as a forcible rape of the victim or threats to one's life. It can be exacerbated by intoxication of drugs or alcohol.
- **Assaultive Self-Harm With Intent to Commit Mayhem (First Degree Self-Assault).** The inmate does not mean necessarily to die, but they do something horrible to themselves, often with

the intent to show others, "See how much I'm suffering!" or "See how much you make me suffer." The distinction between the previous item and this one is a hard call: you may not even be confidently able to make it. However, the mental health professionals who will deal with such an individual would also find this useful information, if you happened to acquire it.

Figure 47.1 Example of Intent to Commit Self-Mayhem (No intent to die)

An inmate has his cell tossed. His possessions are trashed and he finds his daughter's photograph torn and stepped on. He is so enraged he starts beating his head against the wall, so hard that he is knocked unconscious, with his forehead split open. He says, "I didn't want to die. I didn't even think of that. I just didn't know what to do with what was inside me."

- **Assaultive Self-Harm.** This includes any suicidal gestures, such as cutting oneself and other self-mutilating actions **(Chapter 48)**. This gesture is common within jails by inmates seeking the attention of staff. These gestures seldom result in serious harm or death unless the severity is miscalculated by the inmate perpetrator or by staff.
- **Self-Sacrifice.** Rare though it may be, this would include actions that have the intention of helping others—like throwing oneself in front of a friend so he is not stabbed.
- **Self-Execution.** This includes suicide that is primarily directed by a sense of guilt. Such an individual believes that they deserve to die for some unforgivable transgression. We are confining this category to those who have actually done something terrible, not someone who, due to a sense of pathological guilt brought on by mental illness, decides that they do not deserve to live.

Figure 47.2 Example: Self-Execution

One of our consultants described a convicted child molester who hung himself when he discovered his son had been committed to the same jail for child molestation.

Another correctional officer described an inmate who had been arrested for drunk driving and vehicular homicide. He attempted to kill himself when he sobered up.

- **Mercy Self-Killing.** This category includes so-called "assisted suicide" or other suicides in which the inmate is seriously ill and wishes to "die with dignity."
- **"I'm Taking My Body Out of Here."** This is an attempt at final control over one's own fate; something that can range as an act of heroism against intolerable violation or oppression or, more likely, the act of a psychopath in jail whose only way of thwarting the people who hold him against his will is to kill himself.

Figure 47.3 Example: "It's Your Fault"

One of our consultants, while Warden of a California State Prison, came upon a suicide by an inmate who, prior to expiring, had written on his body and cell walls his complaints against the jail system, its staff, and policies and how this contributed to his suicide.

CHAPTER 48

Self-Mutilation

One of the most confusing actions that an inmate can take, at least to those outside the situation, is self-mutilation. When it is potentially life-threatening, but somehow has survival "built in," it is referred to as "para-suicidal behavior." This primarily includes cutting ones wrists or other actions that could, taken to an extreme, have resulted in death. Other actions are not life threatening, and are referred to as "self-injurious behavior" or "self-mutilation." Among self-mutilating behaviors that the authors have encountered are:

- Rubbing an eraser on the wrist until all the skin is peeled away and one has a weeping lesion in the flesh.
- Cutting with a sharp object, or deeply gouging the wrists and forearms.
- Repetitively stubbing out a burning cigarette on one's face and genitals.
- Running a needle in and out of the flesh of one's belly.
- Hacking over one's wrists on the corner of a table, and then, after being stitched up, tearing out the stitches with one's teeth and attempting to spray blood on nearby corrections officers.
- Repetitive incidents of slicing open the abdominal wall all the way to the fascia that holds the organs. (A former nurse did this to herself.)

The hallmark of all of these actions is that the inmate does not intend to die. There are a number of reasons why an inmate would commit such acts:

1. **Self-Hatred.** The inmate punishes himself or herself through self-torture and/or disfiguration.
2. **Attention Seeking.** Attention-seeking cases are usually, *but not always*, typified by less serious wounds. Such inmates, through such acts as superficially cutting their wrists, "require" others to pay attention to them.
3. **Primitive Medicine.** Similar to the historical European and American medical practice of blood-letting to "cure" a variety of physical and mental health illnesses, these inmates are metaphorically "draining out" the poisons in their bodies by bleeding themselves.
4. **A Struggle to Feel Something.** Some inmates in the throes of deep depression or trauma literally feel numb. Absent any apparent emotions, they use these torturous acts help them feel alive.
5. **Stress Reduction.** Physical wounding results in the release of endorphins. These are neuro-chemicals produced by the body that have a pain relieving effect similar to opiates such as morphine and heroin. A common term for this is the "runner's high," that folks experience after a particularly vigorous workout. Inmates can become habituated to this endorphin release, and activities that stimulate it, such as self-mutilation, can become addictive.

Figure 48.1 Example of Stress Reduction by Self-Wounding

A young woman told one of the authors that, after years of verbal and emotional abuse by her father, "I felt like I was walking on egg shells all the time. Then, when my mom and I finally left, it was like I couldn't stand any emotions at all. Even when I was happy, I would still feel like I was going to explode." She described one day cutting herself on the forearm with an Exacto knife, and to her shock, felt a sensation of warmth and peace. Several weeks later she tried it again, and it became an addiction. Now incarcerated, she continues to do the same thing.

6. **Rehearsal.** Some inmates want to commit suicide, but their underlying fears make them hesitant, resulting in numerous "failed" attempts at suicide.

7. **Psychosis.** Inmates in acute psychotic states, particularly when subject to auditory command hallucinations (**Chapters 41/42**) that dictate the inmate's actions, can inflict horrifying wounds on themselves.

Figure 48.2 The Line of Self-Mutilation Has Moved

We must be aware that the line of self-mutilation has "moved." We see individuals with tattoos over the face, multiple piercings, including one's tongue or sexual organs, and others who have voluntarily branded themselves. Many of these people talk about endorphin release. Others claim that they are making their own bodies into works of art. As strange or repulsive as we may find some of these body modifications, this is not an emergency, unless the person puts themselves at medical risk.

The Proper Response to Self-Mutilation by Correctional Officers

You have surely supervised inmates who seem to be in, or seem to create, a constant state of crisis. Everything is an issue, and the most minor problems or setbacks are likely to cause an inappropriate amount of emotional stress and drama. One of the primary outlets for these inmates is repeated suicide attempts, or threats of suicide.

As a correctional officer you should NOT try to manage this type of behavior alone. Instead, you need to consult the other members of the inmate's current treatment team to discuss any concerns for the inmate or their disturbing behaviors. Although the scope of this text does not allow for a discussion of detailed planning for such inmates, let us discuss both the problems they engender and offer an example that gives general principals of case management.

All too often, the focus centers around the person enacting the pathology. Such repetitive para-suicidal actions are, however, acts of violence against the fabric of society, be it jail society or that on the outside. Let us consider the damage they cause:

- **Compassion Burnout.** Quite simply, we get sick of such people. We see them only as manipulative, self-involved pathetic losers. Beyond whatever justification one might find for that point of view, it unfortunately expands. Many officers begin to view all mentally ill people, all suicidal people through the distorted lens that burnout creates. This becomes a safety issue. When we begin to view others with contempt, they can easily respond with their own negative emotions. Therefore, interactions between correctional officers and the mentally ill become increasingly volatile. Remember, too, that a mentally ill, perhaps suicidal person might have a negative interaction with one contemptuous officer, and decide to take it out on another, at a later date.

- **Damage to Operational Effectiveness.** Suicidal threats, alone, can take up an enormous amount of man-hours, not only for custody staff and law enforcement, but also for the emergency medical system. When you have such an inmate, a committee needs to be set up to figure out the best way to deal with the situation. Such a committee, known as an interdisciplinary treatment team (IDTT), should include representatives from correctional staff, case management, and clinical staff.

- **Maintain Contact.** While in custody/jail, it is the responsibility of the mental health system to maintain contact with the person, and begin to work them so that they get a sense of reward when NOT using suicidal threats to get attention.

Comprehensive Plan. A comprehensive plan can be set up so that the individual gets more emotional rewards and attention by NOT engaging in para-suicidal gestures. This planning is a function of the particular inmate's IDTT responsibilities.[41]

Figure 48.3 Example: Interdisciplinary Treatment Team (IDTT) Intervention With a Para-suicidal Inmate

Inmate Mendez is well known in the correctional and mental health communities for becoming suicidal when he does not get his way, gets confronted, or becomes very stressed or upset. Although Mendez has not actually attempted suicide, he is very willing to escalate behaviors from moderate to extreme in a millisecond, and willing to hurt himself or anyone else to get his way.

He is referred to Acute Care after a suicidal statement and moved to a padded cell and placed in a tear-resistant smock. His welfare checks are increased to every seven minutes.

Acute care may need to see Inmate Mendez several times before he is cleared from the padded cell. All of the correctional staff realize that Mendez benefits from the increased interaction from the staff. They don't really like it, but they realize this is the plan that moves him through the process and back to his regular housing.

Once Mendez is cleared from the padded cell, he is moved to a single man cell and remains in tear-resistant materials—smock and blankets. His welfare checks are lengthened to every 30 minutes, but he still has face-to-face time with officers. His care is then taken over by the in-house Mental Health Case Managers and a medication review is completed with the doctor (if it hasn't been already). Cell door visits are completed with Case Managers and with Officers from the Classification Team. Mendez's physical surroundings transform with his continued cooperation with the Mental Health team. He is eventually given a full uniform and blankets as he works with his Case Managers and with the correctional staff. He earns extras such as books, pencils, and paper until he is eventually moved back into his regular housing.

SECTION IX

Recognizing Patterns of Aggression

CHAPTER 49

The Cycle of Aggression

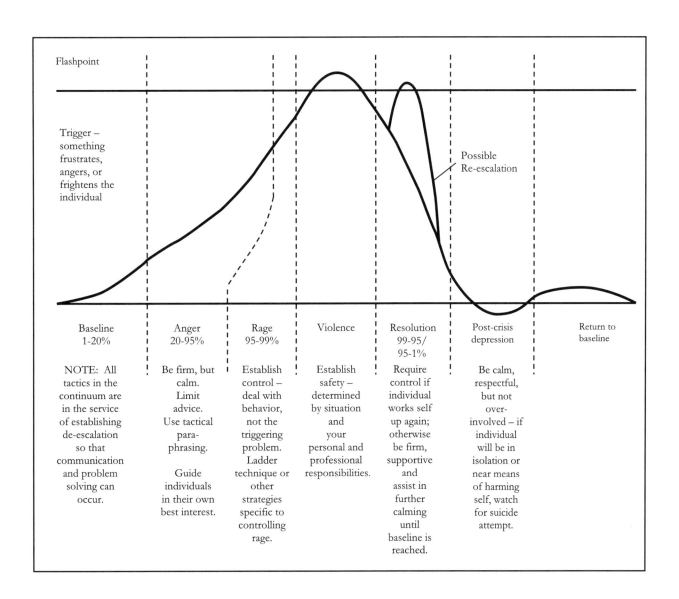

An outburst of aggression occurs in a cycle that starts with relative calm and ends with relative calm. The aggressive cycle often appears to start with an apparent "triggering event" though, in fact, the crisis may have been burning beneath the surface for some time. The reader may recognize the term trigger, being familiar with it in terms of relapse in regard to substance abuse. The same concept applies with acts of violence. Just as many addicts have certain triggers that elicit the urge to use drugs, aggressive inmates have triggers that cue them to become violent.

Baseline: From 0-20

When we are calm, we are at **baseline,** which is represented as "0-20" on the accompanying chart. At baseline, we use the parts of the brain most responsible for our better human characteristics: thinking, creativity, and forming social relationships. The reason that the rating scale goes up to "20" is that we wish to underscore that one can have a little heat and energy, and still be fully rational.

Anger: From 20-95

A triggering event elicits a change in both thinking and feeling. This event can be something that threatens the inmate's sense of safety, frustration at not being able to obtain what they desire, or simply a cue that they are now justified using a skill (aggression) with which they are confident. Once aggression is triggered, the inmate becomes irritable, then angry.

If baseline is presented as being "0-20" on the scale of aggression, with actual violence being "100," anger represents the numbers 20 through 95. Regardless of the numeric value of their anger, the inmate is trying to communicate with you. Because we perceive their attempts to communicate to be loud, obnoxious, domineering, threatening, or just plain irrational, we often don't construe their actions as communication. The inmate, on the other hand, experiences an increasing sense of frustration, and not infrequently, a sense of helplessness, at their inability to make themselves understood (not that they necessarily are making sense), further fueling their anger.

Think of arguments you have had when, frustrated, you said such things as: "No, that's not what I'm saying! Do I have to explain it again?" or "Let me put it another way!" or "You just don't get it! What do I have to say to make you understand?" We become progressively more intense, often raising our voices (as if that will help the other person understand) because we want the other person to "get it." This type of escalation is counter-productive, despite our intentions, because we tend to make less sense when we are angry.

There are several reasons such inmates grow angrier as the perceived or actual conflict continues:
- Many inmates simply can't accept anyone disagreeing with them, especially when they believe they are right.
- When you don't seem to grasp what they are saying, you are perceived as being disinterested, too obtuse to understand, or your lack of comprehension implicitly accuses *them* of stupidity or unreasonableness.
- They may believe you think you are "too good to listen to me."
- When you don't agree or comply with them you are frustrating the inmate in achieving something they desire.
- Many inmates have a distorted and hypersensitive sense of "respect." The inmate often sees resistance, disagreement, or perceived slights as being disrespectful, causing them to lash out in anger or violence in an effort to regain their "street cred."

As inmates become more agitated, the areas of their brain that mediate basic emotions take over. At this point, equity, negotiation, or compromise becomes less and less of an option. In their frustration, angry inmates shift, to attempting to dominate you: to *make* you see things their way, or to comply with them.

For some inmates, anger is accompanied by physical arousal, which functions as a positive feedback loop, driving them forward. As they get more upset, the inmate no longer cares about the truth. They care only about being "right" and proving others "wrong." The disagreement has become a win or lose situation. Such an inmate interrupts more frequently, cutting others off and picking out the flaws in the other person's argument.

To de-escalate and control an angry inmate, the correctional officer should attempt to *"line up"* with them. This lining-up strategy is exactly the same as what hostage negotiators do to eventually get compliance from the hostage taker. When you line up with the inmate, you prove that you understand what they are saying, thereby proving that their concerns are important. This in itself is powerfully disarming, not only calming them down, but also helping the correctional officer demonstrate that he or she will work to solve the problem.

Rage: From 95-99

As you can see on the chart, rage is represented as 95 to 99 on the aggression scale. How can you tell the difference between anger and rage? When someone is angry, you too, may become angry. You might also become concerned, upset, hurt, confused, and/or frustrated. Usually, however, you are not afraid. Why? Although angry people may *later* become violent if they are further agitated, that is not their aim. Instead, their intention is to communicate with you, albeit dramatically, loudly, or forcefully. At worst, they are trying to dominate or intimidate you into doing what they want. As abhorrent as this may be, it is still communication.

When inmates are enraged, however, they are, in effect, trying to "switch themselves on" to becoming violent. Many people slowly work themselves into a state of rage as a prelude to violence. Of course, others can lash out violently with seemingly no prior warning, verbal or otherwise. Usually however, even non-communicative inmates will signal their anger or intentions through their body language and other non-verbal forms of communication. Correctional officers should be aware of these warning signs of impending aggression, as manifested on the intuitive level (**Chapters 16/17**) and based on observable behaviors, as discussed throughout this book.

Most of the time, anger does not result in violence. One reason for this is the various self-inhibitors that work to control our behaviors and prevent us from acting out our baser instincts. But within a state of rage, the inmate is *trying* to overcome those inhibiters, so that they can do what they actually desire: act violently. Some of the prime inhibitors are listed below:

- **Fear of Consequences**. The fear of counterattack, legal consequences, time added on, a new charge or sentence, social disapproval, financial costs, and a host of other possible negative outcomes serve to inhibit one's resorting to violence to settle a dispute.

- **Morality**. Most individuals possess a core set of moral or religious principles that prevent them from harming others. Even most criminals have what could be termed "wolf-pack morality"—if you are a member of the pack, you should be protected.
- **Self-Image**. A man may see himself, for example, as the kind of person who does not hit women, make a public display of aggression, or lose control of himself. Another inmate may have a rule that he never attacks someone, even a correctional officer, from behind. A positive self-image, and fears of tarnishing that image, will often preclude an individual from committing a violent act.
- **The Relationship**. A feeling of responsibility toward the other person, e.g. friendship, trust, respect, love, family relations, etc., will hold an individual from violence.[42]
- **Learned Helplessness**. Some inmates, survivors of abuse for example, have tried to defend themselves in the past and have failed repeatedly. They may believe that fighting back is a futile effort, only leading to further pain and abuse. Their rage, however, is there: inside. There are phrases like, "a cornered rat," or "the worm turns," which describe a person who has suppressed their rage, sometimes for years, before acting out in violence and rage.

Rage therefore, is a set of behaviors, including both physical actions and verbalizations that serve to do away with one's self-inhibitors, so that nothing holds them back from violence. Inmates in a rage state are no longer trying to communicate; they are working themselves up to an attack.

What is the difference, then between rage and violence? Anger is a rocket ship all fueled up with some fumes coming out, and the countdown initiated. Rage is right before lift-off. The rocket has not yet moved, but there are flames and steam billowing out, making a terrible roar, so loud the ground shakes. It is a moment of explosive, tenuous equilibrium. If you cut off the fuel, you can stop the rocket, even now, but there are only a few moments to act, because the rocket is about to lift off. Lift-off is the equivalent of the initiation of **violence**.

What we *should* experience in the face of rage is fear. This is not a bad thing. <u>Fear is just a wake-up call.</u> Fear tells us that we are in danger and that we must do something—NOW! We will most likely be able to handle the situation, but we had better devote every power we have to survival. Fear switches us on, so that our internal emergency response systems are activated. Fear demands attention, but it should not paralyze us into non-action, mentally or physically, in the face of anger and rage. <u>Remember, a sense of powerlessness is not fear; it is a *conclusion* that some people reach when they are afraid, limiting their ability to control the situation, or to defend themselves.</u>

<u>With the enraged inmate, you must establish *control*.</u> De-escalation and control tactics, whether they are verbal or physical, are geared to establish the conditions that make the aggressive inmate no longer dangerous.

Figure 49.1 If You Train Properly, You are Ready to Function in a State of Fear, and Ready to Lead as Well

Early in my supervisory career, a unit of thirty or so violent felons began escalating towards a riot. These inmate were refusing to lockdown, throwing cleaning gear at the windows (mop buckets, etc.) and had broken mop handles to make weapons. They were calling officers names, and were taunting for them to come into the unit. We were at shift change so I had both shifts of officers on the floors.

My first priority was to keep this behavior from spreading to other units, but I didn't have enough radios for every officer. Most of the officers wanted to go into the violent unit first, but since they had done only minimal damage, I knew it was more important to lock all the other inmates down on the floor to prevent the spread of the riot behavior. I started assigning officers in pairs, one with a radio and one without telling them that they had to stay together. I sent them into the calm units to lock the other inmates down.

While this was happening, I was monitoring the violent unit and trying to figure out how many officers I could fit into the elevator, in case the inmates broke through the doors. I was also trying to figure out who to send first and who to send last (besides me—supervisors are the first in and last out.) I was terrified at the thought of losing any of my officers, or of them getting hurt. Luckily, the situation did not spread. I sent officers into the violent unit in forceful numbers. Using reasonable and effective communication, the violent inmates were locked down with no uses of force and minimal facility damage.

Years later, I confessed to one of the officers involved in the event how scared I was. She said that no-one could tell, and was surprised to hear me say it—she had been scared too. She told me she had kept looking at me, and since I didn't appear to be scared or wound up about the event, she calmed down and figured I had it under control.

Figure 49.2 The Difference Between Anger and Rage

Imagine someone hands you a huge plastic container. Through its translucent sides, you can see a dark, hairy shape, a Goliath Bird-Eater, the world's biggest spider. It rustles around the container shifting in your hands like it's filled with mercury. Is it creepy? Sure it is. Is there any reason to be afraid? Not really. As long as the lid is on the container firmly, you are absolutely safe. This is the equivalent of anger. Internally you say, "I'd better keep the lid on this thing."

Now, imagine your 'friend' takes the container back, and to your surprise and horror, takes off the lid. The spider emerges onto the floor right next to your leg. It raises its front legs in threat-display and opens and closes its ¾ inch fangs. There is something poisonous, hairy, and mean in the room, and it is not enclosed in any container! The spider is out of the box. This, metaphorically, is rage.

However, the fear that now arises within you doesn't mean that you are helpless. You can step on the spider or jump up on a table. If you are ticked off enough, you can grab your 'friend' by the neck and make him sit on it! A belief that you are helplessness near the spider is an interpretation, not a fact. Fear is simply the warning cry—the drums at the brink of battle—that demands that you *must* act right now.

To deal with the enraged person, you must establish *control,* especially if, their behavior presents an immediate threat to you, to themselves, or to others. Control tactics—be they verbal or physical—are geared to establish the conditions that make the aggressive person no longer dangerous. In essence, using our metaphor above, we say, "Put the spider back in the box. Now!"

Violence: 100 on the Scale

Violence does not begin when someone is hit or injured. Violence is perpetrated simply through the fear of imminent danger and attack. Some of the legal terms for this are terroristic threats, harassment or harassment by communication, stalking, and menacing. In short, a violent act occurs whenever there is good reason to believe that you or someone else is about to be hurt. In the face of violence, your guiding principle is to establish safety, and you use most effective means of protecting yourself and those around you. Very often, the best thing to do is to escape and get help. In other times, it means to use overwhelming force.

Although actual physical self-defense tactics are beyond the scope of this book, correctional officers should also avail themselves of any offered defensive tactics training, including the less than lethal weaponry you are provided through your individual agencies. As with any skill, self-defense techniques and tactical responses to crisis situations must be practiced regularly to ensure their viability in the event of an actual confrontation. Many officers do extra training on their own, maintaining themselves in peak combat-ready condition.

CHAPTER 50

Why Would an Inmate Become Aggressive?

Aggression is not an alien or unnatural emotion. Without a capacity for aggression, humanity would never have survived. Yet, much aggression seems far apart from the basic activities of hunting or self-defense. Much of it is irrational, self-destructive, vicious, or cruel. Why would someone be swept by rage when it causes so much harm? Why would they be prepared to throw away a future, even a life, driven by emotions that some might be horrified to have expressed even a few moments later? Why would they choose to take on correctional officers, even in situations that they have little possibility of winning? Correctional officers can better control an aggressive inmate when they understand what has driven the inmate to anger. Below are some of the factors that can drive an inmate to become aggressive:

Feels confused or disorganized. Anger and rage can develop because the inmate is confused or disorganized. They cannot understand what is going on around them, or "inside" them, due to cognitive distortions or a chaotic situation (too much information for them to figure out). Among those who experience this confusion are those who are mentally ill, autistic, developmentally disabled, intoxicated, and those experiencing overwhelming emotions.

Feels enclosed, trapped and/or beset with problems. If you are in jail, this is true, by definition. This is often similar in effect to confusion or disorganization, but it is accompanied by a particular anguish. The inmate usually perceives either a person or entity as the agent of their situation, and they fight desperately to get free from his or her oppression.

Has a fear of an attack. The fear of attack elicited by an actual or perceived invasion of personal space is often a precursor to aggression. Each of us has a sense of personal space, a "bubble" within which an outsider is only permitted if invited (**Chapter 17**). A violation of this personal space can elicit aggressive reactions and behaviors. In stressful or volatile situations, you will be perceived as an attacker if you encroach upon another's personal space, no matter your intentions.

Feels wronged or feels a loss of power. An inmate may resort to aggression if they feel they are being wronged, or feel as if they are losing, or have lost, their sense of autonomy and power. Some mentally ill inmates experience a sense of personal violation when they are being limited in their actions or forced to conform to rules, despite the fact that such restrictions are for their own good. This is especially true of paranoid inmates who may believe that they are being oppressed by powers beyond their control. Correctional officers are often designated in such an inmate's mind as the representative of the controlling entity.

Is hallucinating or having delusions. Hallucinations and delusions play a significant role in the likelihood of aggression with mentally ill inmates. The inmate may feel compelled to act as the voices demand or in trying to make the hallucinations stop by any means, become violent. On other occasions, the voices, visions, smells, and/or sensations are infuriating: think how you would react if a neighbor played loud music twenty-four hours a day, shined flood-lights on your house, or left the surroundings smelling like a garbage dump.

Drugs, alcohol, and other organic stressors. The use of drugs and alcohol, along with other organic stressors can also make an inmate more likely to become aggressive, *particularly if the inmate is also mentally ill.* By other organic stressors the authors are referring to a lack of sleep, a lack of regular exercise, and/or an insufficient or non-nutritious diet. Such deprivations can cause changes in perception, mood, and cognition, which can lead to an increase in irritability and/or hypersensitivity.

Feels shamed or humiliated. One of the most powerful driving forces of aggression is a sense that one has been shamed or humiliated. Shame is not a mild sense of social embarrassment; it is a sense of being exposed and victimized by others with no hope of relief. Shame and humiliation are driving forces for revenge-based aggression, and are also prime motivators for attacks when the inmate remembers, correctly or incorrectly, something the correctional officer did that offended them in the past. They may brood about past grievances, their anger slowly escalating until they explode into rage or violence. A particular problem for correctional officers is where inmates may bear a grudge against a previous correctional officer, and they try to take it out on another.

Is acting out of protective aggression. Inmates may act aggressively out of a sense of protective rage. This type of rage is not confined only to parents, but also as expressed by an inmate who is trying to protect another individual from being victimized. The closer one feels to the victim, the more one's identity is "merged" with that of the victim and the more aggressive the person will be in their defense.

Figure 50.1 Example of Protective Aggression

An inmate, a military veteran, feels protective towards another vet, who has brain trauma. He attacks a correctional officer whom he feels treated the injured vet poorly.

Act out of a sense of entitlement or they simply enjoy it. Some inmates may resort to aggression due to a sense of entitlement, or because they enjoy it. In the former case, their attitude is, "If I want it, I deserve it." Others simply take pleasure in intimidating others and acting violently. For them, there is a joy in making others submit and a delight in causing pain.

Anything that elicits profound emotion can cause an inmate to become volatile or aggressive. Emotional stressors include a recent loss through the death of someone close, dysfunctional family dynamics, romantic and other interpersonal relationships, job or housing changes, divorce, infidelity, or feelings of insecurity. Certainly, the criminal justice system elicits strong emotions, and each and every interaction with the correctional officer brings those emotions back, heightening the chances for an aggressive interaction between the officer and inmate. If you go back to the section on suicide, any trigger there applies here, because who is more emotional than a suicidal person? Remember, the only difference between suicide and murder is what direction the weapon is pointing.

Prison gang subculture. Within the inmate gang subculture, violence and acts of violence often play a strong role in defining an inmate's allegiance to the gang, its members and its focus.

CHAPTER 51

What Does Escalation Look Like?

As an inmate escalates in their aggressive behavior(s), they are priming their bodies to posture, to intimidate, to fight, and/or to flee. They can display a variety of different behaviors.

Escalation Behaviors

Physical and Emotional Withdrawal. Some inmates will avoid eye contact, stop speaking, or respond only with short phrases or monosyllabic answers. Of course, some inmates are more naturally withdrawn and reserved; this does not mean that they are readying themselves for an aggressive outburst. Instead, here we are discussing a heretofore friendly and engaging inmate who lapses into sullen hostility or refuses to engage in conversation.

Nervous, Anxious, or Frightened Demeanor. Such inmates usually lash out in defense. They are not looking for a fight; they are trying to protect themselves.

Figure 51.1 Physical and Emotional Withdrawal

If you notice an inmate behaving in this manner you should approach them and engage them in order to elicit a response. For example, you may ask "Inmate Cane, every day, when I see you in the morning, you said hello and ask me how my day is going. But today, you turned your back on me. Something's bothering you today." Note that you did not ask, "What's going on?" Direct questions will merely give the inmate an opportunity to ignore you or reply with simple answers such as "Nothing" or "I don't know." By treating their behavior as a given, you are more likely to get a truthful response, such as "I just heard my uncle died, and I don't want to talk to anyone now." or "You know what's going on! You know what you did!" Such a response is the quickest way of ascertaining if the withdrawn inmate is a threat to you or anyone else.

Overwhelmed or Disorganized Behavior. Inmates who speak in repetitive loops, muttering incoherently to themselves or pacing, are displaying symptoms of either a chaotic mental state or intoxication. Inmates in this state can be unpredictable, and they may react to a correctional officer's attempts to communicate with sudden, unexpected aggression.

Hostility. Any inmate displaying open expressions of dislike or hatred should obviously put the correctional officer on guard.

Seduction. Seduction is not reserved for just sexual expressions or desires. In communication from inmate to correctional officer, the inmate tries to get the correctional officer to collude with them, perhaps in an attempt to convince them to not file a violation report, or perhaps in an attempt to place the correctional officer in a compromising position. The perfect phrase of such an inmate is, "C'mon, officer, you know me…." Seduction is masked aggression, and when it fails, the inmate, who perceives himself or herself to be smarter than you, frequently explodes in rage. You not getting conned is interpreted as "disrespect."

Mood Swings (Chapter 30). These involve rapid shifts in mood and emotional affect, from boisterous to morose, then shifting to belligerence. Such inmates present a particular risk due to their unpredictability and their inability to control their own emotions.

Hypersensitivity. Hypersensitivity is most common in paranoid inmates **(Chapter 33)**, but others can also be hypersensitive. Paranoid inmates in particular, may complain of being stared at, watched, or controlled, and feel perpetually under threat of attack. Ironically, when they have no apparent enemy, they will create one. They feel most stable when targeting someone. The hypersensitive inmate can react aggressively to even the most inoffensive and harmless attempts at communication.

Authority Complex. Many inmates have difficulty with accepting authority. When a correctional officer tries to set limits or say "no," these inmates become outraged, refusing to comply with rules. Their attitude is simply an expression of their hatred for authority.

Electric Tension. This is the feeling you get before a thunderstorm hits: it could be called intuitive correctional awareness. We can't underscore highly enough that you must ALWAYS trust this feeling, this intuitive sense that you are approaching a dangerous situation **(Chapters16 and17)**.

Changes in Cognition

Cognitive Distortions. Cognitive distortions are thinking patterns where the inmate makes broad, negative assumptions. For example, an inmate makes an angry comment to a teacher in a classroom and assumes he will be written up. Therefore, when he sees a correctional officer coming towards his cell, he is already convinced of the injustice he believes will be perpetrated upon him.

Interpersonal Cognitive Distortions. This occurs when the inmate mishears, based on their own negative expectations what the correctional officer is saying. For example, "Kennedy, you have to start complying fully with the committee rules, or I will have no choice but to issue you a rules violation report." And her response is, "YOU ARE WRITING ME UP???!!!!!"

Becoming Less Amenable to Reconciliation or Negotiation. The inmate focuses on dominating the situation, on winning the argument, or on taking out their frustrations on the object of their anger, rather than trying to find a peaceful resolution. The inmate focuses on being "right," and not on the facts. Because only their own ideas and desires have any importance to them, they refuse to consider other perspectives, something typical of almost all angry people.

Deterioration of Concentration and Memory. This causes difficulty in the inmate's ability to communicate, to solve problems, or to recall problem-solving skills. As their information processing skills deteriorate, their **judgment consequently becomes worse and worse**. They can't evaluate what is really in their own self-interest.

Figure 51.2 Example: Deterioration in Judgment

An inmate is being moved to protective custody for a violation. He blames his cell-mate for this, and without thinking of the consequences, blurts out that his 'cellie' is running an illegal business in the jail. Not only is it not true in this case, he is now marked as a snitch.

Changes in Patterns of Verbal Interactions

Silence. Potentially aggressive inmates may lapse into a morose, sullen silence, often accompanied by hunched shoulders, knitted brows, and glaring at the floor or at other people.

Sarcasm. Sarcasm can be considered to be hostility shaded in humor or passive-aggressive phrases. Inmates may jeer at you, or sneer scornfully, demeaning your position. Many inmates don't view correctional officers as true members of the law enforcement establishment. Sarcasm should also be interpreted as thinly veiled threats, and these must be taken seriously, lest the inmate believes that he or she can continue to treat a correctional officer with disrespect without fear of consequence.

Figure 51.3. Example of Sarcasm as Veiled Threats

One of our consultants described speaking to an inmate during a routine tour of the facility. The inmate went on to relate his contempt for law enforcement in general and stated that once released (his parole date was within thirty days), he would be in a position to "educate some of you guys, because being here is worth my own degree in criminal justice, if you know what I'm saying." This inmate was immediately placed in segregation, received a rules violation report for making terrorist threats and received additional sixty days of incarceration as well as a referral to his parole officer for possible high control placement.

Deliberate Provocation. Inmates may deliberately do or say things to upset or irritate a correctional officer. Provocation is a challenge, an attempt to elicit a response from the correctional officer that will justify the inmate in becoming increasingly hostile, or violent.

Playing Word Games. Inmates may deliberately twist or misinterpret what correctional officer says, trying to confuse them or make you question your own memories of previous encounters. Inmates sometimes misremember or "forget" directives, and then try to blame the correctional officer for their position. This is why proper note taking and documentation is vital.

Abusive or Obscene Language. The use of abusive or obscene language should put the correctional officer on guard immediately, especially if the language is threatening or portends a violent act. In these cases the inmate uses language to shock or stun the recipient, causing the correctional officer to focus on what the inmate is saying, and not on what they are doing (such as moving closer, or surreptitiously reaching for a weapon).

Repeated Demands or Complaints. Some inmates will make repeated complaints towards or about the correctional officer for the inmate's derelictions in following established rules and policies, such as arriving to work on time, mail delivery, meal quality and quantity, medical care, or perceived lack of, etc. By making constant demands of their correctional officer, the inmate is looking for a pretext to legitimize their sense of grievance, creating an issue they consider to be worth fighting over, or at least disturbing the correctional officer's composure.

Clipped or Pressured Speech. Some inmates try to hide their aggression by appearing to be overly polite. They often use very formal or stilted language, presenting themselves as being in control when they are actually seething with aggression or a sense of injustice. A typical phrase would be, "What do you mean, officer. I-am-not-angry." This is often the hallmark speech of someone with paranoid traits **(Chapter 33)**.

Implicit Threats. As with threatening sarcastic remarks, any implied threats made by an inmate must never go unanswered or ignored. An inmate who boasts of past acts of violence, or who warns a correctional officer that they might not be able to stop themselves from reacting the same way in the future, must be dealt with quickly and directly. If the situation is threatening enough to warrant the inmate's removal from the general population for a period of time, it should be documented and the inmate placed into temporary segregation pending a review of the circumstances and the potential threat persecuted by the inmate.

Changes in Physical Organization and Disorganization

Facial Expressions. Facial expressions can vary a lot, depending on the mode of aggression. The following list is not hard-and-fast, but there is real likelihood when the following facial expressions are displayed, the person means:

- **Clenched Teeth.** An attempt to contain or control intense emotions.

- **Bared Teeth.** A threat display. You may have noticed certain people smiling who are really baring their teeth.
- **Frowning.** Is often associated with anger.
- **Staring Eyes.** Particularly if there is tension <u>all around</u> the eyes. Can be an attempt at intimidation or manipulation; targeting the other as prey.
- **Biting or Compressing the Lips.** Is associated with barely controllable intense emotions.
- **Quivering Lips.** Is associated with fear or unhappiness.
- **Tightening the Lips.** Is associated with an attempt to control or contain intense emotion.
- **Pulsating Veins in the Neck.** Is associated with building anger and rage.
- **Dilated Pupils.** Is associated with drug intoxication.
- **Avoiding All Eye Contact.** When coupled with other expressions of aggression, this can be associated with planning an attack, hiding intentions of an attack, or, paradoxically, an attempt to disengage so that they won't be forced to fight. Remember that this kind of avoidance may simply be that, particularly in the case of mentally ill individuals or those with rigid personalities—it should be considered one component in a larger picture.

Voiding. When angered, some people have an urge to void themselves, clearing their bodies for the fight. Nausea and vomiting can occur with reduced blood flow to the gut. Other people feel a need to urinate or have an onset of diarrhea. These behaviors occur when an individual is in a state of intense fear or otherwise full of adrenalin.

Breathing. Different breathing patterns are indicative of different modes of aggression
- Inmates who are gearing themselves up for an attack often take deep breaths, which can be slow or fast, depending on how quickly their anger is building.
- Those going into defensive aggression, fearing they will be harmed, usually breathe in a shallow, rapid, and irregular pattern, almost like panting or gasping. Some hyperventilate, breathing so fast that they go into a panic state. They may become violent out of a terror-induced panic.
- Inmates who *want* the confrontation (the belligerent), and are looking forward to it often breathe very deeply, from the abdomen through the chest.
- Psychopathic inmates and others who are "professionals" at violence often maintain a smooth easy breathing pattern throughout.

Changes in Actions

As an inmate becomes increasingly tense and agitated they may try to discharge the tension by pacing, often typified by rapid jerky movements. However, more predatory inmates tend to relax when they are preparing for an attack (leopards are relaxed when taking prey).

Deliberate Rejection in Word and Deed. Some inmates simply pay no heed to any directives by the correctional officer to enforce compliance. Their behavior makes their intentions abundantly clear, and nothing a correctional officer does will change their non-compliant behavior and/or criminal activity.

Posturing. As an inmate becomes angry, they will begin to posture, inflating their chests and spreading their arms to make themselves look bigger, invading their victim's personal space, pacing, smacking their fist in their hand, breathing faster, etc. They may move in quick jerky starts and stops, moving toward their victim and then back again repeatedly, as if working themselves up to attack. These actions are an effort to intimidate, prior to adopting a fighting pose.

Positioning. Inmates looking for a fight or confrontation square off directly in front of their target, while those looking for a victim tend to move to the corner of the person, trying to obtain an angle on them so that they can attack more easily.

Fighting Pose. A combative stance, as opposed to posturing, is often a crouch, with the chin tucked in and the hands raised. In some instances the inmate may brandish a fist or a weapon. Be aware, however, that those most skilled at violence can often attack from a position of complete relaxation. One subset of aggressors, the predatory **(Chapter 70)**, tends to **relax** when they are preparing for an attack. They are at home with violence, like a tiger or a snake. Predators sometimes smile while making eye contact with you.

Figure 51.4. Experience: You Don't Have to Look Tough to Be Dangerous

Those best at being dangerous often don't act dangerous. One of the authors was acquainted with a man with a reputation in some circles as the best street fighter in a section of Tokyo. He was middle-aged, short, pudgy, and out of shape. He couldn't box or wrestle. However, every morning, for one half hour, he would stand in front of a mirror, and practice smiling, relaxing or gazing with a puppy-dog-like apology—perfecting utter harmlessness. Right beside the mirror was a small leather bag at head height. That was how he practiced his nearly perfect sucker punch (which was always followed by a head stomping).

Trespassing and Power Testing. An aggressive inmate will intrude on their victim's personal space, "accidentally" bumping into them, spitting on the floor, faking a punch with just a hitch of a shoulder, or waving their hands close to the other person.

Visual Sexual Assault. Male inmates, in particular, will use their eyes to trespass on female correctional officers, running their gaze over their bodies in what can only be considered a "visual rape." This is one reason why all staff in jails should have the inmate lead the way to the interview room or office. Female officers, especially, should never allow a male inmate to follow them back to their office. A good correctional rule of thumb is to never escort an inmate or enter an office with an inmate without at least one additional staff member for back-up purposes and to notify central control as well as your supervisor as to your intentions.

Displacement Activities. Aggressors may hit, kick, or throw objects in an effort (that always fails) to discharge tension, as a threat display, or as a "warm up" to an attack.

Making a Dramatic Scene. The inmate "acts crazy," either to get closer to you than you would let someone who was purposefully targeting you, or to get you so preoccupied with calming them down, you lose sight of larger tactical concerns.

Diversion. The inmate purposely engages the officer's attention through acting out or other gesture to divert the officer from a pre-planned activity by inmates in another or adjacent location. The activity might be an assault or drug/contraband transaction, escape, etc.

The Edge of Attack

Skin Tone. An angry inmate has a flushed face—the pale skinned turn red, and the dark skinned turn even darker. In essence, blood at the surface of the skin is a threat display, as if to say, "See how angry I am!" Note, however, that flushing occurs for other reasons: some drugs, meth among them, are associated with flushed skin. Do not, therefore, over-value flushed skin as an indicator that the inmate is "only angry."

If they blanch—light skinned people turn bone-white, and dark skinned people get a grayish tone—this indicates RAGE. The threat is not potential—it is NOW.

Pacing. Increased pacing, while muttering to oneself, is arousing, bringing oneself closer and closer to the edge or attack. Some inmates engage in more and more displacement activity: hitting, kicking, and throwing things.

Internalize All Signs. Other inmates will **internalize** all signs of incipient assault, and thus, when the assault does occur, it seems to appear instantaneously. Right before an attack, however, the inmate often stops breathing for a moment. This is often accompanied by stillness, the "calm before the storm," as if you aren't there. In the latter case, the inmate will sometimes have a "thousand-yard stare," where he or she seems to look beyond or through you. Some inmates, particularly, the psychotic aggressors, get eerie smiles on their faces, that hold no mirth. As the attack is incipient, these inmates can "lose it"—shaking, yelling, and acting berserk.

Explosion and the Aftermath

The crisis will be some form of assault, either verbal or physical. As discussed throughout this text you must do whatever you must do to ensure your own safety and that of those around you, up to and including the use of force to control the inmate and the situation.

After the explosive episode, the aggressive inmate moves to the *resolution* phase in which they gradually, sometimes *very* gradually, return to baseline. Their body relaxes, cognitions improve, and their actions are less stilted and threatening. After resolution, there is often a *post-crisis depression*, which is due partly to the physical depletion one experiences after the rush of adrenaline that accompanies any threatening situation, and which is partly psychological. The inmate may be remorseful, apologetic, resentful, or merely withdrawn. In some cases, they are happy, as if blowing out tension from their body, and demonstrating to themselves, at least, that they are not a hundred percent controlled by the jail and it's staff.

SECTION X

The De-escalation of Angry Inmates

CHAPTER 52

Preemptive De-escalation

In many instances the correctional officer can use the tactic of preemptive de-escalation to calm an inmate who seems to be brooding or obsessed with anything from a legitimate grievance to a delusion. An early intervention can enable the correctional officer to avert a crisis before it happens. This technique may be more useful with an inmate with whom the correctional officer is familiar as he or she will be familiar with characteristic changes in the inmate's demeanor, although the correctional officer should certainly be able to recognize any inmate's escalating irritability and frustration.

Perhaps an inmate, mentally ill or not, is a little heated, but still rational. Nonetheless, they are upset. Simply ask what they want or need. If you have a solution to the problem, explain it clearly to them. Always try to explain the process. <u>Give them an idea how long it will take and what they should do in the interim</u>. Many inmates in this state will brood and then flame up if they don't know how long they have to wait or what to expect. With the proper information they de-escalate on their own. This is particularly valid with service-level complaints. This may even work when the answer is not the one they want as long as you explain why and what their options are.

If you notice that the inmate is truly irritated, however, you should not necessarily attempt to address their irritation immediately. In many circumstances, try and draw them into a conversation about a benign subject such as the weather, or another area of interest to the inmate. Such seemingly harmless topics can be used as an assessment tool. If they resist your trying to help them refocus, this tells you immediately that the situation is becoming serious, and your primary goal becomes one of preventing an escalation of the inmate's anger and frustration.

Begin by stating impartially that you believe something is upsetting them, and that they don't appear to be themselves today. Don't pose your concern as a question, such as "What's wrong with you today?" or "Why do you seem so upset? Is there some sort of a problem?" Remember, when you ask a question, you give the inmate an opportunity to simply "close the door" and deny that there is a problem. Instead, use phrases like, "You are really down today. Something is going on." or "You looked really pissed off after your talk with your case manager." These phrases give the inmate an opening to present their problem to you without feeling they are being interrogated.

If the inmate does reveal what's upsetting them, and is willing to discuss the issue, you can use open ended questions regarding possible solutions that require them to respond, such as "I see why you are so upset, but how do you think you can take care of it?" or "What do you think can be done to resolve this?" Open-ended questions are intended to bring the inmate into the conversation by making them consider their options and offer their own solutions. This also gives the correctional officer an opening to suggest other potential solutions to their problem, or to discuss the possible ramifications of the inmate's suggestions.

> ### Figure 52.1 Example: Open-ended Questions as a Threat Assessment Tool
> **CORRECTIONAL OFFICER.** "So how do you think you can take care of the problem?"
>
> **Inmate.** "I'm gonna cut his throat. I told them not to cell me with no sex offender."

Please note however, that even open-ended questions should only be addressed to an inmate who is mildly upset or agitated, not to one who is extremely angry, much less enraged. Questions are used to "slow down" the inmate to make them think. Enraged inmates are beyond thinking. Likewise, if you notice that your questions are *making* the inmate angrier, stop asking them, because questions demand an answer, and an angry or enraged inmate will view your continued questioning as an interrogation or a failure to understand their problem.

Correctional officers can sometimes assist inmates in developing positive outcomes by reminding them of any negative consequences that may have resulted from previous crises or problems when the inmate resorted to anger or violence. Encourage them to use the strategies they have learned to deal with difficult situations: everything from walking away, exercising, writing a kite, etc.—whatever has worked for them in the past.

Sometimes the situation can be resolved simply by allowing the inmate to tell their story in order to get "it" off their chest. There is no need to problem solve and no need to interrupt. In such cases, listening with attention and respect is all that is needed.

Figure 52.2 Caution: Getting Something Off Their Chest Versus Venting

Correctional officers must differentiate between an inmate "getting something off their chest" and venting. Venting can be viewed as a form of verbal aggression, albeit toward someone who is not present. The danger is that venting in and of itself becomes arousing to the inmate. Then, because he or she has allowed it, the correctional officer will have to step in and de-escalate the inmate, perhaps directing the conversation on to another topic, before the inmate has worked themselves into a state of rage. In that process, they may turn on you.

In addition, venting is used by some inmates to elicit a sympathetic response by other inmates in the area, which can lead to a dangerous, possibly riotous situation (**Chapter 72**).

CHAPTER 53

Physical Organization in the Face of Aggression

In **Chapter 17**, we discussed the study of body spacing as a means of honing intuitive skills. In this segment, the authors will discuss the subject of body language, body spacing, and positioning on a tactical level.

Tactical concerns such as whether to sit or stand when interacting with an inmate(s), the time and location of the interview, the issues being discussed, and the history of the individual inmate all have a direct impact on a correctional officer's ability to defend himself or herrself. These questions should be considered before each contact, no matter their previous history of compliance and cooperation. How you stand, how you breathe, your eye contact, and your gestures are all essential factors in calming aggressive inmates. You can say all the right things, but if you look like you are afraid, irritated, or angry, your verbal interventions and commands will have little to no effect, and the situation will only get worse. An unshakeable calm, the knowledge that you can handle any violence the inmate might offer, gives you the power—and therefore, credibility—to negotiate a safe resolution **(Section IV)**.

How to Organize your Body

Breathe With Your Entire Torso, Not High In The Chest. When you breathe rapidly with your chest, you tend to hyperventilate, which "tells" the brain that you're in trouble because you need more oxygen now! Deep, powerful chest breathing, where you pump the air in-and-out, on the other hand, excites the more primal areas of the brain: not flight, but fight. We strongly recommend that you master "circular breathing" (Chapter 21). However, for those who aren't able to effectively use circular breathing, or when one has to teach people in a short time, a more simple method[43] is to inhale on a four count, pause your breath on a four count, and exhale on a four count, People tend to calm around people who are powerfully calm themselves. Proper breathing is the quickest avenue towards that end.

Figure 53.1 Concerning Breathing Patterns

Think of officers in your agency who walk into volatile situations and everyone simply calms down. Think, also, of officers who escalate the situation the moment they arrive. Were you to track their respective breathing patterns, you would probably be able to predict what was going to happen observing two or three breaths.

Standing or Sitting. You always have to judge if you should be standing up or sitting down as you converse. In the office setting, you will most likely be seated, and your office furniture should be arranged to facilitate your safety. However, remaining seated when someone is menacing you is unwise. You will be standing in the yard or the tiers, and of course, in any tactical situation. At these times you should be aware of potential avenues of escape, and not allow yourself to be maneuvered into a position where your exit route is blocked.

Move Slowly and Smoothly. Agitated inmates, particularly those who are mentally ill, startle easily, and any sudden movements or gestures on your part may be interpreted as an attack, or simply surprise the inmate into a physical reaction. By breathing slowly and moving smoothly, you are trying to get the inmate to mirror your actions and attitude. Not surprisingly, overt frustration, anger, or hostility toward the inmate will cause them to become more fearful and/or aggressive, increasing the likelihood of a physical altercation. Don't make any sudden moves, unless the fight has started.

Establish Eye Contact. In most cases, try and establish some type of eye contact. As with the other aspects of body language discussed above, you must be both non-threatening and non-threatened. Glaring at the inmate with hostility or darting your gaze around nervously will just serve to make the inmate more ill at ease, and may actually cause them to attack preemptively.

1. Some psychotic inmates find eye contact to be very invasive. When they are calm, or only slightly agitated, angle your body ("blade stance") in such a way so that they don't feel confronted, and limit eye-contact (while still being aware of their hands and feet). Even with these inmates, however, you must make eye contact to establish control if they escalate into real aggression.

2. Some inmates may be so intimidating that you feel apprehensive about making eye contact with them. Others are so chaotic, manipulative, or disorganized that you find yourself unable to focus on what to do or say when your eyes meet. In situations like these, look between their eyes, at the bridge of the nose or the center of the forehead. You will find yourself far calmer, and the inmate, *if aggressive*, will not be able to tell the difference. You will just appear very strong.

3. There is a disinterested "no-eye-contact" that can be used with *aggressive-manipulative* people **(Chapter 62)**.

Regardless of the exact nature of the situation or the inmate's mental state, never look away from the aggressive inmate. If you turn your attention away from the inmate for even an instant you have given them an opportunity to attack undetected. An attack takes but a split second, especially in close quarters, despite your body positioning and spacing. The inmate must be aware that *you* are aware.

Stand at an Angle. This is sometimes called a "blade stance," because you stand with one foot in front of the other, the back foot at a forty-five degree angle with some space between, thus angling your body. Don't line your feet up, heel to heel ("T-Stance"). There should be at least a fist or two spaces between where your heels fall on the "east-west" axis. Interestingly, this combatively effective stance is calming, because the inmate can tolerate your proximity better than if you were standing squarely in front of them, a more confrontational posture.

You should also sit with a "seated blade stance." Sit on the edge of your chair, with your lead foot flat on the floor, and the other placed on the ball of the foot. You look interested and attentive, but in fact, you can easily get up without the use of your hands, or need to lean forward to get back on your feet.

Space Between You and the Inmate. Don't stand too close to the inmate, particularly one who is mentally ill. Correctional officers can't lose sight of the fact that inmates also have a sense of personal space, and some inmates, especially those with a mental illness, may have an *extreme* view of personal spacing issues. Some of these inmates will see any intrusion into their zone as an attack, and may respond with violence. Correctional officers have to carefully consider how close they get to an aggressive or disorganized inmate. You should be able to define, tactically, why you are close to the inmate. If there is not a good tactical reason, give them more space, so that the inmate doesn't feel pressured or intimidated. Finally, do not get so absorbed in communicating with them that you are not aware of their agitation at your proximity.

Don't Allow the Inmate to Stand Too Close to You. Just as correctional officers must be aware of proper spacing between themselves and the inmate, they must also warn the inmate when he or she approaches too closely. If an inmate keeps trespassing into personal space, tell them calmly something like, "Inmate Rigaki, I know this is important to you, but you are standing too close. Step back three steps and you can tell me the rest of the situation." You should not display any signs of fear or unease. By responding calmly and firmly, you are letting the inmate know that you are alert and aware of danger, as well as able to take care of yourself. Of course, if they do not immediately comply, then you must shift to commands and prepare to defend yourself.

Keep Your Hand Quiet. When communicating with an aggressive inmate, correctional officers should minimize hand gestures and other movements that could be misinterpreted as an attack. When adopting a comfortable stance, clasp one wrist with the other hand. Don't clasp one hand in the other because you may begin wringing them unconsciously if you get nervous, making you look scared and perhaps evoking the aggression you are trying to avoid. The same thing can occur if you keep your hands "open." The adrenalin may make your hands tremble or you simply won't know what to do with them.

By clasping your wrist, you broaden yourself slightly. You will feel solid rather than nervous. Furthermore, you can easily bring your hands upwards to fend off or block a strike if you have to, without looking like you are ready to do so. There is no apparent fight in your stance, just strength.

Use Your Hands as a Calming Fence. Fences lend a feeling of security.[44] When you place both of your hands, in front of you, palms out, you establish a boundary between you and the inmate. The arms should angle from the body at about thirty degrees, and the hands should be relaxed and curved slightly. Your hands should be relaxed, and not clenched in a rigid, fighting posture. Your hands and arms should express that you are closed off to physical contact, but open to listening. Of course, were an inmate to come close enough their body or hands touch yours, physical contact must be interpreted as assault. You can use your upraised hands to push away or fend off the inmate if necessary.

Another option is to hold your hands at about chest height, palms up, with the back of one hand in the palm of the other. In this case, you can "talk" a little with your hands, moving them in unison. You are moving naturally, but at the same time minimizing your gestures. The advantage of this posture, however, is that your hands are higher, even more ready to ward off an attack. If the inmate amps up, you can turn your hands outwards in a "fence," and as they come back down, turn the palms back inwards.

Figure 53.2 One Hand Versus Two

Paradoxically, holding up *one* hand, although weaker from an unarmed combative perspective, is more likely to provoke the inmate. Rather than a fence, a single hand becomes the leading point of a triangle, your shoulders being the other two points. Inmates may experience this as if your hand is up to shut their mouth. Of course, if you need to keep your other hand on your weapon, that supersedes such considerations.

Don't Touch the Irritated Person Hoping to Calm Them Down. Of course, the only times you will touch any inmate should be to handcuff them, physically control them, or protect yourself.

Try to Get the Inmate to Sit Down. Pacing and stomping around is stimulating, and when you are standing, you are more ready to fight. On the other hand, we associate sitting with peaceful communication. Have the inmate sit down, or a chair or bunk is not immediately available, have the inmate escorted to an area, i.e., watch commander's office, counselor's office, etc. where the inmate can sit and be contained away from the inmate general population. Should the inmate repeatedly rise out of their chair, the situation is obviously escalating. In any meeting when you both are seated, if the inmate stands, you should stand as well, because otherwise you are at an immediate disadvantage.

If Inmate Attempts to Disengage. In situations where you do not need to place the inmate in custody or restraint, and they try to disengage to cool down—let them. Assaults frequently occur when the inmate tries to disengage, but the correctional officer insists on working things out *right now*. Of course, if they must be detained for institutional or safety reasons, if the inmate is too enraged, or has overtly threatened to commit an act of violence *after* they leave, then safety becomes the correctional officer's more immediate concern, and the inmate must be detained until the issue is resolved satisfactorily.

Figure 53.3 Author's Experience: Inmates Waving their Hands or Standing When They Should Be Seated

Honesty is usually the best way to go with inmates that are not out of control but are agitated. There have been many situations in which I have told an inmate that I can't concentrate on what they are say if they wave their arms around while they are speaking. If they ask if I am scared (about them waving their arms around) I tell them I'm not scared but I am careful! But mostly I want to hear what they have to say and for me to be able to concentrate I need to not have their arms waving around my face.

I use the same logic to get inmates to sit down while they talk to me. This gives me (a five foot two inch female) at least a second of get away time from a larger, agitated, potential adversary. When they ask if I'm scared, I tell them: "I'm only five foot two and I prefer to look people in the eye while I listen rather than get a crick in my neck—everyone is taller than me." If they won't sit down or quit waving their hands—these are signs that I need to leave or get back up.

CHAPTER 54

Tone and Quality
of Your Voice

Use a firm, low pitch. When facing an aggressor, try to pitch your voice a little lower than is usual for you; it should also be firm and strong. An angry person will focus on your tone rather than the content of your words. Don't betray any negative or angry emotions. A bored tone with either impatience or condescension is guaranteed to evoke more anger, not less. A calm, low-pitched voice communicates to the inmate that you are in control of yourself and the situation.

When you pitch your voice lower, you feel a little vibration in your chest. Under stress, our voices tend to go up in pitch. When you feel the vibrato of your voice in your chest, you get immediate feedback that you have taken control back of your own body, restoring your sense of power.

Also, throughout the animal kingdom, a low vibration in the chest is a signal of dominance.

Slow down. Generally, you should speak a little slower than the inmate you are de-escalating. By slowing down, you are trying to get them to resonate with your slower energy, and also to keep yourself from being swept up in their aggression. However, don't speak with an exaggerated slow motion quality, or they will think you are trying to hypnotize them.

Don't be condescending. When communicating with an angry inmate, don't use a condescending or patronizing tone. Talking to inmates, even those with a mental illness as if they were children, will cause them to become even more angry and agitated.

When necessary, give loud firm commands. For inmates who are very disorganized or angry, the use of a low-pitched voice may not be effective, because it won't penetrate through the fog of their hysteria or agitation. Whenever necessary, correctional officers should give the inmate clear, firm, and loud commands to cease and desist. You let the inmate know that you are in command, while at the same time offering them an opportunity to negotiate a safe resolution to the crisis.

Use of a dramatic voice Sometimes the best tactic is to use a dramatic voice, loud and somewhat enthusiastic, using charisma to grab attention. This is particularly true with some childish mentally ill, demented-elderly or mentally retarded inmates.

Figure 54.1 Example of the Use of a Dramatic Voice

A developmentally disabled inmate is upset because she thinks people in the dining area are laughing at her. You say, "Dobson, I SEE you are upset! Now COME ON over here and tell me about it!" Indicate with your body where you want her to go, moving as if you are absolutely certain she will comply. "C'mon. I want you to tell me EXACTLY what happened! EVERY word! Let's go over here where no one can bother us!"

Show her that not only are you giving her your complete attention, but the drama means that she is important, the center of the action. By moving her somewhere else to talk, you remove her from the scene that is upsetting her.

When to use the "battle cry." When the inmate is moving toward you to attack, or is otherwise presenting immediate danger to another you should roar like a lion to startle and freeze the inmate's motion momentarily with commands like "STAY BACK" or "STEP AWAY," so you can evade, counter, or escape. The way you do this is as follows:

- Open your eyes WIDE!
- "Slam" your stomach BACKWARD to try and connect your navel and your spinal column.
- Tighten your throat. (This will be a little painful to some people, leaving a raw throat for the next day, but it's worth it if it saves you or someone else from harm.)
- **ROAR** a command.

Figure 54.2 Choice of Words for a Battle Cry

When an inmate, already close to you, is moving toward you with hostile intent, don't command that they "Stop" Or "Freeze" They may comply and still be too close. Instead, command that they **"Step Back"** or **"Move Back"** or **"Back Off."**

The commands **"Stop"** or **"Freeze"** should be used to arrest an action that will, in itself, result in harm; for example, if an inmate is about to assault another person, throw something, or simply run out into traffic, or to shock them into momentary immobility, so that you can effectively deploy a weapon to stop their threat.

"Get down on the ground!" or **"On the floor, now!"** are combative orders, with immediate negative consequences for non-compliance.

CHAPTER 55

Across the Spectrum
of Anger

All of the de-escalation techniques outlined in this section are for an inmate between 20-95 on the aggression scale. They are contraindicated with an enraged inmate who is between 95-99.

Figure 55.1 Strategies for Angry Inmates Versus Enraged Inmates

To Underscore: Strategies used to de-escalate angry people don't work with <u>enraged</u> inmates. In fact, they will very likely further escalate the situation. Imagine trying to "validate" a berserk drug intoxicated psychotic, "I see you want to rip my brains out of my skull and smear them on the walls. You've been having a rough day today."

Conversely, using strategies that are suitable for enraged people (control tactics) with angry ones will flame them upwards *into* rage. Imagine coming home and your spouse tells you that he or she is not happy at all that you forgot the groceries in the trunk of the car, and you say, "Step back. Give me five feet right now!" It's all about using the right tactics.

The correctional officer must always center themselves before stepping into the conflict and establishing control of the situation and the inmate. (If you have properly trained in the procedures in **Section IV**, centering is an almost instantaneous act.)

If you don't establish safety for yourself and others, you can be of no assistance to the inmate, or anyone else. This does not mean that you should cease talking with, reassuring, or negotiating with the inmate. What the authors mean is that everything you do must have a tactical basis. In the sections that follow, the reader will be introduced to a variety of de-escalation techniques, some of which may appear to be polar opposites of each other. Some are applicable over a wide range of circumstances, whereas others may only be useful in very specific situations. You use them like a jazz musician uses notes and phrases: to improvise as best fits the scene.

Mentally ill inmates present a somewhat different problem regarding de-escalation as opposed to "regular" inmates, because their fears, concerns, and outbursts may be due to their mental illness, and not necessarily their desire for something specific. Here are some guidelines for handling the angry inmates, particularly those who are mentally ill:

De-escalate, and then solve the problem. Your focus should be on what the inmate is doing, not the cause of their anger. You can't solve a problem with an angry person. First eliminate the anger, and then engage in problem-solving.

Officer presence. The correctional officers' presence can sometimes be enough to calm an inmate down. "Presence," however, does not merely mean that you are "there." It means that you have established, through your stance and demeanor, an authority that can't be ignored.

Watchful waiting. A crisis always requires a moment-by-moment decision on the best course of action. Sometimes, all that is necessary is that you remain centered and ready, as the inmate calms himself or herself without any assistance from anyone else. This does NOT mean that you ignore them, but sometimes the best control tactic is letting them control themselves.

Trust your hunches. As the authors have noted several times throughout this book, correctional officers should pay attention to their "gut feelings." If you have a vague sense that something is wrong with the inmate, you are probably right. Assess the inmate's behaviors, both verbal and non-verbal. What do you see? Have you seen this pattern before? How is the inmate interacting with other people? Have they been having any problems recently? What is different now from the way they act normally?

One point of contact. When de-escalating an inmate, only one person should be communicating with them. This becomes more relevant the angrier they become. Trying to talk to two or more people at once, particularly if *they* are not in complete agreement, will cause the angry inmate to become more and more confused, as well as making him or her feel surrounded and overwhelmed. <u>This does not imply that only one person should be present with the inmate—of course you have back-up. Just make sure that one officer, only, should be talking.</u>

Be what you want *them* to be. Speak calmly, control your breathing, and maintain an upright and non-threatening posture, all the while remaining ready to respond to any attack. Your intention is that the inmate will *template* to your behavior and demeanor. This is not an unattainable goal. In a crisis situation people tend to mirror the behavior of the most powerful individual with whom they are interacting. If correctional officers are out of control, the inmate will feel even more threatened, and become even more aggressive. If you are calm, however, you can imbue the situation with that calm.

Tell me—don't show me. As elementary a suggestion as this might sound, the following illustrates the power of this intervention. An inmate, very upset, begins swearing at a correctional officer. She replies, "Inmate Clifford, it is absolutely clear that you are upset. Furious! And I am <u>able</u> to help you with this. But I won't do that when you swear at me. You can tell me why you are upset; you don't need to show me."

Demonstrate empathy. Empathy is not the same as sympathy, that feeling of sorrow for the person's plight. Empathy simply means that you understand, approximately, what other people are feeling based on their physical organization, what they say and how they say it. Use phrases such as, "I understand you are…" or "What you are saying really makes sense." Or "I imagine I'd feel the same way…" We thereby demonstrate that we grasp what the inmate is experiencing without necessarily agreeing with it.

Figure 55.2 Caution: DO NOT Overuse Empathic Techniques

Don't overuse this, or you will sound like a parody of a therapist. Like everything else we have discussed, it is tactical communication, to be used sparingly at just the right time.

Be professional. Some officers act in far too friendly and informal a manner. Professional distance gives the subject of your attention a clear understanding of the true nature of your relationship with them. Correctional officers should not allow inmates to call them buddy, pal, dude, babe, or any other form of casual address that implies a friendship or intimate relationship. Furthermore, you are not CO's, much less "guards" or "screw." Conversely, the officers should address inmates with human respect. Use their name, not just "Hey you."

Team up with them. Incorporate them into your "team" by using the word "we." When they accept this unconsciously, they begin to feel that they are working with you, not against you. Such statements as listed below are helpful in teaming:

- "Let's you and me go over here."
- "Yes, we do have a problem. Let's see what we can do to figure this out."

Give praise for their good ideas and/or positive acts. Don't be over-effusive, but highlight any positive moves the inmate makes. Seriously: many of your inmates have had so little positive feedback in their lives that they can perceive a little praise as a major thing. This will encourage them to offer more productive solutions. However, praise is not a "put up," to make them feel good, as if a few mere compliments will solve everything. "Ride" the praise into a problem-solving solution. Note the examples listed below:

- "I like that idea! I think we can make it work. You have a few phone calls to make."
- "I'm impressed how you decided to ignore that guy. You are making some good decisions lately. If you can bring that attitude home with you, you could conceivably get out of here on time. Honestly, if you can handle the kind of b.s. that guy was trying to give you—you can handle the last few months here."

Humor. This is the ability to see a situation from another perspective, can sometimes work like magic. However, you must be careful—it only is helpful when the inmate is at low levels of escalation—irritation—rather than strong anger. If they are too upset or agitated, their response to a joke or humorous comment is likely to be, "You are making fun of me," or "This is serious. You think this is a joke?"

> ### Figure 55.3 One Author's Experience (Not in a Correctional Environment)
>
> Many years ago, one of the authors was a member of a mixed-race group when one of the men, an ex-con with a history of assaults, started singing a little song, "I got a bullet for every white man here, because everyone should die." I smiled at him and said, "That won't work on me. I can only be killed by a silver bullet, followed by garlic and a stake through the heart." I looked at him blandly, and he gave me a momentary hard stare. Then we both broke into laughter, and the atmosphere in the room lightened considerably.

Distract. Particularly with cognitively impaired inmates, it is often best to simply distract them. Their anger is driven by feelings and sensations, rather than by what they are thinking. If you can change the focus of their attention, their anger often dissipates.

Honesty is golden. In any interaction with any inmate, correctional officers must be honest and forthright, never making promises (or threats) that can't be kept. This is especially true when de-escalating an angry and potentially aggressive inmate. Don't try to fool the inmate or agree to their demands in the heat of the moment. If you do suggest a solution, be clear as to what the limitations are, and exactly what your legal responsibilities are as a correctional officer. The last thing you should do is leave the inmate feeling betrayed after the incident has been resolved. In fact, should the inmate receive an adverse action, the correctional officer has a responsibility to advise them of the violation process (after the crisis has been resolved safely), and of any recommendations you will make for evaluations, treatment options, or transfer to an appropriate facility.

You will never get "X," but "Y" is a possibility. If you think of de-escalation as negotiation, then you have the opportunity to achieve a compromise solution to the problem. Because the inmate is very unlikely to realize their original goal, whatever it is, you can offer them a secondary goal or solution. However, since many inmates take negotiation as concession, believing they will get everything they demand, you must be absolutely clear with them, "You want X, but X simply can't happen. I'm going to offer you Y."

Keep in mind that with de-escalation of *angry* inmates, you are not trying to intimidate them into compliance or capitulation, but rather to have the inmate *choose* a second or third option because they eventually realize that they are not going to accomplish their original intentions. (The tactics and intent are different with an enraged or violent inmate.)

Preserving the inmate's self-respect: A safety tactic when in negotiation mode. Regardless of the inmate's motivations, correctional officers should allow the inmate to save face. Try to resolve the situation so that the inmate can separate with pride intact. Even if they have not achieved their original goal, the inmate should at least have a certain amount of respect for the professional way that the correctional officer handled the situation.

Another point the authors would like to make here is that word of your behavior as a correctional officer travels quickly through the jail. Indeed, one of the authors can recall a number of occasions when, on meeting a new inmate for the first time, they said something like, "yeah, I heard about you. You are stand-up." On the other hand, if you treat an inmate in a disrespectful manner, lie to them, or go back on your word, your reputation will precede you when dealing with other inmates, leading to confrontational relationships where you go.

A private space. As a general rule, de-escalation is best accomplished without an audience, although this is often unavoidable. Crowds always make things worse.

- Disorganized inmates may be frightened by onlookers.
- Enraged or more predatory inmates may become excited by the crowd or begin to attack others who are present.
- "Bluffers" may be afraid they will lose face. Therefore, in front of others they feel they have to remain aggressive or obstinate.
- Manipulative inmates will use the crowd to their own advantage, by acting out to an even greater degree in an attempt to turn the onlookers against you.

Correctional officers also need to judge when to intervene with an inmate who is either violating a rule or policy or is clearly not following staff instructions. As an example, an inmate who takes an extra helping of dessert in a crowded dining hall should be dealt with late when he exits the dining hall rather than being confronted over a relatively minor infraction in front of scores of his peers where he may feel compelled to act out, thus escalating a minor incident into a major occurrence.

CHAPTER 56

Diamonds in the Rough: Essential Strategies for De-escalation of Anger

Codes for Living: Following the Access Route

Inmates, perhaps even more so than others, have a set of codes by which they live. Some of those codes are based on the culture into which they are born, and others are based on the culture or lifestyle they adopt. Some of these codes are passed down within a family, or inmates may create a code in reaction or resistance to the social codes they were handed. Then there are the codes of whatever jail gang they may affiliate with, while other inmates develop their own credo, unique to themselves. Mentally ill inmates may develop an eccentric set of rules congruent only with their mental illness or character disorder.

The heart of their code is often a phrase or two words that sum up their deepest values. When people talk about themselves, their codes of living are often woven throughout their speech. This is especially true with an angry person, whose reason(s) for their outrage is often their belief that their code is being threatened or compromised:

- They perceive that others are demanding they violate their code.
- They believe they are facing a choice that, if wrongly decided, forces them to violate their code.
- They take offense when others don't conform to their code.
- They think another's actions require them to respond, lest they violate their code.

Angry inmates will very often proclaim their values and code for living in their explanation or tirade, and correctional officers should be able to identify that core value in 1 or 2 words or phrases.

Figure 56.1 Examples of Personal Codes

Inmate 1. "I'm a man. He can't talk about me that way."

Inmate 2. "Think of how I feel. If someone did that to you, wouldn't you be upset?"

Inmate 3. "Are you saying I'm not going to get transferred? I did the job and you owe me. Whether you like it or not isn't the issue, you owe me!"

Inmate 4. "I was standing there all alone. Everyone was looking at me. Talking about me!"

What is most important to each of these inmates in the above examples? Inmate 1's is pride. Inmate 2's is empathy. Inmate 3's is mutual obligation. Inmate 4's is fear of being shamed.

The code is an access route to the inmate. **Use the code to reach the inmate.** When you incorporate their code in your response, you are recognizing (not approving!) the inmate's values, however misguided or anti-social they may be. This is what the inmate often means by "respect." This connection, however tenuous, allows you to work with the inmate toward a resolution. Take note of the following:

1. If you perceive that personal integrity is a core issue of concern to a male inmate, frame your responses with the same theme. "I wouldn't want people talking about you as a man who can't control himself."

2. To the young inmate who believes someone treated him with disrespect (an enormous source of conflict and violence within any jail): you can say, "Man, I can see how angry you are. I'd be angry too if someone said that to me, but if you try to hurt him, you'll end up losing. You'll lose your program, your "good time," your job and your visiting privileges. Yeah, I know you think he *disrespected* you, but if you assault him, you would be letting him *own* you. He says three words, and your response means you lose your chance at getting back to your family in less than three months! Is that what you want?"

3. Sometimes a code is situational, something as simple as the weather. "Look, Frank, it's a hot day, I'm tired, and I guess you are too. I don't care who's right here, really. I just want to finish this paperwork so you can get that appointment with your psychiatrist. The computers are down and so is the air conditioning, so we have to figure out some other way to get through to them. These days are nasty. Here we are, all stressed out just because we're both hot and tired."

4. A mentally ill inmate can get so focused on an issue that they get "tunnel vision," and it is all they can think about. In effect, the problem defines their existence at the moment. A correctional officer replies, "You are absolutely right, those meds are disgusting. They must taste terrible, but if they didn't work so well, your doctor wouldn't ask you to take such foul tasting things. But they do work, don't they?"

Break the Pattern

Correctional officers often find themselves in the same argument(s) over and over again, and often with different inmates! In order to detect any patterns or behaviors that may have negatively affected your communication with an inmate, you can easily perform a "Self After Action Review" of your own actions and responses in past disputes, noting "hot buttons" **(Chapter 20)**. Honest self-reflection will quickly reveal any patterns of behavior, personal style, even *your* personal codes, that may have had a detrimental effect on your relationship with a particular inmate, or group of similar inmates. As with any occupation, correctional officers can get "caught in a rut" that only deepens with prolonged interaction with inmates, especially those who are mentally ill.

At times however, you may be forced to more dramatically break the pattern of interaction between you and an inmate, by doing or saying something that makes continuing the dispute absolutely impossible.

In many cases, you will use a dramatic voice or display somewhat uncharacteristic or unexpected behaviors. This technique is not recommended for "routine" episodes of de-escalation, and most definitely not as an opening in any encounter. However, breaking the pattern can be effective because many inmates expect their victims, including correctional officers, to react in a somewhat predictable manner to their displays of threat, anger or violence. By reacting in an unanticipated manner, you can throw the inmate off balance. This tactic can work with very angry individuals. It sometimes takes the fight out of the interchange like suddenly letting out the air from a tire.

Breaking the pattern may seem like magic, but instead, this is a highly intuitive skill that is developed with time and experience. Because future behavior is unpredictable, correctional officers can't prepare an array of specialized catch-phrases or tactics, ready to disarm an aggressive or disturbed inmate. This technique is pure improvisation, grounded in the same strong and powerful calm that we have written about throughout this manual. If you *consciously* try to be creative, or if you are excited about what a hilarious thing you are about to say, you may indeed say something funny, but it will be at the wrong time, to the wrong inmate. When you are in control of yourself, with the mainline skills of de-escalation at hand, such improvisation will simply emerge. Below are a few examples of breaking the pattern from one of the authors:

Figure 56.2 "I Know Where You Live"

One correctional officer, new at a jail, was walking across the yard and was spotted by an inmate who went to the same high school. In front of other inmates, he yelled out, "Hey, I know where you live!" Without even turning, she said over her shoulder, "Everybody knows where I live," and kept walking.

The other inmates began laughing at the first one, and she did not have trouble from him subsequently (of course, she upped her precautions, just in case.

Figure 56.3 "Breaking the Pattern" with a Mentally Disturbed Inmate

One severely disturbed inmate had a compulsion to shred his sheets and mattress. When he ran out of that, he began smearing feces on the walls.

One officer gave him a large paper bag, with very strict instructions. He was told to carefully tear the bottom of the bag off, leaving a three inch rim all the way around. He was then told to shred the paper in pieces no more than two millimeters in size, and fill up the bottom of the bag. When he finished, he would receive another paper bag.

In this case, it worked. The inmate was not destroying things out of a sense of malevolence. It was a compulsion, part of his illness, and he was absolutely happy to work on the paper bags, thereby eliminating both property destruction and the feces smearing.

Some Guidelines for Limit Setting

As soon as you draw a line, it will become the main focus of your interchange. Don't ever set a limit that you cannot enforce or one that is not reasonable and simple to understand.

Beleaguered by mental illness, struggling with substance abuse, beaten down by poverty or unemployment, inmates often experience their lives fragmenting into pieces. When the rules shift, they can become profoundly anxious. When dealing with such people, **limit setting** is a kindness rather than oppression.

The following will help in setting a "full stop" limit:

- **Your tone of voice should be matter-of-fact**, rather than critical. Simply <u>remind</u> them of the rule or <u>set</u> a proper limit (a new rule, so to speak).
- **Give clear directives with no wiggle room.** For example, you say in a confident, commanding voice, "Inmate Taylor, lower your voice."
- **Give praise if he complies.** Give him a brief mark of "approval" and continue with the verbal control.
- **If he does not comply with the directive, depersonalize the reiteration.** "Inmate Taylor, you are required to lower your voice. "Don't say, "I expect you to…" The individual should experience what you are saying as the "law," an institutional command or policy, rather than a personal issue between them and you.
- **Don't get them caught up in manipulative word games.** Don't respond to professed ignorance, excuses, or confusion. You are using this tactic because there is no ambiguity regarding the transgression and no ambiguity as to what the consequence will be.

Silence

Sometimes, the most powerful thing you can do is to be silent. Be sure that you are not being passive-aggressive, fuming in silent anger, or appearing to ignore or dismiss the inmate. Instead, you should wait, quietly and powerfully. Keep your facial expressions calm, your posture centered, and carefully listen. Nod your head calmly as you listen, doing so slowly and intermittently. In many cultures, including the United States, nodding your head too rapidly indicates that you want the other person to hurry up and finish, or worse, just shut up.

Silence, however, is not that easy, particularly for the person who is suffering the brunt of another's anger. There are three ways to listen silently, and two of them will make people angrier.

Contemptuous silence. You are tired of the dispute, and tired of the inmate. You fidget, you sigh, and most significantly, you roll your eyes upwards to one side, and twist one corner of your mouth. In almost every culture, this facial expression and behavior express an attitude of contempt, and is guaranteed to provoke anger or rage. (Think of how mad you get when your teenager does this.)

Stonewall silence. When you stonewall, your demeanor shows that you have no interest in what they have to say or why they are saying it. You can to do this inadvertently by entering notes into a file while the inmate is talking, or by taking a phone call during an interview. Other times, it is calculated and deliberate. Such dismissive behavior can evoke anxiety or anger in the inmate who wants to get through to you, only to find that there's a "wall" in the way. As a result, the inmate will do anything to "get through to you," including trying to tear down that wall.

In addition to upsetting the inmate, such indifferent behaviors on your part will also increase risk, and decrease your ability to defend yourself from attack because your attention is improperly focused on your computer screen or your telephone conversation, instead of where it should be—on the inmate.

Interested silence. This is the right way to listen silently. When you have been listening quietly, the inmate often interrupts to ask, "Aren't you going to say something?" or "Don't you have any ideas?" If they don't stop, and continue to talk and talk, you may have to interrupt them. Do this by advancing a hand slightly at waist level or a little higher, fingers curved, palms down. (You don't want the inmate to interpret your hand movement as a "shut up" gesture.) You should also lean toward the inmate slightly, indicating that it's your turn to speak. If they don't notice your hand gesture, put both hands up in front of you in a "fence," and tell them to stop a moment, in a voice that is loud and holds a little humor. "Inmate Schultz, wait a minute. You 'gotta' give me a chance to say something! Listen to me a second!"

After interrupting the inmate, the first thing you should do is to sum up your understanding of what he or she just said. This proves that you were indeed listening to them, and are interested in solving their problem. Once you have summed it up, you can either go into problem-solving mode, or, if they are still heated, shift into "tactical paraphrasing" **(Chapter 57)**.

CHAPTER 57

Tactical Paraphrasing:
The Gold Standard With Angry and
Agitated Mentally-Ill Inmates

What Is Paraphrasing?

Paraphrasing is perhaps the most important technique for calming **angry** inmates. You sum up in a phrase or sentence what the angry inmate has just said in a paragraph. If you paraphrase accurately, you have established that you have "gotten" it that far, so they don't have to repeat it, or try to say it in other words.

If you <u>don't</u> show that you "get" it, the inmate will feel compelled to repeat and/or elaborate that layer of the problem with more and more intensity. As they get more intense, they usually get more irrational, and their ability to communicate breaks down even further. <u>The best thing about paraphrasing is that you don't have to be "smart" and interpret anything. You simply have to listen carefully.</u>

It is like peeling off a single layer of an onion so that you can be shown the next one. As you peel off each layer, the inmate gets to the next layer that is driving them. They might start out complaining about a correctional officer who sanctioned them for an infraction, and that paraphrased, they tell you that their wife lost her job and if they don't get out in time for Christmas, the family will be in financial trouble, and that paraphrased, tells you that their wife is threatening to move back east to live with her parents, and that paraphrased, start talking about suicide.

Paraphrasing establishes that you are truly listening and have understood what they have said. There is another component where we also take a slightly activist approach. We <u>select</u> what we will sum up from the complex, sometimes almost incoherent, communication that the inmate has just given us, choosing the *most rational* aspect of what they have just said.

This method is "self-correcting," whereas passive summation, called "mirroring," can make things worse. If you sum up an angry inmate's worst impulses, they will find themselves in agreement with you. Inadvertently, you have lined up with what desires destruction. If you sum up an aspect of what they have said that is in the direction of conflict resolution, you will draw out of them that which *does* wish to resolve the conflict. On the other hand, if they are, in fact, bent on mayhem, they will correct you by escalating what they are saying, believing that you are not getting the message. Remember, they are trying to communicate. All you have to do is paraphrase up <u>what you understand</u> from what they said. When you get it right, they go to the next layer.

Figure 57.1 Example of Correct and Incorrect Paraphrasing

Angry Inmate. "I am so mad at my daughter that I could just choke her when I get out of here!"

1. Incorrect paraphrase: "You want to murder your daughter."
2. Correct paraphrase: "You are *really* furious with her!"

If you have, in two accurately paraphrased the meaning of the angry father's intention, you will naturally go on to the next layer of his complaint.

Angry Inmate. "You won't believe what she did. My wife comes home and I find her on the couch lip-locking that punk from down the street. You know, one of those scumbags who epoxies his hair in corkscrew spikes?"

If, however, the second example is *inaccurate*, and he really *means* number one, the angry father will correct you with more vehemence.

Angry Inmate. "No, *(not really furious)* I honestly want to loop a belt around her neck and slowly strangle her. Seriously! I'm getting out in a month. She better not be home when I get back there."

Why not simply ask the person what's going on? If they want to tell me, why don't they just answer the questions? Asking questions is usually not a good idea with really angry inmates. They already believe you have to "get" what they are saying, and a question shows that you have not done so. Still angry and now frustrated at their failure, this makes them try harder, albeit with less coherence than before. They experience failure over and over—they can't get through to you! When anger is combined with this sense of powerlessness, the inmate feels like he is "losing" to a more powerful other. In essence, they experience a question, a demand for an answer, as putting you in a dominant position in regard to them.

Figure 57.2 Example: An Illustration Showing How Irritating Questions Can Be

Imagine coming home after a bad day. You are hot, tired, and frustrated. You walk into your house, drop your gear on the floor, sigh loudly, and walk toward the shower. Your spouse says, "Did you have a bad day?" Isn't this irritating? Isn't it *obvious* you've had a bad day? After all these years together, and he or she doesn't know when a bad day just walked into the house! On the other hand, imagine your spouse observing you and saying, "Bad day, huh?" You continue walking towards the shower, and say, "I don't want to talk now. I just want a shower. I'll talk to you later." You are not "forced" to explain yourself.

How to Use Paraphrasing Successfully

It is very important that your voice is strong. You speak to the inmate as someone who has the power within to take care of himself or herself and their problem, not as someone who is fragile or volatile (even if they are). You contact the strong aspect of the inmate, the future looking side, that which is striving for strength, looking for integrity. Sometimes, you can use a dramatic summation: "You are really furious about this!" Here, you sum up the inmate's mood with your voice and posture, in addition to what is being said. If you contact the weak, or the insecure, you may foster regression to a less mature level of action. Childish action is often impulsive or violent.

Figure 57.3 Example: A Successful Use of Paraphrasing With a Mentally Ill Inmate

Inmate. "I never get enough sleep."

CORRECTIONAL OFFICER. "You look really tired."

Inmate. "I don't know how I look, but I feel exhausted!"

When you are inaccurate in your summation, the other usually corrects you. He is not arguing with you, just tuning up the signal.

CORRECTIONAL OFFICER. "You've been up late the last couple days and waking early, too, and now you are really tired, aren't you?"

You can include extra information that sums up the experience the other is having. This is for the purpose of steering the inmate toward problem-solving while not giving advice. It also allows you to assess how responsive he is to you. In other words, if you add a little something, is he even able to hear it?

Inmate. "I am not tired at night."

CORRECTIONAL OFFICER. "You can't fall asleep when you hit your rack, huh?"

Notice the tag lines like, "huh?" or "aren't you?" These are not really questions. They follow statements and give the other an <u>invitation</u> to correct you or give you more information.

Inmate. "I don't even bother trying to sleep. I just lie there looking at the ceiling."

CORRECTIONAL OFFICER. "It seems like a waste of time, and then you wake up early anyway. It'd be fine if you weren't tired."

The second sentence by the officer is an attempt to sum up what he believes is the inmate's feelings about his sleep cycle. It is also another assessment; he offers him something to agree with or correct.

Inmate. "Yeah, I'd be fine if I wasn't tired. I'd just be sleepless and do more. But I'm too tired for that. I wonder if I need to talk to Dr. Montour. I think I need something to help me sleep. When I don't sleep, I go crazy"

Imagine that this inmate has bipolar disorder, is very resistant to talking about his medications, but usually gets in lots of trouble when he doesn't take them. If the officer had responded to his initial statement about being tired by suggesting he go to the doctor immediately ("problem-solving"), the inmate might have angrily stopped talking or argued with him. By listening and showing step-by-step that he understood him, the correctional officer got him to find the "deeper layer" of his concern by himself.

Figure 57.4 Example of Successful Use Paraphrasing With a Mentally Ill Inmate (Who often becomes suicidal when frustrated)

Female Inmate. "I can't believe it. She is so stupid!"

CORRECTIONAL OFFICER. "You are really upset!"

Inmate. "No! I'm really furious!"

Note: When you sum up imprecisely, the other usually corrects you. This is as if she were tuning up the signal rather than arguing with you.

CORRECTIONAL OFFICER. "Inmate Scott, I haven't seen you this mad in a long time."

Note: You can include extra information ("in a long time," for example). This is for the purpose of slightly steering the person in a positive direction. It also helps to assess how responsive she is to you. In other words, if you add a little something, is she even able to hear it? In this case, you are validating that she has shown that she is able to maintain control of herself for awhile

Inmate. "I know. But nobody's ever done anything like this to me!"

CORRECTIONAL OFFICER. "This is something new, huh?"

Inmate. "Yeah, I asked her to hook up after our NA meeting, and she said "yes," and then, in front of everybody, she said she was just joking."

CORRECTIONAL OFFICER. "That must have been embarrassing!"

Inmate. "I was ashamed. It was just like when my mom left. I felt like I wasn't good enough for anybody."

You just got the story without a single question. She even trusts you enough to tell you something real about her past. Now you are in a position to do a threat assessment, to determine if she is either suicidal or has aggressive intentions towards the woman who shamed her.

Using Paraphrasing to Communicate with Severely Mentally Ill Individuals

Paraphrasing can be remarkably effective for communication with severely mentally ill inmates. Given the internal chaos that people experience when psychotic, manic, or disorganized, it is essential that we don't add to their sense of confusion by barraging them with questions or attempting to solve their problems by taking over and telling them what they should feel or do.

Figure 57.5 Example of Tactical Paraphrasing With a Severely Psychotic Individual

Murray is psychotic. After inmates complained about his "strange behavior," correctional officers interviewed him, and found him in what appeared to be a decompensated state.

Murray tells the officer that he was electric and that the other inmates knew he was electric and just didn't understand him. He complains of hearing voices that sometimes told him to do acts that scared him.

CORRECTIONAL OFFICER. "Pretty confusing, huh?"

Inmate. "You are darn right it's confusing. How'd you like to be in my head?"

CORRECTIONAL OFFICER. "I wouldn't want to be in a confused head. It must be hard to think."

Inmate. "Hard to think and scary. The voices say scary things. They tell me to hurt me."

CORRECTIONAL OFFICER. "You are telling me about it now. I think you want some help."

Inmate. *(Nodding)* "Yeah, I don't want to bleed."

CORRECTIONAL OFFICER. "Somebody would make you bleed."

Murray. "Yeah, them, in my head. Make me bleed and other people too."

Notice the officer's last sentence. Realizing that they have reached a "core point" of Murray's concern, he will intervene more directly. Notice that the officer didn't ask one question. Questions could have thrown Murray off track, making his communication more confusing and harder to assess for risk. By making a matter-of-fact statement, the officer takes a lot of psychological pressure off the inmate, and it is easier for him to re-organize enough to be able to communicate.

Remember, though, that paraphrasing is self-correcting. Murray might have replied, "There's no blood out here. I'm holding it in." *It's at that point you see him clamping his wrist with the other hand. He lets it go and the blood from the cut veins starts pouring out.*

Core

We know we have reached the core level when there is no more "progress." The inmate **spins his wheels**. They may use different words, but they say essentially the same thing over and over again. Some inmates express relief at being finally understood. Others exhibit an intensification of emotion, because you have reached that which is most upsetting to them. When you reach core, and it is clear that you are on the same wavelength, you can begin problem-solving. This can be:

- Further paraphrasing, where you show greater and greater understanding about what they are upset about.
- A summation of the core problem. For example, "You trusted him, and he stole your cigarettes. I can understand why you'd be so mad at him. You are due out of here in two months. You know he did this to mess up your release date, but you tell me if you don't do something, you will not survive two months. Yet you want to go home. We have to figure out a way that you can really win without getting into trouble."
- By paraphrasing them every step of the way, you establish that you are a person of trust. In some cases, you can now be quite directive, because most people are willing to accept advice or even instruction from people they trust.
- With others, we are ready to engage in a collaborative process of problem-solving, trying to figure out a way to solve the situation that is in the best interest of everyone involved.

Don't Waste It

Paraphrasing is almost a cliché, so much so that we can imagine some of you rolling your eyes when you read the title of this chapter. <u>This technique is too important to abandon, and at the same time, it must be used carefully, i.e., *rarely*</u>. If mentally ill inmates get too used to you using paraphrasing, they will cut you off, because you will appear to them to be giving nothing back, except mirroring. It is "cold fare" compared to a dialogue. If the individual is not angry and requiring you to use de-escalation tactics, don't use paraphrasing. Simply talk with them.

If there is a crisis, however, and *if* the inmate does not believe they are understood, now paraphrasing comes into its own. Paraphrasing can have an almost electrifying effect with an angry individual. Imagine the feeling when you try to pull a splinter from under your fingernail, and after ten long minutes of aggravating struggle, you get a hold of it finally and pull it out of your nail bed. That is the sense you get when, angry and desperate to be heard, you realize that the other person "got it."

CHAPTER 58

Big Mistakes That Seemed Like
Such Good Ideas at the Time

De-escalation requires on-the-scene improvisation, in a very fluid and dynamic setting, often with volatile and unpredictable inmates. In such a highly charged atmosphere, where clear communication is necessary to prevent any misunderstandings that may worsen the situation, correctional officers must think quickly, but calmly, before speaking.

By maintaining a professional emotional distance, and not reacting personally to anything the inmate may say, you will be less likely to escalate an already heated situation. Nobody is perfect, however, many mistakes are very obvious, and the moment something leaves your mouths you think, "Uh-oh. I shouldn't have said that!" Fortunately, taking a moment to gather thoughts before responding to what the inmate has said can often prevent this. Sometimes holding up your hands to give them pause, will also give you time to gather your own resources, and then reply.

Some mistakes are subtler. On certain days, you may be tired, not feeling well, or be distracted by family matters perhaps, and de-escalating an angry inmate is the last thing you wish to do. Not surprisingly, risk increases when you are at less than your optimum ability and awareness, and you are more likely to make a mistake in your communications at these times. You actually need to be more alert when you are not at your best.

The following topics are areas the authors feel correctional officers should take special note, so as not to make innocent blunders that may lead suddenly to escalating encounters with angry inmates:

Ingratiation. Don't try to ingratiate yourself with the inmate; don't pretend that a potentially aggressive situation or encounter has not developed; and, don't ignore the aggressive behavior or language while calmly going about your business in the hopes that the inmate will eventually tire himself or herself out.

<u>We usually see this with people who really shouldn't be correctional officers</u>. They are too nice, too naïve, or too intimidated. That said, everybody has leverage points, and any one of us can slip up.

One of the paradoxes of ingratiation is that correctional officers who allow the inmate to control their interactions often present themselves as having a "special rapport" with an inmate who, in fact, intimidates them. Oddly enough, these same officers, who try to avoid conflict, or "make nice," are often suppressing a lot of anger at being controlled. They displace this on those who call them on what they are doing.

Thus, one of the first signs that the correctional officer is ingratiating himself or herself is an attitude of self-righteousness, a defense mechanism that enables them to avoid questioning the violations of their own integrity. The following factors are also signs of ingratiation toward the inmate:

- You worry about "how things are going" between yourself and the inmate, and react accordingly.
- You are sometimes ashamed of your actions, or believe that you act in a cowardly fashion in the way you interact with the inmate.
- You believe you are caring and nice, so you react with shocked outrage when an inmate is blaming or aggressive toward you, as if you and the inmate made some sort of transaction that they have now betrayed.
- You allow the other inmate to speak to you in overly familiar or rude terms.

The mistake of trying to find common ground. Sometimes, correctional officers will try to connect with an inmate by telling them how they must feel, by confessing to having the same issues, or claiming to have gone through a similar situation. Statements like, "I know how you feel," "I know you love your son," or "When I…." are statements that the angry inmate may not agree with at all. They then decide to prove you wrong by demonstrating that they are NOT what you just said they are. Not only that, most inmates will perceive an officer talking this way as "sucking up" to them, or if paranoid, trying to soften them up by pretending to be alike.

The mistake of allowing venting. Pure venting is an expression of energy, such as going for a run after a difficult day, or chopping wood until fatigued, so that you can "let go" of an unpleasant incident, or just a bad day at work. However, generalized aggression expressed verbally in front of others (tantrums), or aggression expressed about one person to another is also designated by the same term.

We previously referred to letting an inmate "get something off their chest" **(Chapter 52)**. This is not the same as venting. The purpose of the former action is to get finished with something by talking about it; the purpose of the latter is to stoke oneself up into higher levels of aggression.

Many people have a false idea about aggression, and imagine it to be some kind of psychological fluid that builds up pressure inside of us. When we vent (hence the word), these people believe that we get rid of the anger and then become peaceful, similar to a valve releasing pressure from a water line. Aggression, however, is not a fluid; it is state of arousal. Just like any other state of arousal—sexuality, happiness, excited interest—additional stimuli elicits more arousal. When you shout, yell, complain, kick things, or the like, you are stimulating yourself to greater and greater aggression. Therefore, if you allow an inmate to vent, the angrier they will become.

Don't attempt to make any distinctions between venting directed at other people, and either anger or rage. Simply consider it for what it is—aggression. When you let an inmate vent about other people, they perceive that you are giving implicit approval to their verbal complaints and abuse. If you listen to their venting silently, without de-escalating or controlling their verbal escalation, they believe you are on their side. However, when they get so angry that they start to become dangerous and *then* you object, they will turn on you. Thus, whenever an inmate begins to vent, de-escalate and control them.

Obvious mistakes we shouldn't make but do anyway. Although some of the items included in the following list have been discussed elsewhere in this book, they are repeated here as a reminder to the reader of the seemingly minor, yet crucial, details of de-escalation. Correctional officers should not:

- Make threats or promise consequences they can't keep. False promises or implied threats, which the inmate may know the correctional officer is incapable of keeping, will lessen your credibility. The failure to follow through on promises made or consequences threatened will also serve to undermine your authority with the inmate after the incident has been resolved.
- Bombard the inmate with choices, questions, and solutions, as this will only overwhelm the inmate, especially if they are suffering from mental illness.
- Ask an upset inmate "why." Asking a "why" question demands an answer or an explanation from the inmate, something they may be quite unwilling, or unable, to do. "Why" questions should only be used when you have used paraphrasing to reach the core problem successfully **(Chapter 57)**.
- Talk down to the inmate as if they were stupid or ignorant. Don't roll your eyes or sigh heavily while the inmate is trying to communicate with you. Don't interrupt as they speak, particularly to correct what they are saying. On the other hand, interruption of aggressive verbalizations or pointless monologues on the part of the inmate IS the right thing to do.
- Analyze their behavior while de-escalating. Problem-solving and evaluations can be completed after safe de-escalation.
- Share the inmate's private information in front of others.

Figure 58.1 Concerning Inmate's Privacy

Be mindful of "hallway consultations" and consider who may be within earshot of your conversations, either with other inmates or with your fellow officers. If inmates overhear you discussing the details of another inmate's case they may think, "If they talk about that person like that, they are probably talking about me in the same way." Paranoid inmates—and there are a lot of them—will perceive you as putting them in danger because, if you are talking about them, or even someone else, other inmates will use the information to hurt them (which, by the way, may be true).

- Take things personally when the inmate attacks your character or professionalism. The measure of the true professional is NOT taking things personally **(Chapter 20)**.
- Allow the inmate to trespass on your personal boundaries, or violate theirs. The safety issues inherent in personal spacing issues are quite obvious. Safety is enhanced when one enforces a strong, professional hierarchical relationship with the inmate.

- Adopt an authoritarian or demeaning attitude, particularly in front of their peers or other on-lookers, including fellow officers. Authoritarian attitudes and behaviors are some of the most common precipitants of assault by inmates.
- Tell an angry or enraged inmate to "calm down." It never works.

Figure 58.2 The Worst, Stupid, and Unethical Mistake: "Lighting the inmate up"

Let's be honest here. Correctional officers are not all paragons of humanity. Even most of you, the good guys, are not perfect. We are certainly not at our best in periods of high stress, and even less so when we are in danger, when we are demeaned, and when our best intentions are sometimes spit on or worse. When you have an inmate who is, for example, smearing feces on himself, even devouring it, and nothing you can do can stop the foul odor and behavior, it's easy to soon view the person as less than human. (This is quite apart from the fact that something is going terribly wrong that such an inmate does not receive adequate psychiatric intervention to help him or her from this debased condition.) Without effective leadership and a strong sense of both esprit d'corps and personal integrity, a group culture can arise in which correctional officers devolve into "guards." Group culture can lead people to egg each other on, and mild incidents of teasing can escalate.

To be quite blunt about it, it can start to get funny to "light an inmate up." By this, we mean to say or do things to inflame the mentally ill inmate, because you, as a group, get off on" f**king with him." Blunt enough for you?

It happens and it's wrong. Not only is it unethical, as what is right about provoking an individual who, due to their illness, is helpless to stop their reactions and sometimes painfully ridiculous responses. Beyond that, it is unprofessional. If you rightly state that beyond all else, officers must focus on safety, how is this served when officers act in a way that justifiably would cause anyone to view them as enemies. Remember, too, that it will not only be the officer who provokes the inmate who is so regarded. Anyone wearing the uniform will be seen the same way. Not only are other officers at risk in your facility, so too, will other officers in the facility the inmate is transferred to be at risk, or police officers out on the street, and they do not even know they've been set up in this manner. Furthermore, so, too, will the officer out with his or her family in the community who is recognized by the now-released, only semi-compensated but 100% hating individual who, as far as he or she is concerned, was psychologically tortured during their last incarceration.

It is, therefore, not only a mark of a professional to keep your own dignity and integrity. It is equally the mark of a professional to assist the inmates, even the most mentally disturbed, keep theirs as well.

SECTION XI

A Consideration of Communication With
Mentally Ill, Emotionally Disturbed, and
Drug Affected Incarcerated Youth:
For Correctional Officers Who Work
with Juvenile Offenders

CHAPTER 59

Working With
Incarcerated Youth

Figure 59.1 A Note Concerning Youth

Generally speaking, you will use the same de-escalation strategies with youth as are outlined in the rest of this book. The differences are often more on nuance than on major details. We have, however, "sub-divided" youth in some general categories based on behavior that will help both in understanding young people as well as using the best strategies to help stabilize and calm them when they have become aggressive or are otherwise in crisis.

General Concerns

The youth described in this chapter are young *now*, but they will grow up to be adults, perhaps living in your community. Youth today don't just face "coming of age" growing pains. Despite all the prosperity and opportunity in our society, youth face many dangers. Drugs are everywhere, and not only do they affect children directly, but also, far too many have been affected *in utero* by their parents' drug abuse, and not just by their mother; there are questions about genetic changes in the sperm of male drug/alcohol user as well. Furthermore, when one's parents use drugs and alcohol, their attentiveness and caring towards their children is lessened in the "best" of such circumstances; abuse of all kind increases exponentially in drug/alcohol abusing homes.

Gangs metastasize within a community, just like cancer. There is a putrescent vitality to gang life that is both charismatic and compelling. Despite the terrible things one may do, the gang offers solidarity, and a life committed to something bigger than oneself, however damaging it might be. Once initiated, one crosses a line that is hard to cross back over. This charisma, by the way, isn't only attractive to children from broken or abusive homes; the vitality of a warrior culture, no matter how violent and destructive, seduces children from loving families as well. It is only when "the good" has a power and charisma greater than that of gang culture that youth find it easy to turn away.

Youth and young adults show mental illness in much the same manner as adults. If a young person is displaying psychosis, mania, latency, or any of the other behaviors described in other sections of this book, the strategies offered there are fully applicable. In this section, we will be describing the character traits that are often related to aggression in youth; you can view these traits as the youth's fundamental attitude towards the world. A reader might reasonably ask when dealing with an aggressive sounding youth, how could one tell what mode they're in?

View each chapter in this section has a quick step-by-step process. If the approach on impulsive youth **(Chapter 60)**, doesn't work, quickly move on to the next. It is quite likely that you will, intuitively, grasp that a youth is in one or another mode, and start with the tactics appropriate to that behavior. Of course, the next time you have to deal with this particular youth, you will know the second time around where best to start. At any rate, this section will take things as a quick (matter of moments) step-by-step process.[45]

CHAPTER 60

No Brake Pads: A Consideration
of the Impulsive Youth

Per orthodox theory, attention disorders come in two major forms. In the first type, the main manifestation is a short attention span Attention Deficit Disorder (ADD). In the second type, hyperactivity is also present Attention Deficit Hyperactivity Disorder (ADHD). We all believe that the diagnosis of ADD/ADHD, now so astoundingly common, deserves more controversy than it is currently receiving in both media and clinical sources. We strongly recommend that everyone concerned with youth read two contrarian books: one by Leonard Sax and the other by Richard Louv.[46] Whether you end up agreeing with all of what either of the authors proposes, they will require you to think afresh about these issues. And in an era where medications are slung like candy at children, often with little clinical assessment or sound treatment, this is absolutely necessary.

Figure 60.1 Note on ADHD

This type of problem isn't only endemic in America. One of our colleagues wrote to us that in Northern Ireland, "There are various allowances payable to parents of kids diagnosed with ADHD, so many parents lie to their doctor to get the kids on the various drugs, or at least, get the diagnosis."

Let us here consider the impulsive child (ADHD or not), as one who tends to act before he or she thinks. Below you will find some examples of actions by impulsive youth.

- He is in a store and sees a video game he wants, and without considering the consequences, shoplifts it right in front of the security camera.
- She gets in an argument with one of her friends and, her feelings get hurt, she assaults her friend right in front of their teacher.
- Another boy bumps him in the hall and he stabs him in the hand with his pencil; he is as surprised as the victim—both of them looking at the bloody pencil tip with their mouths open in shock.

The impulsive young person gets angry or aggressive for the same reasons as any other person, but they get particularly upset and frustrated when someone interferes with the gratification of an impulse. Paraphrasing **(Chapter 57)** can be particularly valuable with these kids because you demonstrate that you "get" their desire and frustration, rather than argue with them. (NOTE: This is a tactic, just as is done in crisis negotiation, NOT approval for their outburst.)

Impulsive youth track very little of what you say, particularly when they're angry. If they're too escalated for paraphrasing, it isn't the time for explanations, attempts to elicit empathy for the other person, or moral preachments. **What usually works best is a calm demeanor and simple short commands.**

How would you know that they're not merely impulsive or upset? If the following strategy doesn't work, go on to the next strategy. Remember, we're talking about an approach that takes only a few moments—this is NOT a counseling session!

Figure 60.2 Review: Dealing with Impulsive Youth

Until proven otherwise, when dealing with an upset or aggressive youth, assume that he or she is in "impulsive" mode.

- Paraphrase if mildly angry.
- Give them firm, brief commands, if they are at higher levels of anger.
- Help them regain control by directly telling them what to do.

CHAPTER 61

Conduct Disorder:
Fierce Youth

> **Figure 61.1 Definition of Conduct Disorder**
>
> Conduct disorder is a term that delineates behaviors in children and youth that, in someone over the age of eighteen would merit the diagnosis of anti-social personality disorder, or even psychopathy. Because the child/adolescent brain is still so changeable, we <u>properly</u> don't give them a diagnosis that would suggest that change is unlikely, if not impossible. **The majority of children who fully merit the diagnosis of conduct disorder don't grow up to be psychopaths.** Nonetheless, the chapters on manipulation and psychopathy **(Section VI)** are essential in considering any youth who is conduct disordered, because a correctional officer must deal with the behaviors that the conduct disordered youth is showing NOW, however they may become in the future. This section focuses specifically on youth who display ferocious, manipulative, or predatory behaviors, whatever the cause may be.

Conduct disordered character traits can develop from myriad reasons, some of them heart-rending. However, although this may be very important for psychological treatment, it is not relevant for control of their potential violence. If you contextualize or excuse their behavior, someone will be seriously hurt.

The fierce youth typically displays rages in three major categories: fury, manipulation, and predatory behavior **(Section XII)**. It is almost always a mistake to try to establish a "sympathetic" or "nurturing" connection with such youth at any time, much less during a rage state. They experience these gestures as an attempt to soften their defenses, and/or a sign of weakness on your part. Fierce youth children/teenagers lay extreme importance on protecting themselves from "invasion." Your sympathy is experienced as manipulation or an attack.

They try to defend themselves against any need for other people, as well as building up a callous attitude in which they extinguish caring about other people's pain. In the most basic sense, such youth are profoundly isolated. Without human ties, pride and respect are their most important "possessions," something they will live and die for. This pride, however, can be considered an access route for communication and de-escalation. For tactical reasons, meet such pride with "respect." <u>This is NOT approval for what they're doing, or even what they "are."</u> It simply means that you're letting them know where they stand: that they're in violation of the rules of our society, and you, as the agent to enforce those rules will, with no personal agenda, make sure that they aren't allowed to transgress. You're saying, in essence,

"Your job, at least right now, seems to be breaking the rules, and my job is to stop you." **The formula for communication with such fierce youth is "Respect outweighs sympathy."**

In other words, enforce the rules with calm gravity and strength. Never try to ingratiate yourself, or prove you're a "good guy," because all you will get back is contempt. However, if you manifest yourself as a strong and dignified individual who doesn't make it "personal" when you do your job, you will, sometimes, draw their attention, even respect.

If there is hope for such youth, it lies in their fascination with power. You present to them a world they can't imagine without you—that power and decency can exist together and that one actually acquires more power through treating others with respect. If you don't manifest this yourself, such a young person will be unreachable.

Figure 61.2 Author's Example: The Power of Dignity and Respect

Some years ago, I was requested to provide stress reduction training in a very "hot" youth facility—they had forty beds and averaged seventy youth, so overflow slept on mattresses in the hallways. Rather than psych discussion groups, which, in the circumstances, I thought would be useless (the population of the youth changed on a weekly basis), I actually taught some exercises from Chinese martial arts, called *qigong* (NOTE: they were combatively useless, something I made very clear, but they look cool and, as I will describe, and had a beneficial collateral effect). These exercises work a tension-release cycle, something that is at the core of controlling your own emotions. Each week, with each group of kids (some who'd been there before, some new), I'd say, "Don't you hate it when people make you mad? If they *make* you mad, they control you. *I'll teach you how to get mad only when you want to.*" With this population, often gang affiliated, simply suggesting that I'd help them be peaceful or nice-guys, wasn't going to cut it. Then we'd start the exercises.

It was guaranteed that one or another youth would try to provoke me, to see if I "walked my talk." Usually, I'd roll with it, but sometimes, I'd have someone escorted back to their cell—and I'd do it calmly.

There was one young man there, week after week. Always quiet, always apart. I'd been told that he'd nearly killed someone, he'd been tried as an adult and at seventeen years of age, was awaiting placement for a sentence of twenty years. I'd been told that he was a cold, emotionless, potential killer. He did his exercises quietly, never made any trouble.

One day, the staff told me he was going to be sent up after my class. He'd requested to take my class one last time. He worked the exercises quietly, and then, the class over, walked with the others back to his cell. He paused, as he passed me, looked around to see that no one was listening and whispered, "I wish you had been my dad," and walked on.

His passing statement just about broke my heart. It's a tragedy that so many youth have to meet someone in the correctional environment to conceive of what respect and decency is. But we have more power than we sometimes know. The image of the tough, but fair correctional officer or other staff may, in some cases, be the model that leads that particular youth, to take another path.

Figure 61.3 Review: Dealing With Fierce Youth

You first approached the youth as if their aggression is impulsive and you tried to exert authority over them. That didn't work—instead, the youth becomes more focused and directed in his or her aggression towards you. In this case do the following:

- Let them know where they stand—that anything you're enforcing isn't "personal," that you're doing your job and dispassionately enforce your authority.
- Respect before sympathy! Don't try to prove you care.
- Deal with them on a professional, slightly disinterested basis.

CHAPTER 62

Dynamite Under a Rock:
Explosive Kids

The hallmark quality of these kids is that once their fiery tempers are unleashed, it is very hard for them to stop. They rage and rage. Many of these young people can pay attention just fine *until* they lose their temper. Others, such as the child with Fetal Alcohol Disorder or a history of head injury, have learning disabilities, including problems of attention in addition to explosive tempers. Regardless, they're the kids of whom one says, "Billy lost it again today," and everyone nods, imagining the explosion at the judge, along with slung chairs and thrown fits, the young person raging for over an hour *after* they were restrained in hand cuffs.

If you're trying to verbally control them, loud orders and other shouted commands don't work well. They can be unbelievably violent, and they react to commands as further provocation. They flame up at the sound of your voice, particularly if you're yelling. The watchword, instead, is **containment**.

Give commands, but your voice must be very firm and calm. The command is to get their attention. It is to focus everything on one being—you. In favorable circumstances you, and however many others are necessary, escort (or convey) this young person to a containment area, padded cell or the like where they calm down on their own. Your task is to stay nearby so that they don't injure themselves or damage property. You can't however, problem-solve or otherwise work things out while they're still on fire. If you're unable to accomplish this, you should avail yourself of the strategies in **Section XII** on rage and violence.

Some explosive youth, particularly those with neurological damage, suddenly shift into an "organic rage," apparently unmediated by any thought processes. However, these kids often show small micro-changes of behavior right before assaults. You should definitely learn these signs to help the youth shift gears into another activity or process, thereby heading off the explosion. Two examples come to mind:

- A girl in one facility had enacted a number of apparently sudden severe attacks against other inmates, particularly in the school setting. We found that when she focused on an intellectual task too long, she would begin scratching at her forearm. The "sudden" explosion of aggression followed a few minutes after this "tell."
- Another youth would knit his brows and glower in a stubborn manner when he didn't understand a conversation. He interpreted this as people "making me feel stupid," an attack, in his view. This facial expression was a clear sign to the officer to slow down, lighten up, or change the subject.

Figure 62.1 Review: Dealing With Explosive Youth

You're dealing with a young person and attempt to exert authority, and then, when that doesn't work, you try the professional respect, command presence, and distance that you use with the fierce youth. If such a youth continues to ramp upwards into further aggression, assume you're dealing with an explosive youth. They get more and more aggressive as if they don't have a "circuit breaker" that helps them turn off. They become very reactive to anything.

- Rage is usually explosive. They often have no fear of harm when in an explosive rage state.
- Don't get flamed up yourself, no matter what they say (which will frequently be pretty bad!).
- If you speak at all, use paraphrasing **(Chapter 57)**, if they are still at low levels of anger. They ramp up so fast; however, that this usually doesn't work.
- Silently, implacably, take them somewhere safe, where they're contained and unable to harm anything. Wait them out, so to speak.
- Containment is the watchword. The behavior of "explosive youth," in particular, may necessitate physical control.

CHAPTER 63

Opposition-Defiant Kids:
"Even If You Make Me,
I'll Still Make You Miserable"

Oppositional-defiant (OD) disorder is considered a behavioral disorder of childhood. These young people, before their behavior was "made" into a mental health diagnosis, were often referred to by such terms as 'brats." It usually develops with upbringing typified by poor boundaries (too invasive and/or too lax). Aggression is typically against "family;" those familiar to the child. Dictatorial parents, who try to break the child, often "create" OD kids among those who are too strong-willed to crumble. The motto of such kids seems to be, "You won't break me. Furthermore, even if you make me do it, I still say 'no,' and ruin your day in the process." Other parents who aren't consistent nor enforce coherent reasonable discipline (overly permissive or chaotic) also elicit such behaviors. In this case, the child is implicitly saying, "I will act out until you're forced to give me some limits." Not every such child is a product of ineffective or failed parenting, however. There are also parents who haven't raised their children poorly, but the kids have bonded with other young people or with an image that they absorbed from media, either of which encourages defiant behavior. Finally, exacerbated by drug or alcohol abuse, many previously loving young people turn nasty indeed.

Negative reinforcement, only giving attention for negative behavior, will elicit more negative behavior. Reinforcement through punishment that is both out of proportion or inconsistent teaches the child that discipline is an attack, that the parent is unpredictable, and that acting out at least gets the parent's focus on them. The child experiences a kind of "social power" when punished. They see the punisher as having the right to define good and bad, but at the same time, they see themselves as having impact (if they aren't utterly broken in spirit or body by the punishment).

Unfortunately, once power is acquired in this manner, the youth gets a grandiose sense of his or her own importance, and frustrating and defying adults becomes its own reward. They apparently thrive on argument; they look for any pretext to continue the argument, fighting over fine-points, trying to knock the adult off center. This is often not a search for truth; it is simply a power tactic. <u>If you're losing your temper, they're winning, and they hold you in contempt for it.</u> This need to argue, *at its extreme end*, seems related to Obsessive-Compulsive Disorder. Their brain, apparently, won't let go of their place in the argument. Right-and-wrong don't matter; only what they want, right now.

Although the behavior of OD youth can be violent, it seems engendered by the contradiction of resistance to authority against an implicit plea that a clear, trustworthy, consistent authority be exerted over them so that their place in the world is truly defined. Perhaps the most important recommendation we can make is that all people involved with such youth must maintain consistent boundaries with NO deviations. The oppositional youth will test these boundaries over and over again to see if the limits have changed.

The watchword in dealing with these kids is to pick your battles. <u>Don't waste energy arguing about anything that isn't important. When it is important, become implacable</u>. They put energy in their argument; you put quiet steel in yours. *You, an adult, don't argue with such a youth as an "equal."* You tell them what will be, with no negotiation whatsoever. If you're correct in what you require, it should be experienced as a force like gravity: not a debate.

These youth are used to a lot of attention for negative behavior. This drains the adults responsible for them and they're often ignored when they aren't making trouble, much less acting positively. Therefore, be sure to notice when they're acting with integrity, agreeableness, and/or respect, so that they experience positive attention for these actions. On the other hand, do not over praise them when they act well. They will reject this as undermining their sense of power. Instead, simply recognize it and move on (e.g., "I see you are doing your homework." NOT, "That's great! I'm so happy you are doing your work."

Figure 63.1 Review: Dealing With Oppositional-Defiant Youths

These young people argue for argument's sake. Their reward is the negative attention they require from adults, and the sense that they have you—at least your moods—under their control. They believe they've won if they anger you or get you upset. Pick your battles—those not worth arguing, disengage, change the subject, or ignore. Don't argue; require them to follow your instructions. **Be like gravity**—no argument with that. Whenever possible, give a little extra energy (positive attention) when the young person is doing something worthwhile or worth respecting, without it being either praise or a "put up."

CHAPTER 64

Post-traumatic Stress Disorder in Youth

For both children and young adults, post-traumatic stress disorder, caused by either the experiencing or witnessing acts of severe violence, is often physically enacted rather than verbalized. Many males in particular, would adamantly deny ever experiencing trauma, claiming to live by Nietzsche's adage of, "That which doesn't kill me makes me stronger."

There isn't a unique de-escalation method for use with traumatized youth. They can display aggression and violence in a variety of modes, from terrified and chaotic rage to purposeful predation. If you were to take apart any aggressive or violent episode by such a youth, you would have, in symbolic form, the story of their own trauma, not only what happened to them, but also what was created *within* them in response. Traumatized children, in particular, often display **Terrified Rage (Chapter 68)**. The predatory or hot rage states that some traumatized children and teenagers display is a kind of reaction formation. They have found through violence a way to cease experiencing the pervasive dread of the victim. It's only as a victimizer that they feel safe.

One mistake that even seasoned officers may make is to be "disarmed" by the horror that some children have suffered. When we understand that they have already been to hell and barely made it back, we sometimes let our "understanding" direct our response to the youth. The kindest, most respectful thing that you can do is to hold them to the highest standard of behavior. If you allow a traumatized youth "off the hook" because of what may be, admittedly, a horrible history of abuse, they will begin to use their "abuse excuse" to license violence and predation on others.

Figure 64.1 Review: Dealing With Traumatized Kids
- Whatever their history, de-escalate based on their behavior at the moment.
- Don't let them "off the hook." Hold them to the highest standard of behavior.

CHAPTER 65

Pseudo-Nihilism

Such a youth, who may affect a posture that includes boredom, self-destructive behaviors, or disinterest, is, in fact, striving for power. Their sense of power increases when they can horrify, disgust, or offend others. Taken further, they achieve power when they experience themselves as untouched by other people.

You shouldn't be emotionally bland with such youth. If you try to show that their provocative behaviors don't affect you, they will escalate until they do evoke a reaction. However, beyond a "human reaction," you must demonstrate that you don't *need* them to change. Your ability to be at ease with what they are, embodies what they profess they desire. In particular, don't follow the "self-esteem" model, the fantasy that all they need is someone telling them how special they are. These youth are often cynical precisely because people have confused the good feelings that might be elicited from praise, with genuine success in life. They know it's not true.

One is most concerned about youth of this type by what they hide inside. These kids, in particular, need an adult who is able to provide feedback in a way that he or she doesn't feel compelled to resist. They need someone with more life experience to talk with. Without this, their fantasies and unhappiness festering inside—they become more and more destructive, either to themselves or others. Therefore, community safety is served when such youth have someone that they can respect and check in with to provide an alternative viewpoint to the one they, alone and isolated, came up with.

Figure 65.1 Review: Dealing With Pseudo-Nihilism

This youth is cut-off. They may be aggressive, but their primary goal seems to **NOT** make a link communicating with you. They may be very much at odds with you; they may even rage or curse at you or treat you with contempt. One way or another, these kids try to cut themselves off from you.
- Don't try to make them change or feel better. "No put ups." They may try to repel you with what they say, or what they say they have done. Give them a human reaction, but not an over-reaction. In other words, a Great Dane doesn't get off the porch when a little dog is yapping at him.
- They're most dangerous when left alone to stew in their own juices. Be the adult that they almost surely don't have in their life, so they have a moral touchstone. Of course, a correctional officer can only do this in brief contacts. Nonetheless, your impact can be profound.

SECTION XII

Managing Rage and Violence

CHAPTER 66

Preface to Rage
and Violence

Rage and anger are not merely different in degree; they are different modes of being, just as water, once past the boiling point, becomes steam. Frustrated inmates posture or otherwise act angrily to establish dominance, or to force agreement or compliance from others. If nothing else, their goal is to communicate their feelings, although, due to their lack of interpersonal skills, their mental illness, or the effects of drugs and/or alcohol, they often resort to anger in an attempt to make themselves heard.

The reader will recall that anger is denoted as falling between 20-95 on the aggressiveness scale (**Section IX**). This represents a very broad range of arousal, ranging from mildly irritated to truly irate. Rage however, occupies a much smaller fraction of the scale, from 95- 99. When in a state of rage, the inmate desires to commit mayhem. Enraged inmates are in a "threshold" state, their anger and rage escalating until they have overcome any moral or personal constraints that might otherwise prohibit them from committing the ultimate expression of rage—violence.

<u>Therefore, all of the strategies described in the previous chapters dealing with the angry inmate are more or less useless with one who is truly enraged</u>. Sometimes the only viable option for the correctional officer is to remove himself or herself from the situation until reinforcements can be summoned. In others, you are suddenly in combat.

There are various types of rage, and correctional officers need to recognize what type of rage the inmate is expressing, because there are different verbal control strategies to deal with each type. Fortunately, an enraged person's behavior is quite obvious, and after reading this section of the book, you will be able to identify what type of rage the inmate is exhibiting rather easily, allowing you to employ the appropriate strategies to control them.[47]

Figure 66.1 IMPORTANT CAUTION

Here, and in several other areas of this book, we have used animal symbols to aid in the understanding of various types of rage or other behavior. For example, we use the image of a leopard or a shark in describing predatory rage.

These are thought devices, and are not intended to be used in either paperwork or communication to describe such inmates.

In our hypersensitive times, such a reference to a specific inmate may be misconstrued as stigmatizing that individual as "being an animal." Nothing could be further than the truth—the images are to assist in understanding modes of behavior, not character. Nonetheless, such images should remain aids of understanding, not terms of reference.

CHAPTER 67

Chaotic Rage: A Consideration of Rage Emerging from Various Disorganized States

Chaotic rage is typified by profound disorganization of cognitive and perceptual processes, and can be engendered by severe psychosis that has "crossed over" into a delirium state, whether engendered from mania, intoxication, drug withdrawal, severe intellectual/developmental disabilities, senile dementia, overwhelming emotions, or as a result of brain injury or trauma. Enraged disorganized inmates are often very impulsive and unpredictable, striking out in all directions. They may not be coordinated in their actions, but they are fully committed, meaning that they have no fear of injury or consequences to hold them back. They are also often indifferent to, or unaware of, pain or injury to themselves. However, not every person in a chaotic rage state is uncoordinated: with trained fighters, combative reflexes are almost instinctive, and thus, even though they are cognitively shattered, in a state of complete incoherence, they can still fight, throwing punches and kicks with accuracy.

Our symbol for this state is TAZ, the fanged, whirling tornado of arms and legs, in the Warner Brother's cartoons.

Unlike a classic psychosis, the most salient characteristic of chaotic rage is the near impossibility of establishing *any* lines of communication. Inmates in this state often can't logically string words together, communicating in ways that are comprehensible only to themselves. They may utter cascades of words making no sense whatsoever, or grunts, moans, and mumbling. Others make sentences based on rhymes, puns, or cross-meanings, their brains capriciously linking words together based on sounds, not meanings. Delirious inmates may laugh or babble, completely at variance to the seriousness of the situation. They may speak in repetitive loops, fixating on one subject, which could be real, hallucinatory, or such a manifestation of their disorganization that you don't even know what they are talking about.

Delirious inmates can easily become quite frightened or irritable, especially if they are overwhelmed with stimuli, such as a large number of onlookers or the presence of several correctional officers. They may begin yelling, screaming, lashing out physically, or engaging in self-injurious acts such as scratching and gouging their own flesh, striking themselves repeatedly, or banging their head against the wall or ground. Such behaviors should be considered medical emergencies, and proper medical attention must be summoned as soon as possible. Ideally, medical staff should stage nearby while the correctional officers are establishing the safe de-escalation and resolution of the crisis. **Even a few minutes delay in medical attention, once the inmate is secured, can be fatal. Chaotic rage can be a sign of a life-threatening emergency, and inmates manifesting it must receive adequate medical assessment and intervention as soon as possible.**

De-Escalation of Chaotic Rage

Disorganized or delirious inmates are among the most difficult to verbally control, because comprehension and coherent cognitive processes are among the first faculties they lose. Because of their impulsiveness and unpredictability, correctional officers must be on guard against a sudden attack. Therefore, knowledge of any triggers that might have set them off in the past is very useful.

One person, usually the supervising correctional officer, needs to take command and control of the situation and direct other officers as to what they should do, i.e., clearing the room of others, providing site security to prevent others from entering the area, phoning for emergency medical assistance, etc.

- **Use calm movements, and a firm but reassuring voice.** Chaotic inmates often experience poor motor control, vertigo, disorientation, etc. Slow movements and a strong, quiet tone of voice can help orient them physically and emotionally.
- **Repetition is the best strategy.** Use simple, concrete commands with no more than a single "subject" in each sentence—short sentences, little words. Use only one thought at a time, as complex sentences will be confusing, and thus threatening or irritating. For example, say slowly, "Sit down, Williams. Sit down. Sit down. Williams, sit down."
- **Deflection.** Disorganized inmates in chaotic rage states are sometimes susceptible to being deflected to another topic, although this is unlikely when they have entered fully into chaotic rage. You can sometimes fabricate a theme that catches their attention and seems to engage higher thought processes, delaying their outburst of rage until help can arrive. Think of this as a momentary "Island of Sanity." The island of sanity we described above (**Chapter 42**) can be thought of as relatively permanent. This is more like a life raft, or a mat of seaweed. It may not be helpful during the next incident, but it helps keep the chaotic inmate focused on one thing—**NOW.**

Figure 67.1 Example of Deflection: Dealing With an Inmate in a Chaotic Rage State

A correctional officer approached a delirious inmate and said, "Jimmy Jones, what are you doing here, I haven't seen you since high school." As he kept rattling off fictitious memories to the man, the delirious inmate gazed into his eyes in confusion, rocking back and forth in rhythm with the officer's words. The officer was successful in capturing the inmate's attention, until more officers could arrive. To illustrate how dangerous this situation was for that single officer, the moment the other officers tried to physically control him, the man exploded into a violent attack, requiring a number of officers to subdue him.

- **Paraphrasing.** Use tactical paraphrasing to validate and acknowledge their confusion and/or fear. For example, use phrases such as, "Really scary, huh?" Or "You are really worried, aren't you?"
- **Use their name.** One of the last things we "retain" is our name, so use their name, repetitively, interspersing it frequently in your commands in order to get their attention before initiating attempts to redirect them to another activity. *This is a situation where their first name, rather than "Inmate Jones" is probably preferable, because the first name is more fundamental.*
- **Physical contact for one reason only.** Be very cautious about body contact with chaotic inmates, as this may be experienced as invasive, or even as an attack. Correctional officers should make physical contact only as a means of self- defense, to take the inmate into custody, or to prevent the inmate from harming themselves or any other people present.
- **No distractions.** Minimize such distracting behaviors on your part as extraneous body movements. Your movements should be calming and also only be those useful in helping the person understand what is going on.
- **Non-verbal communication is paramount.** Because of their difficulty in attending to what you say, non-verbal communication is a paramount concern. A calm reassuring presence, manifesting both strength and assurance is your best hope of helping to stabilize an inmate in chaotic rage.
- **Be ready for the worst.** Be ready at any time to use physical intervention tactics. Inmates manifesting chaotic rage are profoundly dangerous.

Figure 67.2 WARNING: Disorganized Inmates Can Be Unpredictable and Explosive

Disorganized inmates (male and female) are among the most difficult to de-escalate verbally because words and coherent cognitive processes are the first thing that they lose. You must, therefore, be prepared to evade a sudden attack, and further, be prepared, throughout, to use physical control tactics to ensure your safety as well as that of others.

Catatonia: Special Considerations

Catatonia is a very rare, very bizarre condition in which an inmate stays in a fixed posture, not congruent with injury or seizure. Catatonia is caused either by mental illness (schizophrenia) or an organic condition, for example, drug use. The catatonic inmate's posture may be quite awkward or twisted, seeming to require great flexibility. A classic symptom of true catatonia is "waxy immobility," whereby if someone else moves their body or limbs, he or she maintains the posture into which they were moved. Such inmates will often be totally unresponsive to speech, touch, even pain, and there seems to be no way to establish any communication with them. Others are rigid in posture, locked into place. Sometimes profoundly depressed, withdrawn people are also referred to as catatonic, but in this case, the inmate usually slumps down or lies, unmoving in his or her cot.

Considerable caution is needed in dealing with immobile inmates, for several reasons. First, they may be injured or having a seizure and are in need of medical attention. A second consideration is safety. One way to regard catatonia is to view the individual as exerting one hundred percent of their will to *not* interact with the outside world. Trying to help, you may be tempted to make physical contact, yell forcefully, or clap your hands in front of their face, in an effort to get them to respond when they are unsecured. This can be a disastrous mistake. Imagine the incredible exertion of will required to maintain immobility for hours, even days, without movement, without response, without even blinking in some cases. Now imagine disturbing this equilibrium. The result is what is clinically called "catatonic rage." The catatonic inmate shifts from one hundred percent stillness to one hundred percent explosive motion. One of the authors can recall an incident where a law enforcement officer's career was ended by such an individual who, all of one-hundred-ten pounds, suddenly grabbed hold of his arm and yanking as if he was cracking a whip, ripping through all the ligaments of his shoulder and shoulder blade.

Although you may think the inmate is unaware, they *can* hear you. Therefore, speak calmly and respectfully; don't joke around. Inmates can have very long memories of being shamed, and if you speak about or treat the catatonic inmate as an object rather than as a person, you may evoke a terrible sense of humiliation. In their frozen state, they may not be able to respond immediately, but months or years later, someone or something may trigger an episode of postponed rage. Beyond that, everyone, even a person in a coma, deserves to be treated with respect. Even if it seems that the person can't hear a word that you are saying, act as if they are listening to every word.

Whenever an inmate is immobile and unresponsive, correctional officers should summon medical attention. If you have any suspicion that the inmate may be catatonic, have them placed in restraints and transported to the medical clinic or a hospital where they can be evaluated safely. <u>As you move them, treat them like a bomb about to go off: firm hands, lots of them, and one person talking. Stay smooth, in control and powerful. Do not grab at their limbs, digging your fingers into their flesh.</u>

Make sure that medical staff are aware that they are dealing with someone who is very likely catatonic and that they should not disturb them any more than is necessary when they are, as yet, unsecured. Testing reactivity to pain, light, or noise (shouting in their ear, for example), should not occur until the individual is safely in restraints. When you move them to a gurney, make sure you have sufficient numbers to safely manage them, just encase they were to explode suddenly while being moved.

Excited Delirium Syndrome

Excited delirium is a rare condition at the extreme end of the hyper-aroused wing of the delirium spectrum. Etiology can be varied, but it is most commonly associated with long-term use of stimulants, particularly cocaine and methamphetamine. Single doses of such drugs as PCP, Ketamine, binges on cathinones such as methylenedioxypyrovalerone (so called "bath salts"), and very rarely, psychedelic drugs such as "magic mushrooms," can cause chaotic rage states. It is also associated with extreme manic or psychotic excitement, and can be precipitated by a variety of purely medical conditions. It is typified by some, if not all of the following:

- A sudden onset of extreme agitation;
- Pervasive terror, often without object;
- Chaotic, sudden shifts in emotions;
- Disorientation;
- Screaming, pressured incoherent speech, grunting, or irrational statements;
- Aggression towards inanimate objects, particularly shiny objects like glass and mirrors;
- Hyper-arousal with unbelievable strength and endurance;
- Insensitivity to pain;
- Hyperthermia accompanied by stripping off clothes;
- Most notably, violent resistance to others, before, during, and after arrest or restraint.

Accompanying their almost unbelievable level of physical arousal and resistance to both physical and mechanical restraints is possible respiratory and cardiac arrest. **These people die!** The usual pattern is that they struggle with incredible power and then, suddenly, they stop moving. Or sometime after becoming quiet, either in a stupor or in seeming normality, they die, usually from cardiac arrest. This can look remarkably similar to a seizure, also a very dangerous syndrome.

Because, these days, most excited delirium is associated with long term amphetamine or cocaine abuse, and jail facilities, with people coming in off the street after a violent police encounter, are more likely to see this condition. However, it sometimes arises with combative mentally ill individuals as well, who are not on any drugs whatsoever.

If they haven't been already called, get an emergency medical team on the scene immediately! Correct protocol demands that emergency medical staff should be staged, and ready to intervene medically the _instant_ the subject is physically subdued.

Such individuals can be appallingly dangerous both to others and to themselves. **We can't emphasize strongly enough that this is a medical emergency manifesting as physical danger, and usually requiring both correctional officer and emergency medical intervention to secure the inmate so that they can be treated.**

You will, almost surely, be unable to verbally de-escalate the inmate in excited delirium, but if they are not presenting an immediate assault risk, make the attempt using the principles delineated above. Why?

- In some rare cases, you may be able to de-escalate them.
- You may be able to gain partial compliance that makes it easier to take them into physical custody.
- If nothing else you will "buy time," allowing sufficient emergency personnel to muster, making the restraint that will be necessary to get them help more feasible. By getting the subject focused

on you, they stop moving. This will make it substantially easier to deploy less-lethal means than if they are running amok.

Figure 67.3 The Longer the Struggle, the More Likely the Death

Individuals in Excited Delirium states die from a number of causes: heart failure, acute acidosis, rhabdomyolysis (the breakdown of muscle fibers into the bloodstream, causing kidney failure), to name only a few. One basic principle that must be remember: <u>the longer the struggle and the more intense the exertion, the more likely the person will die.</u> Therefore, medical intervention that may include, among other things, physical restraint, intubation, IV of chilled saline solution and immediate sedation must occur as quickly as possible. Verbal intervention techniques are for the purpose of minimizing the struggle, buying time to assemble sufficient officers to effectively and immediately put the person under total physical control, or in some cases, to get the inmate focused on one officer so that their movement is stabilized long enough to put them effectively under physical control.

In many cases, however, there is no time for verbal interventions. Their use is dictated solely by safety concerns—what is the most effective way to get the inmate under total physical control while minimizing the duration and intensity of the struggle.

Please refer to Appendix A for a detailed protocol on response to Excited Delirium.

Figure 67.4 Excited Delirium or Chaotic Rage

Most individuals who go into chaotic rage aren't in an excited delirium, but it is possible, even in a jail setting. Furthermore, we strongly urge all individuals involved in crisis response be familiarized on how to deal with such individuals. A joint training of all who may be involved in the restraint and treatment of such individuals is imperative. You need to have an established protocol to ensure other inmate safety, law enforcement safety, and the safety, as best as you can accomplish it, of the delirious subject. **Please refer to Appendix A for a detailed protocol on response to Excited Delirium that can be implemented (and adapted as needed) in your facility.**

Greater knowledge about this syndrome has led to several new problems:

- The protocol for **Excited Delirium** is to subdue the individual as quickly as possible to get them the medical attention they need, as well as protecting everyone from the appalling violence they may enact. As most mentally ill individuals, including severely disorganized people, are NOT in excited delirium states, this protocol can seem to directly contradict the model of verbal de-escalation we have offered in this book. In brief, with most mentally ill individuals, take extra time to talk them into compliance; but with individuals manifesting excited delirium, subdue them as quickly as possible. However, a careful reading of this text reveals a fine-tuned set of interventions, including how to approach a disorganized individual, even one manifesting **Chaotic Rage**. As we have emphasized throughout the text that assessment is behaviorally based, any dangerous behavior on the part of the person of concern should elicit a well-practiced physical response.

- Because **Excited Delirium** has finally begun to be recognized by the medical community as a genuine medical syndrome, this could conceivably complicate things for officers. Psychosis, unlike schizophrenia, is a general term. However, if an officer uses the term Excited Delirium, he or she might be accused of diagnosing the person. Therefore, we recommend the use of the general term, **Chaotic Rage**, in establishing your protocols, because it is fully descriptive, encompassing both the disorganization AND the agitation that such individuals display. Furthermore, the officer isn't required to make a distinction between a person with genuine excited delirium, from a pruno intoxicated elderly inmate who also has mild Alzheimer's Disorder or a distraught grief-stricken inmate in a chaotic state. All parties can use this descriptive term, which will activate a specific protocol, without running the risk of being either over-specific or being accused of engaging in amateur diagnosis. Medical staff will sort out the genuine excited delirium cases, from others, and render appropriate aid in each case. The correctional officers' protocol is the same, whenever someone presents with a chaotic rage set of behaviors.

CHAPTER 68

Terrified Rage

Figure 68.1 Terrified Rage Versus Chaotic Rage

Be aware that the line between terrified rage and chaotic rage can be very fine. The terrified inmate, overwhelmed, can shift into chaotic rage. When facing an inmate in a state of either pure terror or terrified rage, be prepared, therefore, to shift to protocols suitable to assisting individuals in chaotic states **(Chapter 67)**.

What Terrified Rage Looks Like

Terrified inmates believe that they will be violated or abused. They appear apprehensive and furtive, looking halfway ready to run, halfway ready to strike. Their voice can be pleading, whiny, or fearful, and their eyes are often wide-open or darting from place to place.

Figure 68.2 Caution: Do Not Rely on the Inmates Eyes as Your Only Assessment Tool

Wide-open eyes don't always indicate fear. In the case of fear, the muscles <u>under</u> the eyes are also slack, giving the face a pleading look. Even though the terrified person may be looking in your direction, they usually don't look *into* your eyes, nor do they want you to look into theirs. The enraged, aggressive individual with wide-open eyes, on the other hand, displays tension around the eyes. Furthermore, they often look penetratingly into your eyes, or *through* you.

The mouths of some terrified inmates gape open slightly, as they breathe in panicky, short gasps, while others press their lips together in a quivering pucker. Their skin tone is often ashen (if dark skinned) or pale. Some make threatening gestures with a flailing overhand blow, while others primarily use a fending off gesture, as if trying to ward off attack. Their body posture can be described as concave, as they pull away from you or hold themselves tightly in fear. Terrified inmates also exhibit heightened levels of physical arousal, accompanied by panting, sweating, and/or trembling. They may back themselves into a wall or corner. They also may yell, seeming to be threatening and pleading simultaneously, using such phrases as, "Stay back! You get away from me! I will hit you!! I will! You stay back!" There is a hollow quality to the voice as if there is not "foundation." This is due to the tightening of the abdomen and diaphragm, so that not only breathing, but also speech is high in their chest.

Causes for Terrified Rage

Severely frightened inmates often suffer from paranoid delusions, fear of the unknown or terrifying hallucinations. At other times, they are afraid of a loss of control or of being laughed at or humiliated. Some are afraid that they are in terrible trouble with someone based on psychotic delusions. Finally, for any one of a number of reasons, they are simply terrified of you. **Imagine a snarling wolf cornered, backed up against a cliff face.** It is a frightened animal with fangs—do you think that what it really needs right now is a hug?

De-Escalation of Terrified Rage

Your goal here is to reduce the inmate's sense of danger. Maintain a safe, distance, and relax your posture. Make sure your movements are unhurried, and that your voice is firm, confident, and reassuring. If direct eye contact is reassuring for the inmate, do so; if intimidating, don't. How will you know? Notice if their body relaxes or tenses in response to your eye contact or its lack. Of course, you should never take your eyes *off* of them. Do not look penetratingly into their eyes if they are terrified by the eye contact.

Initiate a litany of reassuring phrases, speaking <u>slowly</u>, with frequent pauses: "I know you are scared, that's okay. Put down the chair, you don't need that. I keep it safe here. You can put it down now. I'm way over here. Go ahead. Sit down. I keep it safe here." Don't say, "I'll protect you" or "I won't hurt you." Many inmates who go into terrified rage have been hurt by people who said those kinds of phrases. However, when you say "I keep **it** safe here," you are telling them, "This is my territory and no one, including you, will be hurt on my territory. I am taking responsibility, and because of me, you will be safe."

By saying something similar to what they expect to hear, yet somehow different, you cause a "glitch" in their thought process. "What did he say?" He didn't say, "I'll keep you safe." "What's different in what he said?" You thereby cause him to "re-engage" the parts of his brain that actually thinks things through as opposed that which just reacts.

The inmate's body language will also indicate that they are calming down. Their breathing will get a little shuddery or be expressed in short high-pitched gasps. They may slump onto their bunk or onto the floor as if physically exhausted, even beginning to weep. Maintain your reassuring litany, and slowly approach them. If they show signs of becoming frightened again, pause, move back slightly, and continue to speak to them reassuringly.

As you approach the inmate, move in "half steps." For example, move the right foot a full step, then bring the left foot *up* to the right foot—pause. Move either right or left foot forward, and then bring the other foot forward *up* to the lead foot—pause. The advantage of moving this way is that you stay balanced, in case the inmate suddenly attacks. Additionally, if the inmate becomes somewhat agitated, you can smoothly ease backward, creating more space between you, and continue your verbal control.

CHAPTER 69

Hot Rage

Figure 69.1 Some Good Advice

"Hot rage explodes when officers can't calm the inmate down for a variety of reasons, didn't take the time to calm them down, or the officers themselves were so pissed off that *they* got the inmate into that stage. One out of three is not our fault. Three out of three become our responsibility." Quote from veteran officer.

When you think of an inmate who is on the edge of violence, hot rage usually comes to mind. Think of an individual who is yelling and screaming, brandishing their fists or another weapon, and threatening to do harm; they throw things, tip over chairs, and engage in other forms of violent behavior.

Such behaviors are often thought to be instinctual, a product of our primitive "flight or fight" response to danger. However, instinctual aggression is usually uncoordinated and flailing, and falls under the category of terrorized or chaotic aggression.

Hot rage, however, is coordinated: a learned behavior, trained through repetition, learned through modeling, and reinforced through success. This doesn't mean that hot rage is the equivalent of the actions of a professional fighter, who coolly and calmly prepares his line of attack and focuses his aggression on his opponent. Instead, hot rage is a deeply ingrained combination of primitive drives and trained actions. Such pseudo-instinctual behaviors are actions that have either been repeated so often, or are so ingrained in powerful early experiences that they function almost like reflexes. For example, some inmates with long histories of abuse lash out in rage whenever frightened, with no ability to evaluate whether or not they are currently in danger. At the same time, they target where best to hit, and frequently, choose a time and a place where they believe they have the best chance of success.

On a more functional level, a good street fighter who loses his temper does not necessarily lose his coordination. He does his best to knock his opponent senseless, but he automatically takes a stance with chin tucked in—shoulders rolled forward, and punches with his entire body lined up so that his body weight and the torque of his hips amplify the power of the blow.

General Information About Hot Rage

The more often someone goes into a state of hot rage, the more comfortable he/she is with their rage, and the easier it becomes to be violent. Hot rage is often a behavior that has led to short-term success in the past, such as scaring and beating a selected victim either for criminal gain or just for the fun of it. In a state of hot rage, such an inmate has no concern about longer-term consequences, much less guilt. For some, there is a sense of liberation, even a paradoxical kind of joy when they peak into rage. All one's fears and insecurities disappear, and one is left with only the ecstasy of the pure act. For this reason, some inmates desire rage, because that ecstatic state is, to them, the best thing they ever feel.

Displacement. This is a common factor of hot rage, meaning the inmate's anger is displaced, at least temporarily, toward an inanimate object instead of you, or another individual. This also includes picking things up and slamming them down, throwing things, punching or kicking walls, furniture, or other nearby objects. More predatory inmates use displacement as a tactic to make the target of their aggression more fearful, while warming themselves up for an attack.

Peer Group Influence. Hot rage is also associated with peer group influence and masculine display, a primitive attempt to dominate a group or eliminate perceived competition. This can be especially problematic if the inmate begins acting out ("fronting") in front of a group of onlookers, and then, to save face, he or she must attack anyone representing authority.

Frustration. Frustration does not usually elicit rage in normal people. When frustrated desires are coupled with something personal, the inmate may use rage and even violence as a way of either trying to force what they want, or to destroy what they perceive as keeping them from it. Hot rage can be a "transference" in which the correctional officer is a representative or stand-in for someone else who frustrated or controlled them. In their mind, you are the emblem of everyone who ever controlled them or put them down, an agent of an oppressive society, or simply a legitimate target to express hatred and violence.

There are various types of hot rage, each typified by almost unendurably intense feelings. We distinguish three subtypes: Fury, Bluffing, and Aggressive-Manipulation. These three subtypes will be discussed later in this chapter.

Figure 69.2 Example: Hot Rage Escalates Into Violence

An inmate sees a hardened con select out a young new inmate for sexual assault. He is setting him up, by giving him cigarettes, a debt he will not be able to pay. To the first inmate, this kid looks just like his own son, and he intervenes, saying, "That's just a kid. Let him be." The angry rapist shoves him and says, "Mind your own business, or I'll give it to you, too."

The man later described hearing a high-pitched noise, and his vision turning black-and-white. He comes to finding himself atop the man, pounding his face into the concrete.

General De-Escalation of Hot Rage: The Ladder

The primary method of de-escalation for hot rage is called "The Ladder." This is an ideal technique for someone who is beginning to get threatening. It is used only for rage, that gray zone between anger (even extreme anger) and violence. The inmate is no longer trying to communicate with you, and they are right on the edge of assault—in a sense, doing a war dance to work out inhibitions to committing violence.

The technique itself is simple. Identify the most dangerous behavior and repetitively demand that it cease. Use short sentences and easily understood commands. Once they stop that particular dangerous behavior, identify the next problematic behavior and use the same technique, continuing until the inmate is under control. **This technique is only effective right before, during, and after the peak of the crisis** because it is a control tactic rather than the "Lining Up" de-escalation tactic used for anger. Control tactics will provoke rage in a merely angry inmate, someone we might have over-estimated, due to his loud tone, or dramatic behaviors. **As described earlier, facing an enraged inmate causes us to experience fear in a way that anger does not.** The danger is NOW, not merely a possibility should the situation continue to deteriorate.

Establishing a Hierarchy of Danger

The general hierarchy of dangerous behaviors, from most to least, is as follows:
- Brandishing an object or a weapon in a menacing way (NOTE: If they are too close, or are trying to use the weapon, this is violence, not rage.).
- Approaching or standing too close to you with menacing intent (NOTE: if they are too close, or approaching too fast, this, too, is violence).
- Kicking objects, punching walls, or throwing things around (displacement activity).
- Pacing, stomping, and inflating the body in an aggressive manner (posturing).
- Shouting or talking in low, menacing tones.
- Using language that is intended to violate, demean, or degrade.

The Ladder is not merely a verbal intervention. Like any other control tactic with an aggressive inmate, you must move as needed to maintain the optimum space to both defend yourself, and exert maximum influence upon the aggressor. If they are very close or threatening, not only should your hands be up, prepared to ward off any attack, but also as a gesture that is both calming and dominant. On other occasions, you should, as previously described, clasp the wrist of one hand with the other hand.

Give the inmate a straightforward command to stop their most dangerous behavior. By keeping things so simple, you can use your mind to look for escape routes, where weapons might be, or how to get help. By holding to a demand that the most dangerous behavior cease, you are displaying clarity and strength to the aggressor, as well as helping him or her focus *their mind* on the most problematic thing he or she is doing. You should not scream or shout—that won't get through, and will increase their aggressive energy. Rather, your voice should be strong, low, and commanding **(Chapter 54)**.

After a couple of repetitions, always add, "We'll talk about it when you...." followed by the same command. Once that behavior is stopped, pick the next most problematic behavior (the next "rung" of the ladder), and command/require that it stop. If the aggressor does calm down and stops **all** the aggressive behaviors, including assaultive language, THEN set a firm and direct limit.

This is not the time to try and think of something brilliant or life changing to say. By keeping things simple, you can continue to look for escape routes, identify potential weapons, and attempt to get help. You should intersperse your sentences frequently with their name, using this to pace and break the rhythm of your commands, as well as "calling them back" to a more personal interaction. In addition, by holding to a demand that a specific behavior stop, you are helping them focus *their mind* on their most problematic behavior, then the next, and on down the rungs of the ladder. Continue working your way down the rungs until the inmate is no longer in a state of rage. If the inmate re-escalates to a higher and more dangerous activity, simply return to that rung of the ladder and begin again. Remember to stand and use your voice as described in the previous sections.

The last "rung" is probably swearing or other obscene language. Remember, some inmates swear as punctuation, without any hostile intent. They may be crude, but they are not trying to be verbally violent. If that kind of language offends you, it is something you will deal with at another time, during moments of calm. However, if the swearing is an attempt to violate you, it **must** be dealt with in proper order. However, don't focus on the language, no matter how vile, if the person is *doing* something dangerous. Remember that predatory inmates will use language to shock, distract, immobilize, or terrorize. Their behavior is far more dangerous than anything they are saying.

Figure 69.3 CAUTION: The Ladder Is for Rage, Not Anger
Remember, the Ladder should only be used with an enraged inmate. Using this technique with an angry individual will cause them to escalate into rage. In most cases, de-escalation tactics suitable to dealing with angry inmates are sufficient.

Figure 69.4 Example of the Ladder
Your voice is firm, low pitched and commanding, as you "descend" down the rungs. In the following scenario, each statement is, of course, in response to something the aggressor has done or said. Don't talk too fast. Command presence, not hysteria!

1. "Step back, Step back, Jameson, we'll talk about it when you step back." **Continuing,** "Jameson, Step back, Step back, Jameson, we will talk about it when you step back."
2. "Stop kicking things, Jameson, Stop kicking things. We'll talk about it when you stop kicking things."
3. "Jameson, I can't follow you when you pace around, sit down and we can talk, Sit down, Jameson."

*Notice the paradoxical message, that you can't "follow" him. Of course you could, if you wanted to. This is another example of what we call a "brain glitch," the same as we do with the individual in **Terrified Rage**, when we say, "I keep it safe here." You are trying to catch their attention as they try to make sense of what you said. We want them thinking again, trying to figure out what you said and why you said it. We want the part of the brain that thinks things through taking over from the part that is driving them towards violence.*

Imagine they have stepped forward again, thus ascending to a higher "rung" on the ladder.
1. "Step back! Jameson! Step back and we'll talk. We will TALK about it when you step back, Jameson. Step - - - - -back."
2. "Sit down Jameson. We will talk about it when you sit down. We can't talk when you are walking around. We will talk about it when you sit down."
3. "Lower your voice. I can't hear you when you yell that loud. Lower you voice and we will talk."

Here is a second paradoxical communication. Of course, you can hear an aggressor who is shouting loudly. Once again, you are trying to create a "glitch" where he tries to figure out what you mean when you say you can't hear him when he is yelling.

"Talk to me with the same respect that I talk to you. We will talk about it when you stop swearing. Stop swearing. Jameson. We will talk when you talk to me with respect, the same way I talk to you."

Remember, people often swear as punctuation. They have no hostile intent whatsoever. If the individual is swearing in this manner, it is not a problem. For example, "Officer, I'm sorry, I was just mad at my f**king case manager, and s**t, you happened to arrive at just the wrong damn moment."

*However, if the swearing is an attempt to violate you, it **must** be dealt with in proper order. However, don't focus on the language, no matter how vile, if the aggressor is doing something dangerous. Remember that predatory individuals will use language to shock, distract, immobilize or terrorize. What they are **doing** is far more dangerous than anything they are saying.*

Hot Rage Subtype #1: Fury

What does fury look like? Furious inmates are very tense, looking as if they are about to explode. **For a mental image, if they are of big stature, think of a grizzly bear; if they are smaller, think of a wolverine.** In either case, the image suggests an animal that will tear you to pieces if it perceives danger, if provoked, or if cornered. Many inmates, both with a mental health diagnoses and without, display fury, and it is particularly common among those who have suffered head injuries. Furious inmates may show some of the following physical manifestations of their rage:

- Their skin tone is flushed as they become angered, turning red or purplish in color. As they become even more enraged however, their skin blanches, and they turn pale or gray (depending on their skin tone), as the blood pools in the internal organs.
- Their voice, whether loud, or low and quiet, has a menacing and belligerent tone.
- They often pace, inflate their upper body, hit or kick objects, or strike their hands together ominously, punching one fist into the other hand.
- They tend to stare into your eyes directly, glowering from under their brow, with a furious and hostile look on their face.
- Their eyes will appear red or inflamed; usually their eyes are wide open, with tension around the eye sockets and facial muscles.
- Physical arousal, blood pressure, and muscular tension all increase. You may notice veins popping out of the skin, particularly around the neck.
- They may display a smile that shows no humor or joy. Others snarl, or compress their lips with a twist, as if they have a foul taste in their mouth. Still others bare their teeth, or clench their jaws so tightly that the muscles stand out in bunches.
- They are very impulsive, and unconcerned with possible consequences.
- Their breathing is often loud and strained.
- They may claim to be disrespected, humiliated, or shamed. Others will allege that they are not getting their questions answered and their problem solved, or that no one listened or cared. They may rant about "the system" and claim that they are out of alternatives or solutions. This is not "communication." They are doing this to "jack themselves up," to justify the violence they desire to enact.
- At their most dangerous point, they may become calm, break off eye-contact, or adopt a thousand-yard stare.

When confronting a furious inmate your posture and tone should be confident, commanding, even imposing. Maintain direct eye contact, and frequently use their name. Stand directly in front of the inmate, using a blade stance, but out of range of an immediate blow. This best prepares you to escape along tangents to his attack, to ward off blows, and if necessary, to fight back. With the blade stance, you are already "chambered" to do this. As described earlier, your hands are either up in a fence, or the wrist of one arm is clasped in the hand of the other in front of you at waist level, or in many situations, you already have your weapon(s) in hand.

Stand too close and you will appear to be challenging them, too far and you will be seen as fearful—a potential victim. You may have to move forward or backward to maintain this spacing. In either event, move smoothly, without flinching on the one hand or any sudden or threatening gestures on the other. When you move with a relaxed body, you are more ready to protect yourself, yet you don't appear as if you are trying to initiate a physical altercation.

Your voice is strong and forceful. Don't, however, shout. Instead, keep your voice low-pitched and calm, dropping it into your chest where it resonates, as enraged people, in particular, react violently to threatening or angry vocal tones. The only time you would shout is a "battle cry" that you use only when you are trying to stop an actual attack.

You will use the Ladder in its most orthodox form—with your voice pitched low and powerful. You should feel it vibrate in your chest. The inmate will exhibit one of only three actions:

- They keep on coming—you will do what you have to do ensure safety.
- They get close and when you tell them to step back, they say, "make me"—you will do what you have to do to ensure safety.
- They comply—when individuals in hot rage comply with the command to step back, they usually do so yelling and screaming—"you can't tell me what to do." You will continue down the ladder, step by step.

Once you have them de-escalated, you must maintain control. This can mean anything from taking them into custody to simply "reading them the riot act" and putting them on notice that they came dangerously close to being hurt. Only <u>after</u> setting very strong limits would you shift into problem-solving, even with a mentally ill individual. Otherwise, they will assume that the best way to get a reward—your attention or help—is to abuse you.

Hot Rage Subtype #2: Bluff Aggression

In keeping with the animal analogy when describing the furious inmate, **the aggressively bluffing inmate is like a gorilla beating his chest, a display of aggression designed to keep you at a distance.** There is a sense of bluster rather than the pent-up pressure of the enraged inmate. However, their manifest behavior appears much the same as the individual displaying fury, hence the image of the enraged gorilla. At fifty yards, could you tell the difference between a charging gorilla and a charging grizzly bear? Both are huge, hairy beasts that apparently mean you harm. In all likelihood, the gorilla would prefer to be left alone, rather than engaging in combat, but he postures as if he wants nothing more than tear you to pieces: if he perceives no other alternative, he will.

How can you tell the difference between a furious inmate and a bluffer, if their behaviors are so similar? When facing a furious inmate, fear/adrenaline is your natural and likely response. You instinctual mind, that part of you that places survival above all else, demands your immediate attention, and it uses fear to accomplish this. An aggressive bluffer, in a state of hot rage, may also elicit fear, but this fear will be accompanied by another emotion. You will find yourself a bit irritated, thinking how stupid (yet potentially dangerous) this incident has become, and that if the bluffer was not in front of other inmates, or in another case, if someone had not chosen to taunt him as being less than a man, this dangerous situation would never have developed.

The enraged bluffer *often* displays aggression for the benefit of friends or other onlookers. On many occasions these people have provoked him or her to "prove" they are tough. In reality, they are actually *frightened that they will be found out as being frightened, intimidated, or succumbing to authority.* These inmates can become quite violent if they feel a strong sense of peer pressure to resist your commands and efforts to de-escalate them. Because they are performing in front of an audience, they will often attack to protect their image. Sometimes bluffers are alone, but they still have an audience, an image inside their own head to which they believe they must conform. You will often hear this in their self-talk as they amp themselves up. "You don't know who you are talking to. Do you believe this guy? Do you have any idea who I am?"

Many bullies, having a long record of violence, actually function day-to-day in "bluff mode." They are in a perpetual quest to prove to others, and even more so, themselves, that they are not frightened or insecure. As a result, they repeatedly solicit situations where they must either intimidate others or resort to violence. Correctional officers must short-circuit this behavior.

One thing which lone correctional officers simply shouldn't do is to try and "out tough" the inmate by refusing to back down or leave the scene. This is merely bluffing behavior *on your part*, and the inmate's audience will only amplify their calls for the inmate to be even more resistant. As the authors have stated many times throughout this book, don't personalize any of your encounters with your inmates, and if professional prudence dictates that you should retreat, then do so!

Correctional officers need to recognize that the aggressive bluffer is not really in confrontation with you; they are *pretending* that they are, and are dangerous because they may believe they need to prove themselves by refusing to back-down. Another aspect of bluffing is that when frightened, the bluffing inmate will move towards you, so that no one will see how frightened they truly are.

When you have sufficient force, or there is no retreat possible, control using the Ladder, much as you would with an individual in fury, but with a much more <u>matter-of-fact tone</u>. Your eye-contact, too, is matter-of-fact, as if you are having a conversation rather than a confrontation. Rather than having your hands in front of you (either clasped or in a fence position), open your hands, slightly to the sides, palm up. You can still protect yourself just as easily, but your posture appears non-threatening, more open and relaxed. Your body language expresses, "there is no *need* for a fight here." Remember, these inmates will attack out of the fear of being "found out" by their peers. Your task becomes one of *helping them to save face*, rather than issuing forceful commands and instructions. In doing so, you will greatly reduce the risk of violence. However, correctional officers can't allow the inmate to *win the encounter* with concessions or agreements, and there must be some form of consequence subsequent to the resolution of the crisis. The imposition of punishment or consequences can come later, especially if the inmate is *not* taken into immediate custody.

When exerting verbal control on the enraged bluffer:

1. Don't point out their fears in front of others. They will feel the need to defend their honor.
2. Don't try to be more forceful than they are, or appear overly domineering or condescending, as their self-image may require them to strike out. <u>If they are not responsive to a more low-key approach and continue to escalate, you may have a furious inmate (see above) who happens to be in front of other people or a bluffer who has shifted into fury</u>. In this case, you **"turn up the dial,"** adopting a more powerful tone and stance, and shifting into the more forceful version of the Ladder technique for the furious individual.
3. Remember, the inmate's audience is what makes them dangerous. If possible, removing them from their audience will often result in the inmate calming down on their own.

Figure 69.5 The Bluffer's Strut

When you tell such an inmate to step back and do it well, aggressive bluffers often strut back with a smirk, sometimes glancing around and making eye-contact with onlookers. This is for the benefit of the audience, and their own self-image. They are trying to show that they are not afraid, and in control of the situation.

Figure 69.6 The Bluffer

Speaking to a person who was in Bluff-Rage after you have them under control:

"Morrison, I'm glad this worked out with no one getting hurt. Had you not chosen to sit down and talk, you very likely would have ended up being face down on the floor. No. Listen to me for a minute. I'm not disrespecting you—that's why you and I are over here talking instead of in front of them *(indicating the onlookers)*. I'm telling you, it was a very near thing. Again, I'm glad this has worked out that you and I are standing here talking."

"Next time, though, don't do this in front of <u>them</u>" *(referring to the other inmates for whom he was on display, and actually put a little contempt in your voice when you say the word 'them' as if to indicate that Morrison is better/cooler/stronger than those people he is trying to impress.)*

"Come to me and talk to me one man to another" OR "one woman to another" ("one adult to another" in male-female conversations). "You shouldn't put your personal business in front of them." You will observe him "puff up," feeling himself to be flattered. You then continue, "Okay. Are we clear for next time?" "Good. Now as for this time...." Then set the same types of limits as you did with the individual in a state of FURY, which will often include the phrase, "You are going the "hole. You can walk or you can be dragged. I'd prefer that those guys don't have to see you getting dragged. But that's up to you."

They are more likely to accept the disciplinary action when their ego is built up enough to take the hit.

Hot Rage Subtype #3: Controlling Aggressive Manipulation

Aggressive manipulation is a *strategy*, not a symptom of illness. Such inmates are calculating, trying to monitor the effects of their actions. They are not constrained by feelings of honor, integrity, or pride; their goal is win any way they can. Sometimes, you can tell when you are being manipulated ("played") because you are confused about why the inmate is upset, or the purpose of his argument. The aggressive manipulator changes either his mood or the subject of the complaint frequently, displaying some or all of the behaviors of manipulative and psychopathic individuals **(Section VI)**.

Aggressive-manipulative inmates may have a long history of losing control, particularly when their desires are frustrated, or when they believe they are not given what they feel they are entitled. They frequently have a history of various character disorders (habitual behavioral styles that make others miserable).

These inmates may approach you with flattery, or a plea for something, explaining their dilemma in great detail with talk of their suffering. Once their request is denied, however, they blame or criticize you for their troubles, inferring that your refusal will result in furthering their suffering or cause them irreparable harm. They might try to make you feel guilty, or begin to demean you, shifting to subtle threats of violence. They may talk in an arrogant manner, trying to make you look incompetent to others or stupid to you. They often claim to be victims, basing this on either real or imaginary issues. Furthermore, they may use their "status" as a member of an oppressed or victimized class of people as a means of intimidating others, making their demands in a whiny, accusatory voice. Such inmates will recall past grievances, adding their current crisis to the list of prior accusations. They will tell you how you are just like someone else who wronged them. They ask frequent or repetitive questions.

Manipulation does not mean false threat, and manipulative inmates will often harm others. The difference between an aggressive-manipulator and those in a state of pure fury is that the furious inmate's inhibitions are swept aside by their rage. You will often hear terms like "He just lost it" to explain such behavior. The aggressive-manipulator, on the other hand, attempts to monitor your responses and the situation as a whole to assess if his actions and behaviors are successful. Although the inmate's behavior may be calculating, that does not mean he is in control. As he becomes more and more agitated, his judgment deteriorates, and he may concoct a rationalization for violence that makes sense to him in the moment.

Control tactics for aggressive manipulators. Inmates who use this strategy attempt to twist your feelings and emotions, making you doubt yourself, making you ashamed or scared, for example, to get what they want. Don't buy into it. <u>If you recognize this strategy early on in your interaction with the inmate, the best strategy is to cut it off at the onset.</u> **The symbolic image for these inmates is a large rat——NOT because it is meant to be demeaning, but because rats are survivors. They are all about winning, not honor, not image, winning by whatever means they can. Dealing with the aggressive-manipulator is like being placed in a maze. Your task is to walk right through the walls.** If, however, the manipulative inmate begins to escalate his or her strategies, you may have to use the Ladder as a means of control and de-escalation. In this case, however, your tone of voice should be matter-of fact and slightly detached.

Making eye contact enables another person to truly see you as you are, and in return, see them as well. Aggressive-manipulative inmates don't care about you, and they use apparent feelings of contact and intimacy to "read" you and control others. They are interested in gaining information that they can use to their benefit. Similarly, they will use their own eyes to create a false sense of trust or intimacy, as it suits them to confuse you, misdirect your attention, or dominate you. Rather than making eye contact, look past one ear.

Figure 69.7 Don't Look Away

Don't look away. While looking past an ear, you can still see what they are doing. If you look away, you will be assaulted and not even know it is coming. This disengaged look, done properly, indicates that you won't participate in the degradation that manipulation creates.

The Ladder for aggressive manipulators. If your attempts at control and de-escalation of their manipulative strategies are unsuccessful, the inmate may escalate into a rage state. What distinguishes this from pure fury is that, even now, they continue to read and monitor you for advantage. Internally, they are asking: have they succeeded in intimidating you; have they succeeded in distracting or throwing you off balance so that you are open to an attack; have they got you trying to "bargain" your way to safety? At the same time, they begin to "lose it," as it becomes more apparent that their strategic application of intimidation is unsuccessful. Furthermore, they get increasingly frustrated because they believe their manipulation *should* be working, primarily because it has worked so well for them in the past.

In essence, aggressive-manipulative rage is a merger of hot rage and predatory rage (see other chapters in this section). When dealing with such inmates, correctional officers should:

- Stand relaxed and ready to evade a blow and counter the attack.
- Express flat disinterest in their demands, accusations, and complaints.
- Use the repetitive commands of the ladder technique. Your vocal tone should be flat. Don't negotiate. Don't discuss other matters as long as the manipulative behavior continues.

Several things can happen with the aggressive-manipulative inmate when you attempt to control their rage:

- Your flat disinterest indicates that they can't "get to you." After trying several different avenues, they give up, or shift to another strategy.
- In more heated situations, they will flare into a fury (or pseudo-fury).
- When you "lock in" eye-contact, they may "bounce" off into another tactic—sudden tears for example.
- If the behavior does not stop immediately upon being "hit" with your eyes, this means that an attack is imminent. You will shift into the de-escalation techniques used for controlling fury, or take appropriate action to ensure your safety in the event of violence.

Figure 69.8 Locking Eyes (THE LOOP)

If the inmate escalates into *fury*, or if they continue to be otherwise non-compliant, turn from looking past the ear to looking right in their eyes, accompanied by a firm command to stop what they are doing. When you turn your head to look directly in their eyes, roll it slightly up and then down as if sighting a weapon. Speak powerfully and directly, just as you do with the inmate who is in a state of fury. If you have ever raised a teenager, you have almost surely done this. In essence, once you make eye-contact with the aggressive-manipulative inmate, treat them as you would the furious type.

CHAPTER 70

Predatory or Cool Rage

Inmates with this type of rage are intimidators who threaten with either vague innuendoes or explicit threats. Their aggressive behavior is calculated, but unlike the manipulator, violence is often their first choice rather than one of many options. The predatory inmate may deliver threats in cool, dangerous tones, often *after* a clear and strongly stated demand. Then they offer you a chance to avoid injury if you comply. A variant tactic is to pretend being out of control. This is in contrast to a genuine attack, an action that they are eminently capable of and willing to carry out. Our symbol for them is either a leopard or a shark, depending on if they present as "warm-blooded" or "stone cold."

While these inmates seethe with hostility and contempt for others, they have developed these emotions as a deliberate weapon of terror, perhaps even enjoyment. Paradoxically, their physical arousal is often low. Their heart rate can actually go down and they can be charming and engaging, even as they prepare to commit an act of violence. This disconnect between appearances and intentions can cause some correctional officers to lower their guard because they may have a hard time believing that such a seemingly nice guy is ready and willing to terrorize others psychologically, or hurt them physically.

These inmates actually have no inhibitions regarding their aggression other than tactical calculation or self-interest. They have no capacity for sympathy or guilt, and many experience low-levels of anxiety in situations that would frighten ordinary people. Every time they intimidate someone successfully, their behavior is reinforced, and they view non-action on your part, either during the confrontation or afterward, as either weakness or tacit approval, thereby increasing the likelihood of similar behavior in the future.

The best response is a combination of overwhelming force and respect.[48] The former is obvious. Never be in a situation where you are vulnerable with such an individual. "Respect" means, simply, that you make your control "institutional," not "personal." When you are dealing with them, they should not have a problem with you, personally—their problem is between themselves and correctional facility, whose rules they are breaking. As a correctional officer, you are merely the agent of that institution.

What to Do When You Don't Have Overwhelming Force

Your basic task is to demonstrate that you are not prey, and that the inmate's attempts at intimidation will simply not work. **Symbolically, they are like a leopard or a shark, depending on if their style is warm-blooded or cold.**

Most predatory inmates don't wish to interact with someone whom they *don't* intimidate or otherwise control through emotional abuse or physical posturing. Instead, they seek more conciliatory and subservient victims, where their chances of success are great. When engaging a predatory inmate correctional officers should remember the following:

- Stand or sit ready to move. Be poised, but don't appear fearful or too defensive.
- Avoid gesturing or expressive movements. Fear often causes your movements to be awkward, and the inmate will see this as confirmation of their control over you.
- Be open and strategic in everything you do: the way you position your body, your voice, and your posture. The predator is skilled in reading body language and assessing weakness. Protect yourself openly, and don't change your actions based on what they say, i.e., their efforts to put you at ease or promises of compliance. Another tactic the predator may use in these circumstances is to use anything you do against you, either deriding you or pretending that you are out of control, paranoid, or acting strangely. Ignore all that, and openly act to keep yourself safe. For example, "Do you really think you can get to that Taser before I can get to you?"
- Don't make explicit or unrealistic threats, such as, "If any of your boys come near my family, I will kill you!" To the predator, that tells him what you won't do. In his mind, if you really meant it, you would do it now. An explicit threat is an empty threat.
- Don't over-react to vague threats, or he or she will interpret your reaction as a victory. If however, the inmate makes an explicit threat to harm you then they should be taken into custody immediately or shortly after the encounter (after you have removed yourself from the situation safely and returned with sufficient force). Correctional officers can't allow *any* inmate to threaten them with physical violence without the swift and sure response of punishment.
- Don't comply with any of the inmate's orders or demands that you *should not* carry out your professional duties and responsibilities.

Cryptic Consequences: Your Strategic Response to the Predator When You Don't Have Overwhelming Force and Need to Extricate Yourself From the Situation

Keep your voice matter-of-fact, and give clear and direct statements of *potential* consequences. If you can, smile. **These consequences are of a special type, clear, but cryptic,** e.g., "You know what would happen if you did that." In this case, don't tell them what would happen. Let their imagination take over. These vague consequences are a mirror of their own method of intimidation, and they may react to you as "not prey, not edible, not worth the trouble."

- If they say, "What are you talking about?" you should reply, "You know exactly what I am talking about." When the predator responds to your cryptic consequence with questions or with confusing statements that would make your statement illogical, simply say, "You know what is going on here. You know what is happening."

- You may have to intersperse your vague consequences with Ladder commands if they escalate their behavior.

- Try to minimize eye contact. However, you need to look directly at them, so look between their eyes, or look with an empty stare. Imagine turning your eyes to buttons. They will look like a cut-out or silhouette. Your eyes are flat, with no attempt to "penetrate" or make contact. (You should make sustained eye-contact only if in a fight for your life. Then, you must shift focus, trying to penetrate his or her eyes as if you were a laser beam).

- Don't over-react to threats, or they will interpret your reaction as a victory.

- Your entire goal is to convince them that it isn't worth it to hurt you. Once you have succeeded and are free, you need to get help.

To reiterate, you don't have to prove that you're bigger, tougher, or more dangerous. You're establishing that you're merely on to their game and aren't, by nature, someone to victimize. Like a leopard who chooses *not* to chase an antelope because it is moving too smoothly, showing that it is healthy and strong, the predator is likely to disengage if you don't give him anything to discount (an attempt to intimidate them with a direct threat) or if you try to negotiate (something they have no interest in).

Figure 70.1 Example: Interaction With Predatory Inmate When the Officer is Without Back-up and Cannot Escape

Predator. "Look, this is very simple. I think you and I can agree that you misinterpreted what I said about payback. Look, I understand. You must have been having a bad day, and you over-reacted. This can be fixed very easily. Just call the captain and tell them that you didn't quote me accurately, that you've been overworked lately and misjudged the situation. See, I bet you love your family as much as I do. You've got your child in a good school over at Echo Lake. Actually, it's amazing, that's one of the last schools in this area that still lets the kids out for recess. Oh, sorry, I'm a little off track. What I'm saying is that I bet you would be devastated if anything happened to your family. I'm the same. I am really worried that a misunderstanding could cause me to lose my "good time," and my child will be deprived of his father that much longer. You are the problem that is happening to my family! And this is a problem you could fix, unless you are really sitting there telling me that you want to destroy my life and that of my child. IS THAT WHAT YOU ARE SAYING??!!!!"

CORRECTIONAL OFFICER. *(With a little smile and a strong, confident voice)* "I am really glad we are having this conversation, because it's good that we both understand each other."

Predator. "So you'll make the call."

CORRECTIONAL OFFICER. "Oh, you know what's going to happen."

Predator. "Suppose you tell me."

CORRECTIONAL OFFICER. "There's no need to do that. You know exactly what's going on."

Predator. "Are you threatening me?"

CORRECTIONAL OFFICER. "I don't know where you got that idea. In fact, we both know the situation here."

Predator. *(Walking away)* "You think this is over. You better watch your back."

To reiterate, you don't have to prove that you are bigger, tougher, or more dangerous. Merely establish that you are on to his game, you are not someone who will be victimized, and that there will certainly be consequences for their actions. Predatory inmates are likely to disengage if you don't react to their threats as they wish.

Figure 70.2 CAUTION: Cryptic Consequences Are Only for the Rarest of Inmates in the Rarest of Situations

You ONLY use this strategy with the openly predatory, ONLY when they are escalating into predatory rage, **and only when you don't have sufficient force or backup to place them immediately under full control.** In other words, it should never happen, but you need to know what to do if it does.

CHAPTER 71

De-escalation of
Developmentally Disabled Inmates

Developmentally disabled inmates present a special situation. The preferred de-escalation tactics are not remarkably different for other inmates, but one must be aware of their cognitive deficits. If you use language that is too sophisticated, you may elicit more frustration and anger within the inmate by making them feel stupid. In addition, many developmentally disabled inmates are subject to magical thinking, and their beliefs about the world, and their own powers and vulnerabilities often don't conform to reality. Sometimes, correctional officers can use these beliefs to help calm this type of inmate—as you would with a child. On other occasions, one must be aware of these beliefs to keep the situation from escalating out of control.

If you try to control a developmentally disabled inmate based on their physical age and appearance, say a 250 pound, 35-year-old male, for example, things can go wrong very quickly. Most of our associates have found that once we make eye-contact, we can usually estimate the emotional age of the developmentally disabled person very quickly, among young kid or pre-teen. Then you can speak to them at their emotional age.

However, regardless of the inmate's emotional age, you can't permit their apparent childishness to compromise your physical safety. As with children, developmentally delayed inmates can be quite impulsive and unpredictable. Unlike a child however, they have the physical strength of an adult, and even more dangerously, may not recognize their own strength. For this reason the tactics for evasion, self-defense, or taking the inmate into custody are unchanged.

Correctional officers can still use tactical paraphrasing (**Chapter 57**) with an enraged developmentally disabled inmate. In this case, however, don't just sum things up calmly. Use a more dramatic voice, and over-emphasize certain words. For example, "YOU are REALLLLLY upset about having to go back to court! You really don't want to go!" Your tone is a combination of drama and enthusiasm. In essence, you are trying to catch their attention with charisma, a kind of energy in which you change the dynamics of the relationship through your voice and demeanor. Your dramatic voice validates how important the situation is to the inmate. They will find themselves in an interaction where there is no "fight" coming from you, but they perceive you as really taking them seriously.

Following the crisis, which was undoubtedly frightening and confusing to the developmentally disabled inmate, correctional officers can certainly acknowledge and validate their feelings. For example, "Mark, that was really scary. I'm glad that's over. I want you to sit in this chair now. Yeah, know you were scared, but it's over now." A detailed critique or discussion, however, may be a mistake. Because of developmentally delayed inmates cognitively impairments, their memory after an incident is usually sketchy. They are unlikely to recall or retain detailed information. Emotionally, they may react to your debriefing as a new attack. Your concern should be behavioral stability (no new attack) and reassurance because they are very likely afraid that you will punish them for their behavior.

Figure 71.1 Author's Experience With an Assaultive Developmentally Disabled Individual

A developmentally disabled woman once grabbed my finger, trying to break it. I neutralized her attempt by shifting the angle of my hand as she yanked, and as she was at the emotional age of about eight years old, rather than commanding her to "let go!" I said, "I know you want to hold my hand. You don't have to twist my finger. We can hold hands as much as you like. Sure, we can hold hands." She suddenly let go and dropped to the floor, crying.

Figure 71.2 Review: De-escalation of the Developmentally Disabled Person

Speak to them at their emotional age, not their chronological age. Use tactical paraphrasing, summarizing not only what they are apparently thinking, but what they are doing.

CHAPTER 72

Mob Rage: Feeding Frenzy

Figure 72.1 Rage State and Possibility of Violence

This discussion covers both the rage state and the possibility of violence. Pack behavior can easily escalate and therefore, it is impossible to separate rage from violence in this discussion. The discussion here concerns situations where you don't have sufficient forces to manage the mob.

Mob behavior amplifies hot rage exponentially, with one person's behavior and arousal amplifying that of those around them. The more people there are, the more likely that they will coalesce into an enraged mob, a beast of many heads, but one terrifying, destructive mind. Individually, members of a mob will display any or all of the types of rage that have been discussed throughout this section. An aggressive bluffer may try to entice those he/she is trying to impress into violence. Sometimes, mob frenzy is created and stoked by one predatory inmate who uses the mob as a weapon or distraction. When faced with such a situation the best possible solution is to escape and summon help. However, if escape is impossible attempt the following to control the mob:

- Overwhelming force. Quite simply, the most powerful method of de-escalation is a demonstration to the mob and its members that they will be stopped. Each member of the mob suddenly feels alone: "the first to go down."
- Isolating the leader as the one individual who will face the consequences. All of your psychological energy should be focused on the leader. This is particularly effective when the leader is hiding behind the power of the mob. If you perceive that the leader is manifesting manipulative, bluff, or predatory rage, make it clear that whatever happens, they will be destroyed. The goal is definitely not to shame them, especially before the mob. Instead, presenting yourself with a quiet, grave, yet powerful calm and allowing the leader to save face are essential if you have any hopes of causing him to draw his forces back. However, in most jail mob situations, there are "many leaders" and the situation is chaos to begin with. Therefore, this is rarely a viable alternative
- Build up the leader's ego by clearly identifying them as one worthy of conferring with. This is for the purpose of either drawing him away from the group, or appealing to his grandiose narcissism. If his goal is to appear important in the eyes of his mob, you may have given him what he really wants, without the need for violence.

- Break the pattern, as Discussed in **Chapter 56**, you do something so unexpected or outlandish that none of the individuals in the mob knows how to react.

Figure 72.2 Author's Experience: Breaking the Pattern in a Potential Mob Attack

About forty years ago, while hitchhiking, I was malevolently dropped off in a very dangerous area of a city during a very volatile period of racial strife. A crowd began to coalesce around me. I grabbed a stick I found on the ground, began cackling and shrieking like I'd lost my mind, hitting myself in the head, and then began dancing and whirling down the street, attacking moving cars with my stick. Everyone pulled back. I continued for about ten blocks until I reached a safer area.

To review, the best option when facing a mob is to escape and summon assistance. If you do intervene, be aware that you may have to fight for your life. Your best hope, were this terrible situation to develop, and go "berserk." Fight like a wolverine in a trap with teeth, claws, and anything else you can use, tear your way free, trying to maim your attackers as savagely as you can. The goal is to become so violent yourself that each member of the group wants to get away from you. As they recoil, hopefully, an escape route opens up.

CHAPTER 73

Deceptive Rage: Snake in the Grass

As is obvious by the subject of this book, many criminals have concurrent mental illnesses; others have spent time in a forensic unit somewhere for evaluation purposes; still others are there because they were able to fake mental illness so that they could be moved to a hospital either for a more attractive environment, or for the purposes of escape.

What do you think such inmates do, particularly the manipulative and sociopathic, while in the hospital? They victimize more vulnerable inmates, either directly, or indirectly. They have an opportunity to play with other people who easily influenced and victimized. The opportunities to torment the genuinely mentally ill are endless.

Beyond such predation, they study. Perhaps the behaviors of a truly mentally ill individual may prove advantageous someday. Perhaps it will prove useful in convincing an evaluator that they are genuinely mentally ill and of diminished capacity, not responsible for the crime they committed. Furthermore, perhaps it will give such a person an opportunity to catch someone, even a correctional officer off guard.

Such an individual obscures his/her intentions behind a screen behavior: the imitation of genuinely mentally ill individuals whom they have observed. They pretend to be psychotic, in a state of terror, distressed or needing your help. All this is for the purpose of either conning you into leaving them alone, or more dangerously, drawing you close enough so they can harm you.

Imagine a snake coiled in the leaves, pattern almost indiscernible from the ground, ready to strike.

The "de-escalation" strategy here is simple: deal with the behavior, not the cause! Imagine you have stopped a confused, psychotic appearing inmate walking down one of the hallways. What you don't realize is that a moment earlier, he was walking smoothly. Spotting you coming, he began walking in a gimping fashion, his head lolling. When he gets close, he looks frightened. You tell him to identify himself, and he replies, stumblingly, that he was just released from a crisis unit and transferred from another jail, and he's on D block, and his eyes are a little teary, and he looks so intimidated and he hunches over a little as he cries and you can't see his hands (!!!!!!!!!). What should you do? <u>Obviously, you get some distance between you, and either put a hand on your weapon</u>

<u>or your weapon in your hand, depending on your best judgment and you order them to show you their hands.</u> One of two things will result:

- As predatory individual, they slowly remove their hand and exercising due caution, you pat them down and find a shank.

- They are genuinely mentally ill or developmentally disabled, and at your sharp command, they begin crying in terror. You are now in the position of helping them. Once you ascertain everything is safe, you kindly but firmly tell them that you are going to teach them the rules of how to talk with correctional officers. "I'm sorry you were frightened. But you did something that looked dangerous. I'll tell you right now how you should act so something like this won't happen again."

CHAPTER 74

The Aftermath: What Happens to the Aggressive, Mentally Ill Inmate After an Aggressive Incident?

Rage and even more so, violence, are exhausting experiences—both emotionally and physically. Many people get the "shakes" after such an incident. So much blood has "pooled" inside the core of their bodies to prepare for combat that they feel cold and start to tremble. Most inmates have a significantly impaired ability to remember what happened in sequence. They may have a patchy memory of a few events. Much of the rest of the incident is a blur. Although they may even be remorseful, they usually don't remember what happened, how it started, or who was responsible. Even more drastically, they can lapse into a state of defensive confusion where they no longer recall what happened at all, or they distort the incident in their memory completely, thereafter taking no responsibility whatsoever.

Others may feel profound guilt. This might be positive, were it to lead them to reflect on their own responsibility, but for most inmates, this guilt is so unpleasant that they project responsibility onto the person who "makes" them feel guilty. Thus, they soon shift to resentment and begin to blame the other person.

Humiliation, the feeling of having one's faults or vulnerabilities involuntarily or forcibly exposed to others, is quite common, and here, too, many people become defensive. One humiliation is the almost inevitable loss of the fight with the correctional officers. People describe humiliation like being flayed alive. Many respond by becoming enraged all over again. Their thinking seems to be, "If I feel this bad, someone must be doing it to me." What is almost universal is a post–crisis fatigue, a combination of the depletion of energy stores in the body and the cumulative effect of all the mood and cognitive changes described above.

Managing Risks Post-Crisis

In some situations, consequences or punishment will be required. In this case, correctional officers must clearly convey the processes and procedures of detention to the inmate. Dependent on the nature of the arrest, correctional officers must try and arrange for the transfer of the mentally ill inmate into treatment facility or segregation unit as appropriate.

Once the crisis has been resolved and the inmate is stable and willing to talk, clear and unambiguous limits regarding future behaviors must be imposed. Without the imposition of limits and the reiteration of consequences for violating those limits, the inmate will simply repeat their aggressive behavior. Through de-escalation you have established control over the inmate, and you can't relinquish that control simply because the crisis has passed. Reassure the mentally ill inmate that you are not out for revenge, but neither will you pretend that nothing serious happened nor are you going to reward them just because the aggression is over.

Consequence must be imposed swiftly, and can include more restrictive incarceration, or a sanctions hearing. This depends on the nature of the actual incident, and the judgment and discretion of the correctional officers.

If the mentally ill inmate is really frightened or devastated by what happened, the first priority is **reassurance and orientation**. For inmates who are disorganized, psychotic, or otherwise in a fragile mental state, you may have to explain to them what has happened, what is going to happen, and why. With inmates who don't have the mental capacity to really understand the details or implications of what happened, the best approach is to be calming and reassuring, and not detail attempts at problem-solving.

If the inmate has the cognitive ability to understand, then an **educative follow-up** is necessary. Of course, this may be delayed until the inmate has been released from custody, or hospitalization for their mental illness. Still, the incident should be reviewed with the inmate in order to clarify and reiterate the consequences of similar behavior in the future. Discuss with the inmate what other tactics they might have used to get what they desired, assist them in recognizing patterns that lead to aggression and how to avoid such situations in the future, and return the inmate to a sense of dignity and integrity.

Consolidation of Gains

Another important factor is to consolidate whatever gains you made. Just because the inmate seems to be listening doesn't mean they understood or even heard what you said. There are several strategies you can use to ensure that your statements are heard and agreement established.

- Paraphrase their understanding; "So, John, we've agreed that you will… and I will …."
- Have the inmate repeat your instructions back to you.
- Have the inmate read and sign a written copy of the instructions and stipulations of their supervision plan. Although the inmate will have signed a copy of the rules and regulations at their initial interview, the recent incident may call for a modification of that plan.
- Establish a time frame for follow through with any promises you may have made, such as placement in a treatment program. Failure to uphold your end of the bargain will lead to feelings of betrayal, making future de-escalation more difficult.

CHAPTER 75

Managing Threats to Your Family

Anyone working in the field of corrections is much more concerned with, and disturbed by, threats made toward their family than they are with threats toward themselves. By threatening your family, promising to attack when you are not there, inmates can create a sense of helplessness and desperation on your part. The threat is usually empty, made in the heat of the moment, or as means of additional defiance and meant to terrify you. You must, however, take any such threats seriously, because it is almost impossible to know when the threat is real or not. And, truth be told, a bit of preventative planning, and educating family members as to their need to be mindful and aware is never a bad thing.

Basic safety concepts (**Section III**), are easily transferrable toward enhancing the safety of your home and family, although the authors have also expanded that list with the recommended strategies listed below. Remember, as in the work environment, the development of a safety plan is not enough, and your plan should be reviewed regularly with your family.

- **Inform your family of any threats and of the need to take protective action.** In regard to children, your responsibility is to explain everything they *need* to know, but no more. Furthermore, if you display your own fears excessively, you will only frighten your family members. To this end, we strongly recommend that you acquire two books by Gavin de Becker, listed here for your convenience: *The Gift of Fear* and *Protecting the Gift*.[49]
- **Inform local law enforcement.** Police officers will assist you in drawing up a safety plan as well as considering what, if any, action they can take on your behalf.
- **Review home security.** Are you a soft target or a hard target? A soft target is easily accessible, predictable, and unaware of danger. A hard target is not easily accessible, or predictable. Adequate lighting and the use of quality locks, doors, and windows will limit the ability of an intruder to enter your home. Consult with your local police department, if need be, as to how to make your home more secure. Some departments will be more willing than others to send an officer out to walk through and around your home to inform you of security gaps. There are also excellent books on home security available. Consider having a home alarm system installed.
- **Concerning firearms.** Should you decide to purchase a firearm for home security, each member of your family must attend a firearm safety and instruction course. Firearms should be stored and cared for as delineated in the course.
- **Concerning dogs.** In many ways dogs are a better security option than a firearm. Unlike humans, a well-trained dog, particularly certain breeds, won't hesitate to act when they perceive a threat. Dogs will also provide you with an early warning system, detecting sounds and smells that

you can't. Further discussion of dog breeds and training is well beyond the scope of this book. A good dog can be one of the most important aspects of home security.

- **Scan your surroundings.** Your family members must learn to scan their surroundings and note anything out of the ordinary. Remind family members to report suspicious people and cars.

- **Inform employers and schools so they are aware of the identity of the potential assailant.** Make clear to school officials exactly who is allowed to meet or pick-up your children.

- **Change your routine.** As much as possible, travel by different routes and at different times. Be unpredictable.

- **Safety in numbers.** Neither you nor any of your family members should be the last to leave their workplace or school. Enlist co-coworkers, coaches, teachers, etc., to be part of a team.

- **Notify your office and family of travel plans.** Ask that they not reveal any travel plans or other schedules.

- **Be careful about giving out personal information.** This can be difficult with children, as they happily exchange information with their friends or others. Remind them to be careful of strangers, and to report any such inquiries. Don't forget about social networking sites such as Facebook and MySpace, texting, Twitter, and other dangers of the Internet.

- **Plan an escape route.** Figure out the best ways to escape from your home and rehearse this with family members. You can combine this with fire drills—something the children are already familiar with from school.

- **Plan how to ask for help if in public and how best to call for help if needed.** If your children are alone and there are no nearby police cars, the best stranger to ask for help is a *woman*, as women are far less likely to be a threat. Of course, this is not the case if a woman is the threatening inmate, or if a male inmate has a female associate outside. Nonetheless, on a random basis, women are far safer than men.

- **Concerning code words.** Teach your children a code word or challenge that must be answered by strange individuals. This includes neighbors, and in some cases, relatives. For example, a person approaches your child after school and says, "Tasha, your mother and father were injured in an automobile accident. The police told me to take you to the hospital! Please come with me now." Your child should have been taught to keep her distance, looking for escape routes as she asks, "What's the word?" If the person does not reply immediately with the correct word, the child should run to a safe haven and describe the individual as best they can.

- **Post emergency numbers near each telephone in your home.** Establish safe havens to escape to in times of danger. If possible, enlist your neighbors in your safety plan.

CHAPTER 76

Conclusion

The history of mental health services has intertwined with the work of law enforcement for decades. As funding for social policies have waxed and waned, populations in jails have expanded and mental health facilities decreased. Time has shown that legislation, laws and policies have little impact on the population of the mentally ill in jails and prisons. Sweeping changes in the past sixty years intent on moving individuals with mental illness from state hospitals to community mental health centers and primary care doctors have failed to meet the needs of the people it intended to serve. Thousands of mentally ill people come in contact daily with the jail system from crisis inmates to the homeless, chronically mentally ill. Our jails have become the treatment centers of last resort.

This book and the material covered herein demonstrate the perspective that change occurs when officers recognize the need for training, recognize a problem can be addressed and encourages the search for answers. This starts at the individual level, with awareness and recognition of how an officer responds to the work, how an officer breathes, views the environment, and interacts with the inmates. Recognition is key: being aware of abnormal behavior and having the ability to label and define behaviors creates new opportunities to engage, interact, and communicate. Practice, however, is vital. Once you've made a commitment to change or try a new process be consistent, be persistent, and seek out additional information. If you have questions regarding information discussed or are looking for additional training opportunities please contact us.

If you as a corrections officer have a behavioral health provider in your facility, set a time to meet with them, discuss what they do, who they serve, and the process for referrals. Opportunities to collaborate are key. As discussed earlier there are frequent admissions that are often system "problems:" inmates that are expensive to treat, house, and work with in the community. Identifying who these individuals are and working on a collaborative intervention program using available resources can move an inmate out of an endless cycle of misdemeanant arrests, incarceration, release, relapse, and back to jail again. Correctional officers have a primary mission protecting society from "bad" guys. If this book assists in moving the "sad" guys to a place better suited to their illness than a jail, and assists officers in more effectively managing such inmates when they are incarcerated, then time reading this book is time well spent.

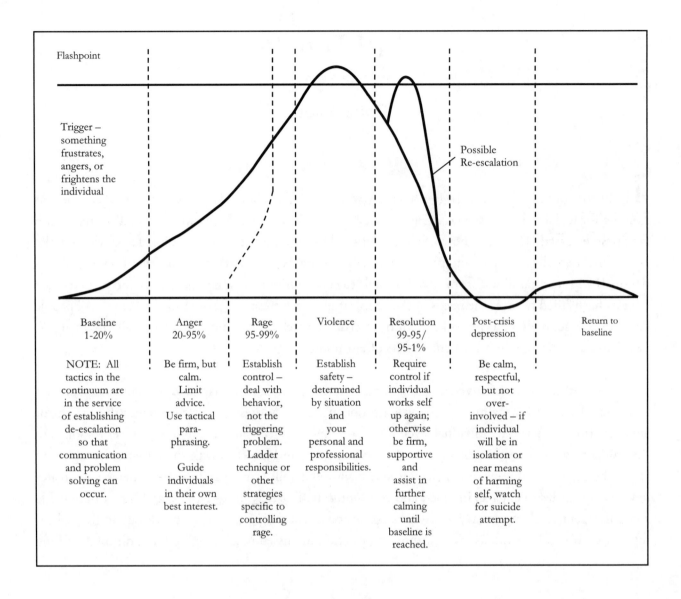

Flashpoint

Trigger – something frustrates, angers, or frightens the individual

Possible Re-escalation

Baseline 1-20%	Anger 20-95%	Rage 95-99%	Violence	Resolution 99-95/ 95-1%	Post-crisis depression	Return to baseline
NOTE: All tactics in the continuum are in the service of establishing de-escalation so that communication and problem solving can occur.	Be firm, but calm. Limit advice. Use tactical para-phrasing. Guide individuals in their own best interest.	Establish control – deal with behavior, not the triggering problem. Ladder technique or other strategies specific to controlling rage.	Establish safety – determined by situation and your personal and professional responsibilities.	Require control if individual works self up again; otherwise be firm, supportive and assist in further calming until baseline is reached.	Be calm, respectful, but not over-involved – if individual will be in isolation or near means of harming self, watch for suicide attempt.	

Appendices

APPENDIX A

The Question of Positional and Compression Asphyxia
by Gary M. Vilke, MD, FACEP, FAAEM

Background on Positional Asphyxia

- The concept of "Positional Asphyxia" was originally based on research that had significant methodological flaws (Reay, et al 1988)
- The premise of positional asphyxia was that if you left a patient in a hobble restraint position, he would tire, go into ventilatory failure and then asphyxiate into cardiac arrest.
- The hobble position is defined as prone with hand cuffed behind the back and ankles restrained with a device that is then pulled up and tethered to the handcuffs leaving the knees bent.
- The original research and dozens of papers since have NEVER shown hypoxia (low oxygen levels in the blood) to develop in the hobble position.
- The original research and dozens of papers since have NEVER shown hypercarbia (elevated CO_2 levels in the blood) to develop in the hobble position.
- In fact, the only paper to report that the hobble position results in positional asphyxia, actually demonstrated that oxygen saturation levels IMPROVED in all subjects who were left in a hobble position.
- Subsequent studies evaluating obese subjects also have demonstrated that when left in a hobble position, they will not asphyxiate.(Sloane, et al 2014)
- All of these studies prove that people left on their stomachs in a hobble position will not die from asphyxiation, which includes both thin and obese individuals.

Best practices

When encountered with a patient in a hobble restraint, certain assessments of a patient are critical and the documentation of the findings in the pre-hospital record is essential.

A. Assess the level of consciousness. Is the patient awake or not and is he verbal?

B. Assess perfusion. Is his skin color good and does he have a strong regular pulse?

C. Place on a monitor as soon as feasible and document first rhythm.

D. Place on pulse oximeter as soon as feasible and document O2 sat. If placing on a finger, make sure the hand is getting good perfusion through the handcuff if the O2 sat reading is low.

E. If the patient can be safely transferred to a supine position with approved 4-point restraints secured to the gurney – this is the optimal position as one has full access to the patient's airway and direct visualization of the face and access to the chest.

F. If the patient cannot be safely transferred out of the hobble position, attempt to transfer the patient in a lateral decubitus position on the gurney – preferably with the face and chest facing the EMS personnel to optimize monitoring.

G. Face down on the gurney in the hobble position is the least desirable position as the patient cannot be easily monitored or accessed if the physical status changes. If utilizing this position for transport, care must be taken to assure the airway is clear and not obstructed by sheets or the mattress.

***Despite all of the data supporting the safety of the hobble position, this is the position that will have the most scrutiny in a lawsuit if a patient deteriorates into cardiac arrest.

H. Ongoing monitoring and vigilance is important. The issue of medical concern is not the actual hobble position, as this is deemed physiologically neutral, but rather the concern is the underlying medical condition (drug induced or not) that required the patient to be hobbled in the first place.

I. These recommendations are meant to supplement, not replace, existing EMS protocols (blood glucose assessment, IV fluids, etc)

Background on Compression Asphyxia

- The concept of "Compression Asphyxia" evolved after the theory of positional asphyxia was essentially debunked. (Chan, et al. 1997, Chan et al 1998)

- The premise of compression asphyxia was that a certain amount of weight is often placed on the back of an individual to get a him into custody and handcuffed. Often this weight is multiple officers holding the person down with hands, forearms or knees. During this time period while the weight is being applied, the theory is that the subject would tire, not be able to breathe (ventilate), go into ventilatory failure and then asphyxiate into cardiac arrest.

- Research with up to 225 lbs of weight on the backs of healthy volunteers has not demonstrated physiological changes that would indicate that asphyxiation is likely with these weights. (Michalewicz, et al 2007)

- Studies with weights on the backs of normal subjects has also shown that cardiac output and blood pressure are not impacted.(Savaser, et al 2013)

- If an individual is alive, moving and breathing after the weight has been removed and then subsequently goes into cardiac arrest, the weight did not cause compressive asphyxia. *There is not a delayed asphyxiation*, it either happens while the weight is on or it does not occur.

- Even if the weight on an individual is so great as to restrict adequate ventilation, if the subject is breathing once the weight is removed, the person will breathe out the retained CO_2 and will recover. The effects of the weight are not lasting and a breathing individual will self-correct very quickly.

- It takes a great deal of weight, consistently placed over the ventilatory muscles of the back, for a significant length of time with essentially complete impedance of ventilation without breaks to breathe in order to theoretically cause a death due to compressive asphyxia.

- If a person is vigorously and repeatedly yelling or screaming, he is moving air in and out of his lungs and thus is not meeting the "complete impedance of ventilation" criteria and thus is not in a position at that time to cause asphyxiation.

  NOTE: That being said, other medical emergencies CAN present with the *sensation* that one cannot breathe, when in fact they are ventilating fine but are suffering from a myocardial infarction or ischemia, for instance. These patients should be carefully evaluated.

Best practices

When EMS encounters a patient who had weight placed on him to get him into custody, certain assessments of a patient are critical and the documentation of the findings in the pre-hospital record is essential. Basically the patient will either be spontaneously breathing with a pulse, or not. If he is spontaneously breathing with a pulse, then he did not suffer from compression asphyxia and should be assessed and documentation should follow as per the "Best practices" for positional asphyxia (above).

If the patient is not breathing or does not have a pulse, treatment is basically standard advanced cardiac life support measures. Documentation optimally should reflect the events that led up to the cardiac arrest. Often EMS is present or staged within viewing distance of the event. If so, some of the following observations can be critically useful in evaluating the case for quality review or a subsequent legal action:

- How many officers where physically involved?
- Where were they located on the subject? (i.e. holding legs, holding head, knee on back, hands on shoulder, etc)
- How long was weight on the subject?
- Was the weight moving and shifting (did the subject arch up, roll over or was he just laying flat on his stomach)?
- At what point did the subject stop yelling in relation to the cardiac arrest?
- Was the change in status sudden or gradual over time?
- Was there weight on him at the time of the cardiac arrest and if so, how much?

Pearls

Careful monitoring – you will likely be unable to prevent a patient who is suffering from Excited Delirium Syndrome from going into cardiac arrest. Additionally, rapid recognition and treatment is unlikely to change the ultimate outcome for the patient, but careful charting and documentation is extremely beneficial for subsequent legal actions that are likely to arise.

ETCO2 - If possible, document the earliest possible end tidal CO2 level. Pre-intubation with bag-valve-mask is best if feasible, as this value if low or normal, will support that the individual did not asphyxiate, as CO2 levels are high in patients who asphyxiated.

Careful accurate documentation with details as clear as possible. These cases in which there is a cardiac arrest often end up in litigation, so clear documentation of what was observed and reported with specific details is incredibly helpful in evaluating the case.

Appendix A CAUTION

Medically evaluate the subject carefully, even if the person is vigorously and repeatedly yelling or screaming. It may be obvious that he is moving air in and out of his lungs and thus is not in a position at that time to cause asphyxiation – however other medical emergencies, like myocardial infarctions or ischemia can present with the sensation of difficulty breathing and should be considered during the assessment.

References

Chan TC, Vilke GM, Neuman T, Clausen JL: Restraint position and positional asphyxia. Ann Emerg Med 1997;30(5):578-586.

Chan TC, Vilke GM, Neuman T: Reexamination of custody restraint position and positional asphyxia. Am J Forensic Med Pathol 1998;19(3):201-205.

Michalewicz BA, Chan TC, Vilke GM, Levy SS, Neuman TS, Kolkhorst FW. Ventilatory and metabolic demands during aggressive physical restraint in healthy adults. J Forensic Sci 2007;52(1):171-175.

Reay DT, Howard JD, Fligner CL, Ward RJ. Effects of positional restraint on oxygen saturation and heart rate following exercise. Am J Forensic Med Pathol. 1988 Mar;9(1):16-8.

Savaser DJ, Campbell C, Castillo EM, Vilke GM, Sloane C, Neuman T, Hansen AV, Shah S, Chan TC. The effect of the prone maximal restrained position with and without weight force on cardiac output and other hemodynamic measures. J Forens Leg Med. 2013 Nov;20(8):991-5. Epub 2013 Aug 30.

Sloane C, Chan TC, Kolkhorst F, Neuman T, Castillo EM, Vilke GM. Evaluation of the Ventilatory Effects of the Prone Maximum Restraint Position (PMR) on Obese Human Subjects. Forens Sci Int 2014;237:86-9. Epub 2014;46(6):865-72. Epub 2014 Feb 14.

APPENDIX B

Suggested Response Protocol for Correctional Facilities Concerning Suspected Excited Delirium Incidents

By Lieutenant Michael Paulus

Appendix B Figure 1: Excited Delirium is a Chaotic Rage State

As discussed in detail in **Chapter 38**, **Excited Delirium** is a medical syndrome that is included within a general category: <u>Chaotic Rage</u>. It should not be incumbent upon either eyewitnesses or first responders to distinguish between excited delirium and other similar, equally dangerous forms of chaotic rage. The authors of this book, therefore, suggest that protocols in your jurisdiction be coded for chaotic rage, with a clear understanding that this term encompasses excited delirium and other similar states, whatever the cause. **Medical staff will sort out the genuine excited delirium cases, from others, and render appropriate aid in each case. The correctional officers' protocol is the same, whenever someone presents with a chaotic rage set of behaviors.**

When considering a response to suspected Excited Delirium Syndrome incidents, it is important to understand what the correctional officer is facing. Dr. Deborah Mash of the University of Miami Brain Endowment Bank has called Excited Delirium, "a medical emergency that presents itself as a law enforcement problem."

Keeping this in mind, correctional officers are presented with a dilemma comparable to dispatching the fire department to a bank robbery. They do not have the appropriate equipment or training to handle the high-risk nature of a bank robbery. By the same token, EMS personnel are only dispatched to domestic disputes in order to tend to injuries to any of the parties—they are not expected to intervene in either legal issues or stopping the violence between the involved parties.

Similarly why would correctional officers be expected to manage to a medical emergency that requires a minimum of an advanced life support ambulance crew to address? There is nothing on the officer's duty belt or in their work area, or normally in their facility that will address hyperthermia, acidosis, cardiovascular collapse, or other life-threatening issues that are common in an Excited Delirium Syndrome (ExDS) incident.

Dr. Michael Curtis, of St. Michael's Hospital in Steven's Point, Wisconsin has said, in reference to Excited Delirium, "The legal issues can wait, the life-threatening medical emergency will not." This points out that, in a very important sense, correctional officers do not have the primary role in these incidents, but they do have a critical backup role. It just so happens that this "back-up" comes first. Unless the individual is under complete physical control, medical assistance cannot be rendered. For this reason, correctional personnel must get the right resources to the scene as quickly as possible. In doing so, the inmate is given the best possibility of surviving.

In order to get the right resources in place, it is necessary to develop a multi-disciplinary approach to adequately respond to this multi-faceted problem. Some of the most common stakeholders in such a plan include: law enforcement, corrections, EMS personnel, fire personnel, telecommunicators, emergency room physicians/nurses, coroners, medical examiners, mental health professionals/consumers, risk managers associated with the corrections facility and the appropriate State/District attorney. Your jurisdiction may have different stakeholders, maybe more or maybe less—but the critical issue is to identify those that are, or should be, part of a best practices response to these, all too often, fatal incidents.

What is proposed here has been a successful multi-jurisdictional response since July 1, 2008 in Champaign County, Illinois. The American College of Emergency Physicians (ACEP) put out a white paper in September of 2009 that expressed the ideas that were in place in Champaign County almost a year prior. It is offered for use as a template to help gather interested parties to the table to establish a protocol that works within the confines of the resources you have available.

Correctional officers are presented with numerous situations to observe the common behaviors of ExDS. Whether it is from drug use, alcohol withdrawal, or mental illness, corrections face the same challenges when dealing with this medical emergency as do law enforcement in the field. The response to suspected ExDS incidents really does not change between the street and the correctional facility. Awareness of the behavioral cues followed by the call for additional resources to be dispatched is of primary concern.

Correctional officers must be vigilant to the signs that may indicate an inmate might be in the throes of an ExDS incident. This should begin from the time the subject is brought to the facility by law enforcement and continue throughout the time the inmate is in the facility.

There are stories of prisoners being brought to a facility for a minor offense and showing no signs of ExDS. Within a few hours, the inmate is in a full-blown ExDS incident requiring isolation, cell extraction, and then transport to the psychiatric ward.

Correctional staff should avoid the tendency to "diagnose" the reasons for the inmate's behavior. Awareness of the common behavioral signs that signal a possible eminently life-threatening medical emergency must be dealt with as soon as possible regardless of the cause.

Like law enforcement, correctional staff must realize that any criminal charges or institutional violations can wait. The medical emergency cannot and will not wait but is moving forward and requires rapid and aggressive medical intervention to give the inmate the best possibility of survival.

The effectiveness of this protocol relies upon correctional officers' understanding of what they are dealing with as soon as is humanly possible, and then, immediately calling for additional backup and medical response. This protocol extends to the dispatcher/call taker as well to reasonably identify incidents that require sending additional resources to the scene as early as possible.

The correctional environment presents both opportunities as well as challenges when dealing with a potential ExDS incident. The opportunities include having inmates generally contained for the most part. This, unlike law enforcement in the field, means that unless there are exigent circumstances present, correctional personnel can develop a plan for how to get control of the inmate prior to any physical contact with the inmate. Correctional staff will usually have some knowledge about the inmate prior to contact that may give them some indication for the behavior as they plan their response.

Video surveillance also allows correctional personnel to possibly observe any sudden onset of behaviors consistent with an ExDS incident. This helps cut down on the time the inmate is experiencing the incident before medical attention is brought to the scene.

Generally, in the correctional environment, there is also enough staff present to be able to gain rapid control of the inmate prior to turning them over to medical personnel. This includes more correctional officers that might be able to go hands-on with the inmate, but also most correctional facilities have some sort of medical resource on hand. This can range from a nurse with basic medical response up to more fully equipped infirmaries. The number of personnel sent to the scene will be defendant on what resources are available, but four to six correctional officers should be dispatched to the scene, when possible. CIT (Crisis Intervention Team) officers should be sent, if available, as well as a supervisor. Interagency agreements are common that allow various departments to share resources in times of emergencies such as these.

When correctional staff is dispatched, EMS should be sent as well. This will save precious time in getting the medical personnel and equipment to the scene as quickly as possible. Some communities have a combined EMS/Fire Department. Those that don't will then need to consider if sending a Fire Rescue truck is a possibility, along with EMS. Some jurisdictions have, as part of their City Ordinance that any "medical emergency" requires a Fire Rescue truck be sent. If this is the case, expect the EMS crew as well as the Fire Rescue personnel to be dispatched to the scene. The Fire Rescue's role will be discussed shortly.

Depending on the situation, it should be considered by correctional staff to create a quick action plan and wait until EMS/Fire Rescue has arrived before making physical contact with the subject. The reason to wait has to be balanced between the safety of the subject, the correctional personnel, other first responders, and other inmates. One of the toughest decisions a first responder will make could be containing the situation until the medical personnel arrive instead of physically contacting the subject. <u>We know we are repeating ourselves, but sometimes emphasis is necessary: whenever possible, correctional officers should wait until Medical has arrived before making physical contact with the subject.</u> Of course, this is contingent on how immediately dangerous the subject is to himself or herself, the correctional officers, other first responders, and bystanders. This is where the role of the correctional officer trained as a CIT officer *may* help the subject and where the verbal control strategies for Chaotic Rage **(Chapter 67)** may prove helpful. There is no guarantee that the subject in the midst of an ExDS incident will be able to be talked down, but the benefit of having staff trained to recognize a person in crisis and then attempt to use the verbal de-escalation techniques to reach an "island of sanity," as the authors of the text call it, is worth the effort.

One way to help officers understand the dangers that individuals in excited delirium states present to themselves is the concept of "capture myopathy," a term from the veterinary sciences that deals with the issues related to capturing animals and the physical stressors that accompany their capture. Capture myopathy is a physical condition that may result in death. Relating this to the capture of the suspected ExDS subject is an easy one considering that <u>the longer the struggle goes on with first responders the greater the risk for the subject. To repeat: if it is possible have EMS on the scene before going hands on with the subject, in order to lessen the potential for making the current condition of the subject worse.</u>

However, correctional officers must not wait for Medical arrival when there is imminent risk of serious injury to either officers or to the subject. First responder safety is of primary importance as it is those officers who are primarily responsible for getting this situation under control. Furthermore, standing by until Medical arrives, while the subject starts to or continues to injure themselves runs counter to the goal of getting them to the hospital as safely as possible.

The EMS unit should stage closer to the subject than is usual in many other situations; however, this is not to say they should put themselves in needless jeopardy. Given that EMS personnel have the training and resources to deal with the medical emergency, it is critical that they be in a position to see the subject, do an eye-sight physical and behavioral evaluation as soon as possible. The important point to remember is that this is a potentially life-threatening medical emergency and the inmate must receive rapid and aggressive medical intervention as soon as possible.

As discussed in the multi-disciplinary approach above, if there is a field sedation protocol in place, it will be important for the EMT's/medical staff to observe the subject to estimate the amount of medication needed, or at the very least, to call in to the Emergency Room to get orders from the attending physician. It is, of course, incumbent upon the correctional officers to keep the EMS personnel safe, as they do not have the means to protect themselves from serious injury should the subject attack.

It might be a good time to briefly discuss the types of medications that your EMS Medical Director could consider using in these situations. To be clear, this is not a medical document, as it is designed for correctional staff. There are no *recommendations* on medication here; whatever medication EMS brings to the scene is *their* choice, not one guided or recommended by non-medical people. Nonetheless, it is essential that all stakeholders understand something about the medications that are used for field sedation, so that they can put in place restraint procedures best suited to facilitate their administration. One common sedative that most ambulances currently carry is midazolam, which also goes by the trade name, Versed®. Another drug that increasing numbers of EMS Medical Directors are currently using on the ambulance rigs is Ketamine. This is a dissociative anesthetic that has been used for a long time, mainly in the Emergency Room, not in the field. This has started to change and is being considered and used in more and more areas. Whatever your EMS crews carry, it is incumbent on correctional officers to know the best way for the Paramedics to deliver the drug to the subject, correctional officers can position the subject to facilitate that delivery.

The role of the Fire Rescue personnel is to support the EMS personnel with the treatment of the inmate. This can be through driving the ambulance from the scene to the hospital, or by helping with the treatment of the subject in the back of the ambulance. If EMS and Fire are separate, it is important to note that the rescue truck does not have to have a code response. It is also important to make sure they don't park too close, which might make it hard for other emergency vehicles to enter or exit the scene.

As the first responding correctional officers arrive on the scene, it is important to assess what is actually happening. This will minimize the potential for missing important information, such as dangerous environmental conditions or other people with injuries that are not recognized because your attention is too focused on the inmate.

As soon as reasonably possible, correctional officers along with EMS/Fire personnel should develop a plan to address the incident. This will mean officers will need to know if the EMS paramedic will sedate the inmate. This decision is the sole discretion of the Medical staff and not correctional personnel. Correctional supervisor or someone designated should be in charge of the incident, a quarterback, if you will, to assign personnel and keep track of what is going on. This does not have to be the highest-ranking person at the scene, just someone who is running the operation.

The quarterback will assign what limb each officer will be responsible for as well as the less lethal weapon officer, if one is available. Advising the capture officers of the EMS decision on whether or not there will be a sedative given, will let the officers know what steps will be taken once control is gained over the inmate.

Once there is a plan for capturing the subject that includes EMS, it is important to consider which less lethal weapon options are available to the officers.
- OC spray may temporarily blind the subject, but it cannot be counted on to incapacitate a subject in this extremely agitated state.
- Electronic Control Devices (ECDs) (i.e. Tasers®) provide a means to knock the subject down from a distance as opposed to tackling the inmate. It must be understood that voluntary compliance is unlikely when a person is in this state, so the number of deployments should focus only on getting the person to the ground, and allowing the officers to get into a position to control the limbs. If an agency equips their officers with ECDs, the subject can best be put under control

and restraint through "cuffing under power." This tactic has been taught as a part of the ECD usage and works well when dealing with resistive arrest subjects and may prove effective with the Excited Delirium subject as well. A clear distinction must be made between this procedure and any attempt to use an ECD device to *elicit* compliance.

- Some agencies have less lethal impact rounds known as bean bag rounds, as well as plastic impact rounds. These could also be used as knock down options, provided they are available at the scene, or close by. However, unless the inmate is incapacitated, they will, almost surely, just get up again.

- The last option would be for a physical takedown of the inmate. There are studies that have shown that going "hands on", physically grabbing, wrestling, or fighting an inmate, has the greatest potential for injury to both the inmate as well as the officers involved. We must get physical control of the subject, and that requires hands on control, but the takedown should be viewed as a last resort in lieu of other less lethal means.

After capturing the subject, they are placed face down with arms out to their sides and feet spread apart. This position makes it the hardest for the inmate to resist or attack the officers. This position is also consistent with the arrest and control tactics used most often by correctional officers. This means that learning a completely new control tactic for an incident that may happen infrequently is not necessary.

The physical control tactic described below is adapted from a method of control originally developed by Chris Lawrence, of the Ontario Police College in Ontario, Canada. I refer to it as **Multiple Officer Control Tactic (MOCT** – see step-by-step illustrations at the end of this section).[50] The tactic isolates the shoulders of the subject by placing the armpits of the officer on the back of the subject's shoulders, raising the subject's wrists, turning their palms to the sky, placing the officers legs in a position so it is the legs (through leverage and positioning) that are keeping the subject's arms raised, and finally moving the arms above the shoulder-line to completely isolate the shoulders. This makes the shoulder a weak joint, and does not allow the subject to bring their arms under their body, which would otherwise enable them to continue the struggle.

The legs are controlled by separating them and having the officers put their chests on top of the subject's legs, just above the ankle. Whether the officers are back to back, or in between the subject's legs, the subject will not be able to keep moving forward, something that could enable them to continue the struggle. If there is a fifth officer available, this person should be up at the subject's head, pushing down on the shoulder blades. This would be the best position for the quarterback, because this person has the best view of the entire control process.

One of the advantages of this MOCT is that there is no one lying on the inmate's back or lower abdomen. Concerns about restricting the inmate's breathing from too much weight on their back are alleviated because it is based on the mechanical control of each limb in such a way that prevents the subject from moving, not weight on the subject's back. Another benefit of the MOCT is that it is gross motor skills based. Because individuals in this condition are often sweating profusely, possibly covered in blood, the fine motor arrest tactics often taught in some academies, are not very effective. The gross motor tactics of the MOCT allow officers to control the arms and legs of these subjects effectively in the sometimes cramped conditions that they face.

This MOCT position can be accomplished with four officers, and as few as three officers. Fewer than that, and there is no reasonable way to prevent the subject from continuing to struggle. The MOCT can be performed by EMS and Fire personnel in coordination with law enforcement. As long as personnel understand the mechanics of how to isolate the different limbs, the inmate can be controlled. In communities where there are only one or two correctional officers available, having two EMS personnel and/or Fire personnel could give you enough people to capture and control the inmate.

Once the inmate's limbs are controlled by the personnel on the scene, this is the point that the sedation can occur, if EMS has a sedation protocol in place. The type of sedative used will dictate the best position of the inmate to administer the sedative. If there is to be an injection of the sedative, the buttocks and the thigh are positioned as to make this possible. If the EMS company uses a nasal-atomized sedative as part of their protocol, it is better for the subject to be mechanically restrained prior to placing the inmate on their back in order to deliver the sedative. As stated previously, the decision to sedate or not sedate is solely the paramedics, not the correctional officer.

There are going to be incidents where either there are not enough officers present or EMS has advised that sedation is not going to take place which will mean the process may have to be adapted to the situation at hand. **It is important to understand that whatever means correctional officers and EMS personnel use to capture the ExDS inmate, there must be frequent training that involves ALL of the participants. This develops the common understanding of what each of the responders will do or can do to assist in getting the subject controlled.**

There have been several recognized emergency medical experts, along with mental health professionals, that suggest that the person in such a state is in need of rapid sedation. The sedation allows the EMS personnel to begin to treat the inmate's underlying life-threatening medical issues as quickly as possible. It has been documented in numerous incidents that the inmate in this state will continue to struggle with the very people that are capable of helping him or her. It is important to understand that the field sedation does not directly address the multitude of medical issues the EMS personnel are facing. It just allows them access to the inmate so they can begin to treat the acidosis, the hyperthermia, etc.

Once the sedation has been given, or if there is no sedation protocol in place, or the paramedic does not choose to sedate the person, the inmate will need to be restrained in such a way as to allow the EMS personnel to treat the subject safely and then transport them. This is accomplished by using multiple sets of handcuffs so as to allow the subject to be placed on their back with their arms down by their sides. This gives the EMS personnel access to the subject's veins in the arms to get IVs started. Remember, that the hands must be cuffed with chain link handcuffs, not hinged handcuffs, as hinged cuffs will torque the wrists when the subject is lying on their back. Once the arms are secured with enough handcuffs, a minimum of three in a daisy chain configuration, then the legs are restrained with a hobble restraint.[51]

There are various types of hobble restraints, but a simple nylon web restraint with a couple of cam buckles allows the legs to be secured quickly together and then tied to the backboard. This will prevent the subject from kicking the EMS personnel in the ambulance, as well as the ER staff at the hospital. It is also easily removed at the hospital by either correctional or nursing staff.

After the arms and legs are secured, the subject should be placed in the "recovery position," on their left side, pending placement of the inmate on a backboard. This position is recognized by EMS personnel as beneficial for the inmate's heart, as well as preventing the inmate from aspirating their own vomit. If the EMS crew is already on hand, the subject will be placed directly on a backboard, and loaded into the ambulance.

The subject should be secured onto the backboard, in the supine (face up) position, with whatever standard restraints are used by local EMS crews. Some will use larger nylon straps with buckles, or they may use "spider straps" to keep the subject secure on the backboard. Once they are secured on the backboard, they are loaded onto the gurney and then placed in the ambulance, where at least one correctional officer will ride with the ambulance crew. The quarterback will need to make this assignment to ensure someone rides with the inmate. The correctional officer's role is to advise the EMS personnel of what occurred with the inmate before the ambulance arrived. The officer is also on hand to be able to release the inmate from the handcuffs should this be needed by the EMS personnel. The officer should take notes on the actions of the EMS personnel with the inmate, while en route to the hospital for future documentation.

Upon arrival at the hospital, the officer should advise the ER staff of the inmate's actions before they arrived on the scene as well as actions taken with the inmate after their arrival. This will give the ER staff a better idea on what has happened to the inmate since correctional staff and EMS arrived to treat the inmate. **The request for a core body temperature should be made as soon as possible.** Subjects with very high body temperatures are consistent with people in this state. Unfortunately, if the core body temperature is not taken, a valuable piece of evidence is missing, which could help to explain the dire state the subject was in, at the time of correctional officer involvement.

There are several other tests, in addition to the core body temperature, that the ER physician can order that will help them identify the medical state the subject is in and what direction the treatment will take. This can be a "work up" of several tests that include:

- Initial vital signs
- Arterial Blood Gas
- Serum Lactate (acid level)
- CBC (red and white blood cells) and Complete Metabolic Panel
- Total CK and CKMB, Troponin (for heart attack)

- ETOH (alcohol)
- TSH (thyroid)
- Ten drug urine (drugs of abuse), urine HCG (females only)
- EKG, CXR
- Head CT without contrast

This is not a complete list, but one that will help the ER physician get an idea on the current status of the inmate. These tests are for the physician to help treat the inmate, but if the inmate dies, they then become critical evidence of the profoundly dangerous medical condition the inmate was in when correctional staff made contact.

One reason that these tests are so important is if the inmate does not die, the opportunity is usually missed for further investigation. The incident may be memorialized in the station house story of the "naked guy who was brought in last winter, who bashed his head against the wall during booking"—this is legend, not data. Neglecting to administer proper medical testing loses a valuable opportunity to document what Dr. Mash has called "flicker events" in which a person gets into this excited state and then works their way out of it. These flicker events could be predictors of future incidents that portend a dire ending.[52]

If the inmate dies, there will most certainly be a thorough investigation. One consideration, made in conjunction with your coroner and your medical examiner, should be to harvest the brain sections from the inmate who has just expired. This must be done, generally, within twelve hours and the samples sent to Dr. Deborah Mash from the University of Miami's Brain Endowment Center for analysis. Dr. Mash is able to test for heat shock proteins and cocaine levels in the brain of the inmate that can help investigators, coroners, and medical examiners in identifying the incident as an ExDS incident. Specimen kits are available from Dr. Mash and should be kept available in the event that a sudden in-custody death has occurred and it has the signs and behaviors that are consistent with a suspected Excited Delirium case. In the case of death, someone should request a copy of the EKG strip, if such an exam was carried out. This will be of value to detectives, medical staff, and Medical Examiner and can be made part of the permanent record as well.

Appendix B Figure 2: Deal with the Behavior, Not the Cause

To underscore one more time, your protocols must not be predicated on the inmate actually being in a medically "certifiable" Excited Delirium Syndrome condition. Just as the Correctional Officer is not required to know if an inmate's gasping for air is due to an asthma attack, aspirated vomit, or a half-swallowed object—the facilities protocol is behaviorally coded for Chaotic Rage. If it turns out to be ExDS and the protocols are properly initiated, very likely the inmate's life will be saved. If it turns out to be some other, similar appearing condition that is caused by other factors, nonetheless, the initiation of this protocol will also very likely save the inmate's life.

All too often the focus of the investigation is on the use of force needed to get control of the inmate, instead of the numerous behavioral cues of a possible ExDS incident. The focus of this investigation should be on recreating at least the last twenty-four hours before the incident, but preferably longer. This will create a complete picture of the various factors that led to the involvement of correctional staff and EMS. The force used to gain control of the subject will be reviewed for reasonableness, but the investigation should not remain at that level.

There are numerous incidents where the subject was demonstrating superhuman strength, seemingly unlimited endurance, and incredible pain tolerance. These behaviors are what have led correctional officers to use force that is needed to get the subject under control and to the hospital. If the inmate dies, then the investigation tends to focus just on the force and not what might have caused the behavior in the first place.

Investigators should attempt to collect as much medical information as possible about the subject. This may indicate the serious medical condition the inmate was in at the time that corrections and EMS were contacted. If the medical tests were done, as previously stated, for medical purposes, then the results will be available for investigative purposes as well. The goal is to completely explain what happened, and what actions were taken in order to give the subject the best *possibility* of survival. This is often referred to as a "Psychological Autopsy," and it should include detailed personal and criminal history, as well as any information that might suggest a pre-disposition for Excited Delirium: this can include a history of chronic drug use, or episodic use of such substances as "bath salts," PCP or so-called "Sherm," which can precipitate such an episode without years of chronic drug abuse, as is more typical with such substances as cocaine or methamphetamine. In addition, investigators are often able to get information about so-called "flicker events," where the individual ramped up, momentarily or episodically, into what appeared to onlookers to be a delirium state, but one that was resolved without injury.

Investigators should attempt to collect information from the subject's criminal, medical, psychiatric, social worker, hospitalization, and jail/prison histories. This could give the investigator clues to other underlying causes for the subject's behavior. Evidence regarding the subject's prescribed medications as well as if the subject was compliant or non-compliant with those prescriptions should be located.

Witnesses and responders should be interviewed as soon as possible for their observations of the subject and the timeline of those observations. This will help the investigator understand the progress of the subject's behavior leading to their involvement with law enforcement personnel. The longer witnesses go without being interviewed, the greater the potential for failed or distorted recollections.

Since the officer was only concerned with the recognition that the subject needed to receive medical attention, and not with what caused the subject's behavior, it is now the investigator's task to seek to identify the cause of the incident. Primary emphasis should be on stimulant drug abuse and then possible psychiatric causes. The investigator will face a difficult task if the medical testing mentioned previously was not done.

The investigator and administrator should understand that it is usually *after* the subject has already reached an out-of-control state that the call goes out for assistance. This puts correctional staff behind the curve on the inmate's condition. If you liken this ExDS process to a "metabolic freight train to death," then if the correctional staff arrives as the inmate is already "pulling into the station," it may be possible that the correctional officers were dispatched to just observe the inmate's demise. The officers are then left in a state of confusion, wondering what could have been done differently.

If the investigation focuses on just what the officers did and not the condition of the subject, the potential for inaccurate conclusions is possible. This will not help the family of the subject, the officers involved, the agency, or the community to understand the incident.

SUMMARY

To summarize, dispatch personnel should gain as much information from the caller, on the condition of the subject, as possible. It is important to understand this could be a *medical emergency* that requires the appropriate number of correctional personnel, EMS, and Advanced Life Support (ALS) to be dispatched to the scene.

If the correctional officers observe the inmate acting in an agitated, chaotic manner *before* the call comes in or goes out from dispatch, they should assume that this is likely a *medical emergency*, and call for additional backup and EMS as soon as possible. The officer should assess the situation and determine the need to make contact with the inmate, dependent upon the circumstances. It is preferable to wait to make contact until EMS is on scene, unless the previously described exceptions are present.

A plan, in conjunction with EMS, should be made as quickly as possible in order to capture the subject. Once the subject is face down on the ground, consider using the MOCT (Multiple Officer Control Tactic) to quickly overcome the subject's resistance. If sedation has been decided upon by EMS personnel, it is necessary to control the inmate until that is accomplished. Restraining the subject with enough handcuffs to keep the subject's hands down by their sides as well as restraining their feet, to keep them from kicking first responders needs to be done in an organized manner. Remember the use of chain link handcuffs on the subject's wrists instead of hinged handcuffs to prevent possible injury to the subject's nerves.

The subject should then be secured to a backboard, face up, and loaded onto a gurney. Correctional staff should assist EMS in loading the subject into the ambulance. At least one officer should accompany EMS personnel to the hospital. It is necessary for the officer to articulate the subject's actions prior to the arrival of EMS, and any and all actions taken by law enforcement and EMS on the scene prior to arriving at the hospital.

Careful documentation of each incident, especially those that survive, can paint a clear picture of the tense, uncertain, and rapidly evolving situation faced by the first responders.

This guide may be used as a template to develop your own multi-disciplinary response to this multi-faceted problem based on the resources available in your community.

If you have questions about this protocol, please contact Michael Paulus at
michael@michaelpaulustraining.com

Multiple Officer Control Tactic (MOCT) – An Illustrated Guide

Figure#1- (Pin#1) Patient's arms are above the shoulder line with the officer's armpit on top of the shoulder. Patient's arms are controlled by officers by use of "figure four" along with a chain-link handcuff. Patient's arms are raised by using the officer's outside leg. Weight is kept off the patient's back to isolate the patient's shoulder.

Figure#2- (Pin#2) Patient's legs are moved out from the centerline of the body to limit their power. Officers wrap the patient's leg with their arms and tuck the heel under the armpit on the outside of their body. Weight is kept low towards the patient's ankles.

Figure#3- (Pin#3) Skeletal isolation is maintained by having two officers on the arms, two officers on the legs and then one officer at the patient's head. The officer at the patient's head is pushing down on the patient's trapezius muscles and monitoring the patient's status. This can be achieved by as few as three officers.

Figure#4- (Sedation#1) - EMS IM injection is achieved after the "quarterback" has confirmed that the arms and legs are controlled enough to allow EMS to approach the patient. EMS will move in from the sides which allow better access to buttocks or upper thigh of the patient.

Figure#6- (Cuffing#2) - If the subject is larger, then four or more sets of handcuffs should be applied so that the patient can be placed in the supine position.

Figure#5- (Cuffing#1) - Once sedation has been given, officers will bring one arm behind the back at a time and apply at least three sets of handcuffs in a daisy chain configuration to allow the patient to be turned to a supine position. This will allow EMS to access the arm to establish an IV if warranted.

Figure#7- (Cuffing#3) - The patient's legs are brought together, ankles crossed if possible, then the nylon hobble is applied and pulled away from the patient. The other officer holds the patient's legs to keep them secured.

Figure#8- (Recovery#1) - If EMS is not on scene when the patient is captured, the officers are advised to place the patient in the left recovery position until EMS arrives on scene. Sedation can still be administered in this position.

Figure#9- (Backboard#1) - The patient is placed on top of the backboard with the series of handcuffs under their back. This starts to limit the patient's ability to resist.

Figure#10- (Backboard#2) - Close-up showing patient on top of handcuffs while on top of the backboard.

Figure#11- (Backboard#3) - Close-up of patient's arms while handcuffs are under the body and spider straps are applied. Notice that an IV could be started while in this position.

Figure#12- (Backboard#4) - Close-up of patient's legs secured to the backboard using the spider straps and the nylon hobble tied to the end of the backboard.

Endnotes

1   In the authors' experiences this can be due to ignorance of the actual law, a fear of lawsuits or an adversarial attitude towards law enforcement.

2   Excessive bail shall not be required, nor excessive fines imposed, nor cruel and unusual punishments inflicted.

3   Some institutions limit mental health training to that dealing with suicidal inmates, beleivng, thereby, that they have fulfilled requirements for mental health threatment. Training in working with mentally ill inmates should not be limited to this subject alone, however necessary it is..

4   Inmates enrollment with Medicaid, Medicare, Veterans benefits or other services are dropped from these services during incarceration. The likelihood of them getting re-enrolled by themselves is very low.

5   State intake facilities receive packets of information for each inmate. Every write up or housing change—whether good or bad—is contained in the packet and this information is used to assign long-term housing. Local jails, however, do not have the convenience of a prepared packet of information sent before the inmate arrives. Intake is the point at which all information gathering begins.

6   See Rhodes, Richard. (1999). *Why they kill: The discoveries of a maverick criminologist.* New York: Vintage, on the work of sociologist Lonnie Atkins, who coined the phrase "violentization," to describe the process in which a victim of violence becomes a perpetrator. Atkins focused on the family, but violentization can also occur later in life. On the other hand, prior incarceration can also work to the institution's benefit. Some inmates are so familiar with the system that they fall into its natural rhythm. They will even ask the booking officer to tell the officer that runs inmate programs that they are back in jail. Some officers are happy to see the "good laundry worker" or "floor guy" back in custody.

7   Ibid.

8   One of the authors observed an informal study by a neurologist at a youth detention facility. He noted signs of closed head injury (through neuro-psych evaluation) in approximately fifty percent of the male inmates.

9   The Religious Land Use In Prison Act (RLUIPA) requires jail administration to develop policy and subsequent training for staff in order to ensure compliance with its tenets.

10 Issues of religion are almost always brought in the medical interview as many religions have dietary restrictions.

11 Eric Silver et al. Assessing violence risk among discharged Psychiatric patients: Toward an ecological approach, 23, *Law and Human Behavior 23* 237-238 (199).

12 Psychiatric Treatment Units (PTU), Psychiatric Service Units (PSU), or Residential Treatment Units (RSU)

13 California cases include Plata vs. David, the largest ever jail class action lawsuit concerning the adequacies of medical care in jail settings; Budd vs. Cambra, regarding the California D.O.C. failing to license jail health care facilities; Coleman vs. Wilson, wherein the Federal Court found the entire California D.O.C. mental health system to be unconstitutional with jail officials deliberately indifferent to the needs of the mentally ill jail population; Gates vs. Deukmejian, which required the improvement of medical care at the California Medical Facility, California, D.O.C.; and Marin vs. Rushen concerning improved medical and psychiatric care at the California D.O.C.'s San Quentin State Prison. While these cases are all located in California, the issue of adequate mental and medical care in jails and correctional facilities is a nationwide phenomenon.

14 See: Skidmore-Roth, L. (2010). Mosby's 2013 nursing drug reference. Philadelphia, PA: Elsevier Books.

15 Another, highly effective model, not described in this text, is the "Criminogenic Risk and Behavioral Health Needs Framework," which is supported by the National Institute of Corrections (NIC), Bureau of Justice Assistance (BJA) and Substance Abuse and Mental Health Services Administration(SAMHSA).

16 Munetz, Mark R. & Patricia A. Griffin, Use of the sequential intercept model as an approach to decriminalization of people with serious mental illness. *Psychiatric Services, 57(4)* (Psychiatry Online: http://ps.psychiatryonline.org/ article. aspx?articleid=96593)

17 Ibid: These two illustrations replicate the information of those in Munetz & Griffin

18 Ritter, Christian, Jennifer L. S. Teller, and Mark R. Munetz. (2005). Research briefing two: The impact of diversion programs on consumers of mental health services." Ohio: Kent State University, College of Medicine.

19   PEW (2012) http://www.pewtrusts.org/news_roomdetail.aspx?id =49696)

20   See Amdur, Ellis & Alan Pelton. (2011). **From Chaos to Compliance: Communication, Control, and De-escalation of Mentally Ill, Emotionally Disturbed and Aggressive Offenders.** Seattle: Edgework Books, Seattle, for a comprehensive discussion on these issues. That book accomplishes for the community corrections system (parole/probation) what this volume does for the jail system.

21   Dauphinot, L. (1996). The efficacy of community correctional supervision for offenders with severe mental illness. Unpublished doctoral dissertation, University of Texas at Austin, and Solomon, P., Draine, J., & Marcus, S. (2002). Predicting incarceration of clients of a psychiatric probation and parole service. *Psychiatric Services*, 53, 50-56.

22   AOT is also referred in some locale as Outpatient Commitment (OPC).

23   "Assisted Outpatient Treatment Laws," Treatment Advocacy Center, 2011: http://www.treatmentadvocacycenter.org/solution/assisted-outpatient-treatment-laws

24   Ohio sheriff closes the 'dumping ground' of jail for some mentally ill," *Treatment Advocacy Center*: http://www.treatmentadvocacycenter.org/about-us/our-blog/115-oh/2023-ohio-sheriff-closes-the-dumping-ground-of-jail-for-some-mentally-ill-

25   Illinois developed a set of evidence-based recommendations for emergency departments to implement when working with the mentally ill. More information is available by following this link: http://www.psych.uic.edu/ijr/pdf/mnaylor/BestPracticesFinalReport_June2007.pdf

26   For more information on service planning following psychiatric hospitalization the following resources are noted. Los Angeles County Jail Overcrowding Reduction Report: www.vera.org/download?file=3381/LA%2520County%2520Jail%2520Overcrowding%2520Reduction%2520Report.pdf; Illinois Hospital Illinois Hospital Association Behavioral Health Steering Committee Best Practices Task Force: http://www.psych.uic.edu /ijr/pdf/mnaylor/Best PracticesFinalReport_June2007.pdf

27   The State of Minnesota, Department of Corrections has implemented a comprehensive Crisis Intervention Team (CIT) training throughout their state corrections system. Excellent information on this program, including youtube videos, can be accessed through a simple web-search.

28   Example: cheeking – http://www.youtube.com/watch?v=DzLFquT2jTQ

29   You will sometimes see the same thing with people for whom English is not a first language.

30   An extremely valuable book regarding OCD is: Schwartz, Jeffrey (with Beverly Beyette). (1996). *Brain lock: Free yourself from obsessive-compulsive behavior.* New York: Regan Books.

31   One of the best books on manipulation, the famous "yellow book," is: Allen, B., & Bosta, D. (1981-2002). *Games criminals play: How you can profit by knowing them.* Berkeley, CA: Rae John.

32   Hare, Robert. (1999). *Without conscience: The disturbing world of the psychopaths among us.* New York: Guilford.

33   In Greek mythology Sisyphus was a king who, as a punishment from the gods, was made to roll a huge rock up a steep hill, but before he could reach the top of the hill, the rock would always roll back down, forcing him to begin again, dooming Sisyphus to an eternity of frustrations. Today, pointless and frustrating activities are often described as Sisyphean.

34   Arieti, Silvano. (1994). Interpretation of Schizophrenia (2nd ed.). Jason Aronson.

35   Other major categories of stalkers are:

    a.   **Relational stalkers**. Often an extension of a controlling or violent relationship, this stalker is either keeping tabs on his/her partner, or pursuing them once they have left.

    b.   **Obsessive stalkers.** The classic stalker—a hyper-focus on the victim as prey, not necessarily to kill or even harm, but always to control. Like ordinary obsessive-compulsive disorder, this stalker can be well-aware that the victim does not desire contact, and may be afraid of or hate him/her. But just as the germ-obsessed obsessive MUST wash his hands 50 times, despite *knowing* that they are clean, the obsessive stalker has to have the attention of his/her victim.

    c.   **Psychopathic stalker**. Such an individual may certainly have been in a relationship with or be obsessed with his/her victim. In addition, there is considerable "ego" involved—this stalker's psychological energy focuses on self rather than the victim. A true predator, he/she is doing something they enjoys—simply because they can (for amusement), or because the victim, in some way, offended them (for revenge).

At least in the professional context, correctional officers are most at risk from obsessive stalkers, who get fixated on them, or psychopathic stalkers, who decide to target one officer for revenge, hatred or amusement.

36   Our thanks to Aaron Fields of the Seattle Fire Department for another version of this intervention.

37   An actual incident. The engineer was killed trying to jump clear when the manic person wrecked the train.

38   Researchers note that a mixture of alcohol and cocaine is particularly dangerous, as the body synthesizes them together into a new substance, coca ethylene. Retrieved from http://jpet.aspetjournals.org/ content/274/1/215.abstract

39   U.S. Dept. of Justice 2010 Key Indicators Strategic Support System Demographics.

40   These same questions can and should be used if the suspected suicidal person is a fellow officer and you, as a friend, are trying to convince them to seek services.

41   This chapter is a brief discussion of a much more complicated issue. It is beyond the scope of this text to go into such planning in detail as this involves a lot of players beyond law enforcement, and gets into a lot of "political" issues on how one responds to the distress of mentally ill or emotionally disturbed people. Those wanting consultation or assistance in dealing with para-suicidal individuals should contact author Ellis Amdur through http://www.edgework.info

42   A remarkable example of "the relationship" saving a correctional officer's life can be seen on this YouTube video: http://www. youtube.com /watch?v=s1FR6YjHbYE As described in an article in "Mail Online," dated November 6, 2009: "Previtera, the commander of Hillsborough County's Department of Detention Services, said the inmates had 'saved the deputy's life'. 'The response of the inmates in this case, I think, speaks volumes as to the fact that we treat these men and women ... in our facilities with a lot of respect,' he added. Letters of thanks were sent to the attorneys of the four inmates who came to Deputy Moon's rescue, to be delivered to a judge on their behalf. Deputy Moon himself was admitted to the hospital for his injuries but quickly released. When asked why they had bothered to help him, the inmates' answer was simple: He was a good guy and they liked him."

43   One of the authors first heard this method presented by author David Grossman. Also see his exemplary book: Grossman, D. (1996). *On killing: The psychological cost of learning to kill in war and society.* Santa Ana, CA: Back Bay Books.

44   The authors owe the image of the hands as a fence to Geoff Thompson, who has authored a number of books on his career as a doorman in violent British pubs, as well as exemplary books on self-defense.

45   We are indebted to John Holttum, MD, Child Psychiatrist from Tacoma, Washington. One of the authors attended a presentation given by Dr. Holttum which influenced us greatly in terms of how to "subdivide" the presenting behaviors of youth and how best to intervene with them. We must underscore that any intervention recommendations are ours, and may be at variance to those Dr. Holttum might offer.

46   Louv, Richard. (2005). Last child in the woods: Saving our children from nature-deficit disorder. Chapel Hill, NC: Algonquin Books. And Sax, Leonard. (2007). Boys adrift: The five factors driving the growing epidemic of unmotivated boys and under-achieving young men. Philadelphia: Basic Books.

47   The authors owe a debt for some of the basic information in this section to a form of training called Professional Assault Response Training (PART), thanks to a workshop one of us attended approximately twenty years ago. We have made major changes in their basic four-part schema, as well as adding a significant amount of new data. Therefore, our approach is, in many aspects, quite different, and it should not be confused with PART's procedures.

48   See: Salter, A. (2004). Predators: pedophiles, rapists and other sex inmates: Who they are, how they operate, and how we can protect ourselves and our children. New York: Basic Books. Our gratitude for the formulation of the overwhelming force-respect concept that she presented in a great story during a seminar.

49   See: de Becker, G. (1997). The Gift of Fear: Survival signals that protect us from violence. U.S. and Canada: Little Brown; and (1999). Protecting the gift: Keeping children and teenagers safe (and parents sane) New York: Random House, New York.

50   Any defensive tactic requires hands-on instruction to execute properly. For those who wish more information, Lt. Paulus' contact information is at the end of this appendix. Having attended one of Lt. Paulus' trainings, one of the writers here states simply – Go to the source. Lt. Paulus is not only the leading law enforcement officer trainer of this method, but has, of necessity, used these methods on a frequent enough basis that he truly is the authority.

51   Many institutions have sets of soft restraints, particularly useful for those who need to be secured for long periods of time. There is a tradeoff here. The individual in a chaotic rage/excited delirium state is very likely to continue to struggle against the restraints. They are less likely to be injured by the soft restraints than they would from handcuffs. However, do not forget the salient characteristic of excited delirium—superhuman strength. They may be more likely to break the soft restraints. If soft restraints are the preferred method of your institution, take into account the possibility of such breakage—which would require you to subdue the inmate all over again, doubling the risk of officer and inmate injury. Consider the possibility of training in doubling or tripling the soft restraints. If such a protocol is decided, then all drills must be on that basis.

52   One of our consultants notes that such events are relatively common, and go undocumented. When needed to support evidence for an excited delirium episode, all they have on file is anecdotes. Therefore, protocols would do well to include recognition and documentation of flicker events.

ABOUT THE AUTHORS

Ellis Amdur

Edgework founder Ellis Amdur received his B.A. in psychology from Yale University in 1974 and his M.A. in psychology from Seattle University in 1990. He is both a National Certified Counselor and a State Certified Child Mental Health Specialist. He has written a number of books concerning communication with mentally ill and emotionally disturbed individuals and the de-escalation of aggression.

Since the late 1960s, Amdur has trained in various martial arts systems, spending thirteen of these years studying in Japan. He is a recognized expert in classical and modern Japanese martial traditions and has authored three iconoclastic books and one instructional DVD on martial arts subjects.

Since his return to America in 1988, Ellis Amdur has worked in the field of crisis intervention. He has developed a range of training and consultation services, as well as a unique style of assessment and psychotherapy. These are based on a combination of phenomenological psychology and the underlying philosophical premises of classical Japanese martial traditions. Amdur's professional philosophy can best be summed up in this idea: "The development of an individual's integrity and dignity is the paramount virtue. This can only occur when people live courageously, regardless of their circumstances, and take responsibility for their roles in making the changes they desire."

Ellis Amdur is a dynamic public speaker and trainer who presents his work throughout the U.S. and internationally. He is noted for his sometimes outrageous humor as well as his profound breadth of knowledge. His vivid descriptions of aggressive and mentally ill people and his true-to-life role-playing of the behaviors in question give participants an almost first-hand experience of facing the real individuals in question.

For more information on books and training by Ellis Amdur, please refer to his website at www.edgework.info

Sergeant Michael Blake

Sergeant Michael Blake earned her Bachelor's Degree in Law and Justice from Central Washington University in 1993. While in College, she volunteered for the local Crisis Line and completed an internship with the Attorney General's Office. That internship included compiling statistics for the FBI's Uniform Crime Reporting and she was introduced to the Homicide information and Tracking System (HITS Program) in which crime statistics are coupled with GPS in order to solve Crime in Washington State. Since 1994, she has been employed off and on in Corrections with the Yakima County Department of Corrections in Washington State.

In 2002, she promoted to Corporal and in 2003, began working as one of the Training Coordinators for the Department. During her tenure as Training Coordinator, she wrote the first training model for corrections officers based on the Reno Model for training Law Enforcement officers. She also co-authored promotional training models for Corporals and Sergeants with her partners in training. All three of these training models were accepted and approved by the Washington State Criminal Justice Training Academy as qualified curriculum for certification processes.

Michael was fortunate to travel to Longmont Colorado to participate in the National Institute of Corrections Training program for Training Coordinators. She also became a Certified Field Training Officer in the Reno Model. In her spare time she began bringing the training records into compliance with the American Correctional Association's standards for records retention and destruction.

While working with the Department of Corrections, Michael was invited to be an Adjunct Professor at Yakima Valley Community College, teaching an Inmate Populations Course, for which she developed the curriculum, guidelines, and tests.

Michael helped implement the first Peer Support Team for the Yakima County Department of Corrections. She was one of the founding Peer Support members and has assisted staff after numerous crisis events. During this time she was asked to teach the Corrections portion of the Crisis Intervention Training course being offered to Law Enforcement by Comprehensive Mental Health.

In 2007, Michael promoted to Shift Sergeant, running a team of thirty plus officers where she remained for two years, helping to guide her shift through several crisis events, including the death of an officer.

In 2009, Michael transferred to the position of Population Liaison Sergeant. This position included the supervision of the Classification Division in the jail as well as helping to manage the population of State Contract Inmates in the facility. Michael was requested to help develop a pre-release program for Yakima County. She, with a team of professionals, developed and implemented the Release Analysis Division. This division provided recommendations to the court regarding the risk and release factors of inmates. As that position was closed, Michael went back to being a Shift Sergeant, adamant that it is the best job in Corrections.

Chris De Villeneuve

Chris De Villeneuve is a happily married father of two young children. He holds an MBA in healthcare management, a master's degree in counseling and a bachelor's degree in Psychology. He has worked in the behavioral health field for 25 years. He is a Director with Comprehensive and works as the Site Director in Sunnyside, Washington. He is a designated mental health professional in the State of Washington and has been a volunteer hostage negotiator for the Yakima Police Department for ten years.

He started work with the Behavioral Health Diversion program during a grant project in 2006 that teamed local government, community mental health providers, and law enforcement agencies to implement a behavioral health intervention program. Presentations on this program have been made at the State and National level.